TECHNIQUES OF FICTION WRITING

Measure and Madness

Leon Surmelian teaches English and literature and directs the Pacific Coast Writers Conference at California State College at Los Angeles. He taught advanced workshops in the novel and the short story in the University of California Extension Division, 1958–64. His work has been reprinted in *Best American Short Stories* and in college and school textbooks, and his short stories have appeared in *Prairie Schooner, University Review, New Mexico Quarterly,* and other literary magazines. Many of his articles have been published in *Holiday*.

Mr. Surmelian's books have received high critical praise. His autobiographical novel, *I Ask You, Ladies and Gentlemen,* the story of his Armenian boyhood, has been translated into several languages. He is the author of *98.6°,* a novel, and has two distinguished volumes in the UNESCO Series of Representative Works: *Daredevils of Sassoun, The Armenian National Epic,* and *Apples of Immortality, Folktales of Armenia.* Mr. Surmelian is a graduate of Kansas State University.

TECHNIQUES OF FICTION WRITING

Measure and Madness

by Leon Surmelian

INTRODUCTION BY MARK SCHORER

Anchor Books
Doubleday & Company, Inc.
Garden City, New York

Grateful acknowledgment is made to the following for permission to reprint material copyrighted or controlled by them:

Harcourt, Brace & World, Inc., for excerpts from *Mrs. Dalloway* by Virginia Woolf. Reprinted by permission of the publisher.

Harper & Row, for excerpts from *Point Counter Point* by Aldous Huxley. Reprinted by permission of the publisher.

Christopher Isherwood, for excerpts from a personal communication to Leon Surmelian. Reprinted by permission of the author.

Harold Ober Associates, Inc., for excerpts from "I'm a Fool" and *Seeds* by Sherwood Anderson. Reprinted by permission.

Oxford University Press, for excerpts from *The Notebooks of Henry James*, edited by Matthiessen & Murdock; for excerpts from *What Is Art? And Essays on Art* by Leo Tolstoy, translated by Aylmer Maude; for excerpts from *Crime and Punishment* by Fyodor Dostoyevsky, translated by Jessie Coulson. Reprinted by permission of the publisher.

Charles Scribner's Sons, for excerpts from *Portrait of a Lady*, by Henry James. Reprinted by permission of the publisher.

Wirt Williams, for excerpts from a personal communication to Leon Surmelian. Reprinted by permission of the author.

From *The Rainbow* by D. H. Lawrence. Copyright 1915 by D. H. Lawrence, 1943 by Frieda Lawrence. Reprinted by permission of The Viking Press, Inc., and Laurence Pollinger Ltd.

The quotations from various works of Ernest Hemingway that appear in this book are protected by copyright and have been reprinted here by permission of Charles Scribner's Sons, and Jonathan Cape Ltd.

From *Ulysses*, by James Joyce. Copyright 1914, 1918 by Margaret Caroline Anderson and renewed 1942, 1946 by Nora Joseph Joyce. Reprinted by permission of Random House, Inc., and The Bodley Head Ltd.

From *The Sound and the Fury*, by William Faulkner. Copyright 1929 and renewed 1956 by William Faulkner. Reprinted by permission of Random House, Inc., and Curtis Brown Ltd.

From *The Razor's Edge*, by Somerset Maugham. Copyright 1943, 1944 by McCall Corporation. Copyright 1944 by Somerset Maugham. Reprinted by permission.

CONTENTS

INTRODUCTION

Leon Surmelian has an infectious enthusiasm for fiction, an irrepressibly effervescent concern with what goes on in the making of it. As one begins his book, it is this quality that one first observes, and it is beguiling. It is more than that, for almost at once one is made aware of another quality, that of the voice of the teacher of writing. But what is striking in this second quality is the tone: it is not that of the organized lecturer, certainly not that of the systematic critic (which he does not claim to be), but rather that of the committed teacher in the workshop, mingling informally with his students. Here is a man, one knows from his own prose, talking to students who want to become fiction writers (or better readers of fiction), and he is talking to us just as he does to them: passionate about his subject, making his points through that passion, not always logical perhaps, sometimes purposefully a bit repetitious—making a point, advancing to another, then circling back to reinforce the first, to restate it in the fuller context—but always caring deeply, as if nothing else were more important than this subject. And one can infer—beyond the mere beguilement—the effectuation. His madness can no doubt be measured in his results.

At the outset he has something to say about the writer's innate equipment, his "madness," that is, his immersion in and his responsiveness to all the turbulence and chaos of experience. This consideration has of course to do with the very roots of creativity itself. At the end of his book he writes at length about the writer's language, the essential means by which measure is imposed on madness or brought out of it, as you will, the resolution of chaos in order. And this consideration has ultimately to do with the effects of art, what one might call the responsibility of the writer. But on the whole these two matters, the before and the after of a piece of fiction, are not the concern of this book; its concern is the multiple means that make for measure.

In an introduction, then, it may not be wholly inappropriate to take up these two matters, as a kind of frame for the substantial, central discussion of the book itself.

The creative process is the process whereby order is brought out of disorder, form out of chaos. That is why James Joyce was being only very literal rather than heretical when he insisted on the artist's role as God-like. For as God brought the universe out of chaos and ancient night, so the artist brings his creative work out of the chaos of his subjective life and out of the disorder of the world. But there is order in the world as well as disorder, and particularly the order of all that has been created before any new creation; and there is *some* order in the subjective life as well, if only that impulse, striated through it, that impels a particular order to emerge. "*Spur in Treibsand*"—trace in the shifting sand: this is the conception of consciousness held by the painter, Kokoschka. We can, if we wish, take this figure of speech, in its most intense and heightened significance, as representative of the creative impulse itself, as that striation through the flow of subjectivity that will fulfill itself in created objectification. And the created object, every truly creative act, transcends in one degree or another both forms of order, the order of the world and the potential order within the subjective life, is new, goes beyond what has been. This is not in the least to say that it is *better*, only that it is *itself*, and therefore in one way or another, perhaps in many ways, different. The bringing of order out of relative disorder and the emergence of the new over the old, over all that has been before—these are probably the two basic facts about creativity.

Men have speculated since ancient times on the power that is prior to and activates the creative impulse. Such speculations are interesting enough but probably vain because they are ultimately undemonstrable. Ancient and later romantic theories of divine fire, of the sudden infusion in the creative mind of a power from without or above, theories of inspira-

tion in the literal sense of being breathed *into,* conceits such as
that of the poetic soul like a harp upon which the wind blows—
all these are probably only metaphors for a mystery that eludes
rational inquiry because in itself it is non-rational. It is because the first movements of the creative impulse toward the
created object are non-rational that many writers have as-
sured us that the work was accomplished automatically,
somnambulistically, as if under hypnosis, in a state of trance.
From these assertions one can only suppose that the intensity
of creative concentration may seem to induce such states or
states analogous to them, but that is not at all to say that such
states are necessary to the beginning of creation or that creation will begin if they are induced.

There are more mundane speculations. There is, for example, D. H. Lawrence's belief that the motive force lies in a
psychic need for therapy. "I always say my motto," he wrote,
"is 'Art for *my* sake,'" and "One sheds one's sicknesses in
books, repeats and presents again one's emotions to be master of them." This is a view not unrelated to André Gide's of
the necessary connection between genius and disease, a view
later explored by Edmund Wilson in the essays he collected
under the title *The Wound and the Bow.* Again, both are
specializations of the theory, widely held, of art as compen-
sation, whether for feelings of inferiority or an unhappy
childhood or a nagging mother-in-law. It is a view that sometimes approximates the idea of art as revenge. One might
mention, too, I. A. Richards' theory of the motive of conflict:
a maximum number of appetites in conflict or in imbalance,
striving to come into balance or harmony.

Behind most of these ideas lies the theory of Sigmund
Freud as he developed it in his paper of 1908, "The Relation
of the Poet to Day-Dreaming." The argument here is that
creation begins in fantasy or reverie or daydreaming, all of
which are simply adult extensions of the play of childhood, in
which the child quite frankly creates a make-believe world.
"Unsatisfied wishes are the driving power behind phantasies;
every separate phantasy contains the fulfilment of a wish, and
improves on unsatisfactory reality." Such wishes are generally

of two kinds, ambitious wishes and erotic wishes, and these two "are often united." This is a considerably plausible theory, and we must, of course, respect it, yet it is, as I believe, incomplete, partial.

We can agree, perhaps, only on this much as to the beginnings of the creative process, that the will, like rational intellectual process, plays probably no part in it at all. And we would wish to add that a given subject chooses its author at least as much as the author chooses his subject. We need not, to make the point, use the violent language of Nietzsche when he said that the subject of *Alzo Sprach Zarathustra invaded* him, although that is a powerful word. I am not now thinking of inspiration, but rather of the necessary limitations that are imposed upon every creative being. Can more come out of the subjective life than transfigurations of what has been poured into it? The objective environment necessarily places curbs on the subjective potentialities. Henry Adams felt that his imagination was undernourished because he had been brought up in the United States. "I am too American myself, and lack juices," he said. And, of course, it has long been argued that the American writer in general has found it difficult to fulfill himself because he is nourished on such barren ground. This was the burden of Henry James's eloquent and sad essay on Nathaniel Hawthorne, and the argument has since been applied to many other writers by other critics. Having examined the work of ten well-known twentieth-century American writers, T. K. Whipple, for example, concluded as follows: "Most of their work has a touch of that gauntness or emaciation, a deficiency in variety, body, mass, which springs from underfeeding of the imagination—from having lived, that is, in a world which affords inadequate experience." The world that we create, I am only trying to say, depends in large part on the world that we inhabit. The power of the man, in Matthew Arnold's phrasing, is not separate from the power of the moment. Even the greatest genius has a collaborator in his environment, and if that collaborator is sluggish, even the greatest genius may fail in the full realization of himself.

Realization is the word toward which I have been laboring.

It is the *need* of realization—and it can take many forms—it is the need of realization, I believe, that impels the creative act. Max Eastman, in *The Enjoyment of Poetry,* many years ago employed the word to define "the poetic temper." "Poetic people, and all people when they are in a poetic mood . . . are lovers of the qualities of things. . . . They are possessed by the impulse to realize . . . a wish to experience life and the world. That is the essence of the poetic temper." Realization of experience, and through that, of himself and of his creative potentialities: this is the basis, and without this, I believe, nothing can begin. On this subject, Henry James wrote tellingly. "What kind of experience is intended," he asked, "and where does it begin and end?"

> Experience is never limited, and it is never complete; it is an immense sensibility, a kind of huge spider-web of the finest silken threads suspended in the chamber of consciousness, and catching every air-borne particle in its tissue. It is the very atmosphere of the mind; and when the mind is imaginative —much more when it happens to be that of a man of genius— it takes to itself the faintest hints of life, it converts the very pulses of the air into revelations. . . . Therefore, if I should certainly say to a novice, "Write from experience and from experience only," I should feel that this was rather a tantalizing monition if I were not careful immediately to add, "Try to be one of the people on whom nothing is lost!"

Potentially, at least, the most creative person is the person on whom least is lost.

It is reassuring to find this quality in Dr. Donald McKinnon's summary of the qualities that one creative person shares with other creative persons: "his openness to experience," including his own early experience, "his freedom from crippling restraints and impoverishing inhibitions." The creative process itself may be described as a movement from the unrealized to the realized. It is itself the highest form of realization. It is a process that begins in the unconscious, yes; but its impulse, beginning there, is to bring that realm into the realm of consciousness, to objectify the subjective, to know and to make known the unknown, to bring the shining new out of the darkness of ancient night.

It is here, I believe, that a distinction made by Carl Gustav Jung—and to use it does not mean that we need follow him back into the darkness of the collective unconscious—is more useful to our subject than the ruminations of Sigmund Freud on daydreams. Daydreams have to do with the fulfillment of our wishes only; but there is also the other part—the containment of our terror and our fears. And, really, if we must weigh one against the other, unfulfilled wishes and uncontained fears, I would say that the latter are much more insistent in their grip upon the creative heart.

I hope that I do not begin to sound like Carl Gustav Jung, who is, of course, so much more "literary," in the suspect sense, than Sigmund Freud, who, not at all "literary" in that way, is quite a good writer. Still, Jung can help me now with his distinction between what he calls the *visionary* and the *psychological* literary creation. The second term, at least, is not very exact: for *psychological* I would substitute *social*. Or, better still, if we are really trying to mark out the extremes, we might call the first *apocalyptic*, the second, to invent a word, *mundanic*. Whatever we call these two literary modes, the distinction, if we know what we are talking about, is very useful.

Jung finds the distinction most clearly exemplified in the two parts of Goethe's *Faust*, and he has other examples of both kinds. The first kind, what he calls the "psychological," takes its material from "the vast realm of conscious experience," from "the foreground of life." But the second kind, the "visionary," "derives its existence from the hinterland of man's mind," evokes either a prehuman or a superhuman world, is "foreign and cold . . . demonic and grotesque," plunges us into chaos, into dreams, into "monstrous and meaningless happenings," into "the unfathomed abyss of what has not yet become." And so on. For his own purposes, Jung is eager to demonstrate that these two modes of creative experience are indeed two modes, separate and discrete. I would suggest rather that the distinction is one of degree, that in the material that is concerned with "the foreground of life," the rational analytical intelligence finally plays a large part, and in the material that is concerned with a re-presentation of chaos and the grotesque, the irrational attempts to reveal itself as directly as possible. Helpfully for this argument, Jung himself writes further that "in the day-time he [man] believes in an ordered cosmos, and he tries to maintain this faith against the fear of chaos that besets him by night." The one externalizes chaos, what we fear, and binds it; the other reaches toward moral or social or psychological order, that to which we aspire. I do not think that there is a dichotomy here, but rather that even the extremes, if they are genuine creations, share in one way or another in the qualities of the other. I find some support here in an essay by Jerome S. Bruner, when he writes of "the literalities of experience and the night impulses of life"—"I would urge that we not be too easily tempted into thinking that there is an oppositional contrast between *logos* and *mythos*, the grammar of experience and the grammar of myth. For each complements the other. . . ." It is in the complementariness, even the interpenetration of the one by the other, in my view, that we recognize what is indeed the creative experience.

At the beginning of his lecture, "The Mind as Nature," Loren Eiseley tells how, as a small boy, he lived "in two worlds."

> One was dark, hidden and self-examining, though in its own way not without compensations. The other world in which I somehow also managed to exist was external, boisterous, and what I suppose the average parent would call normal or extroverted. . . . I was living, you see, in a primitive world at the same time that I was inhabiting the modern world as it existed in the second decade of this century. I am not talking now about the tree-house, the cave-building activities of normal boys. I am talking about the minds of the first dawning human consciousness—about a kind of mental Ice Age, and of how a light came in from outside until, as I have indicated, two worlds existed in which a boy, still a single unsplit personality, walked readily from one world to the other by day and by night without anyone observing the invisible boundaries he passed.

Dr. Eiseley seems to think that this is an unusual experience for a child and one that might easily prove psychologically disastrous. My own feeling is that it is the normal condition of childhood and that it is the condition always of the creative man. As T. S. Eliot has written, "The artist, I believe, is more *primitive*, as well as more *civilized*, than his contemporaries, his experience is deeper than civilization, and he only uses the phenomena of civilization in expressing it." The works of Dostoyevsky and Henry James, of D. H. Lawrence and Jane Austen—I would argue that ultimately they are not different in kind, only in the degree to which the nighttime and the daytime worlds are given some priority. Even such a writer as Sinclair Lewis, whose work seems to depend on accumulations of social notation alone—even such a writer is moved by an animus of pain and anger, a secret world far back and down into which perhaps he never looked with open eyes, but which, now and then, breaks into the conscious and deliberate structure, and then gives us a glimpse into a nighttime chaos that the sun-parched city blocks of Zenith never knew. Or, to take another example, the early and the later works of Truman Capote: the nightmare incursions into surrealism that characterize "The Headless Hawk" or *Other Voices, Other Rooms,* and the comic social extravagances of *Breakfast at Tiffany's* or the direct reporting of a social catastrophe of *In Cold Blood*—these arise from the same creative intelligence and each is concerned to objectify the human experience, no matter at what level. From the point of view of creativity, what is important to recognize is the fact that it all begins at the lower level and it ends up in objective externalization, the created fact.

Yet the need to live largely in the nighttime world has been observed by many writers. "The poet is at the disposal of his night," Jean Cocteau has written. Thoreau writes somewhere of the "sleep" out of which his work came, and even such an orderly and rational man as John Dryden wrote of the inception of one of his plays in "a confused mass of thoughts, tumbling over one another in the dark; when the fancy was yet in its first work, moving the sleeping images of things towards the light, there to be distinguished, and then either chosen or rejected by the judgment."

By the judgment! And now we are at Mr. Surmelian's subject—how the creative literary impulse manages to get itself
expressed. Marianne Moore has said, "Ecstasy affords the
occasion, and expediency determines the form." The seed
sprouts in the dark, from the dark, but most generally the
plant blooms and is pruned in the daylight. And when the
reason takes over, it operates in quite a different way from
the indolent somnolence of inception. Now comes a dedication
that can be nothing less than fanatical, a furious willfulness.
One thinks of Joseph Conrad, writing *Nostromo,* and, finishing
that book, asking his friends to congratulate him "as upon a
recovery from a dangerous illness." Or one thinks of the
agonies of Virginia Woolf, writing *The Years:*

> A good day—a bad day—so it goes on. Few people can be so
> tortured by writing as I am. Only Flaubert I think. . . . I
> think I can bring it off, if I only have courage and patience:
> take each scene quietly: compose: I think it may be a good
> book. And then—oh when it's finished! . . . I wonder if any-
> one has ever suffered so much from a book as I have from
> *The Years.* Once out I will never look at it again. It's like a
> long childbirth. Think of that summer, every morning a
> headache, and forcing myself into that room in my night-
> gown; and lying down after a page: and always with the
> certainty of failure. Now that certainty is mercifully removed
> to some extent. But now I feel I don't care what anyone says
> so long as I'm rid of it. . . . Never write a long book again.
> Yet I feel I shall write more fiction—scenes will form.

Scenes will form! There is a certain helplessness, first as to
inception, then as to the need for execution: or should I say
first helplessness, then compulsiveness. Jung wrote:

> The artist's life cannot be otherwise than full of conflicts, for
> two forces are at war within him—on the one hand the com-
> mon human longing for happiness, satisfaction and security
> in life, and on the other a ruthless passion for creation
> which may go so far as to override every personal desire. The
> lives of artists are as a rule so highly unsatisfactory—not to
> say tragic—because of their inferiority on the human and per-
> sonal side, and not because of a sinister dispensation. There
> are hardly any exceptions to the rule that a person must
> pay dearly for the divine gift of the creative fire.

He pays in frenzy and frustration and in possible deprivation of everything else as he submits to his creative drive to realize itself. It can realize itself only through his language, through what in the most general sense we may call technique.

Technique, I know, is a word that has unpleasant mechanical connotations. I think that it is a mistake to think of the word with those connotations, and if there were some better word, some word that did not suggest mere mechanical manipulation, I would use it; but I do not think that there is a better word. By technique I mean simply the means by which a writer gets his initial impulse to create a work out into the open and over to his readers. Technique, in fact, is the means by which the writer himself first finds out what he is really trying to say, from all those inarticulate impulses that impel him to say it, and then to say it, that is, to make it a creative object. And this is the subject of *Techniques of Fiction Writing*—the multiple means by which a work of fiction is created.

And now, to leap over that entire area that Mr. Surmelian treats so comprehensively, to my second point. Journalists and some critics like to talk about the responsibility of the creative writer to society, his function, and to chide writers today for the perversity of their sense of alienation from society. Many readers will remember a notorious example—a polemical editorial published in *Life* magazine a number of years ago, called "Wanted: An American Novel." Taking off from Sloan Wilson's remark that "These are, we forget, pretty good times. Yet too many novelists are writing as if we were back in the Depression years," the editorial declared:

> Ours is the most powerful nation in the world. It has had a decade of unparalleled prosperity. It has gone further than any other society in the history of man toward creating a truly classless society. Yet it is still producing a literature which sounds sometimes as if it were written by an unemployed homosexual living in a packing box shanty on the city dump while awaiting admission to the county poorhouse.

In my view this diatribe shows an extravagant ignorance of the nature of the creative impulse, of the creative writer, of the created work, and, above all, of the creative function and of creative responsibility.

The first responsibility of the creative writer is to his language and to his technique, because only through these can the creative impulse itself find its realization. His second responsibility is to his own freedom to use his language as he must. He must be free to rebel, and in a profoundly basic sense every real writer is a rebel. The rebel, for so many literary generations the hero, has been largely replaced today by "the stranger," the outsider, the alienated and disaffected wanderer, the human being who declines to participate in the human enterprise.

The creative writer, like his heroes, is also the stranger; but there is always this fascinating thing about the artist: he creates what he describes and, in the act of creation, is superior to the object of his observation, which cannot create itself. And therefore the writer, as stranger, is not doomed to that nihilism in which the hero, as stranger, is caught. The artist, always using his freedom, remains a rebel even when he is a stranger; his basic rebellion, in this time or any other, is directed at the universe itself, and the universe cannot be undone by history, it remains, and it provides the stuff which the artist at once rebukes and celebrates. Every truly creative act is an act of rebellion against the universe and a celebration of the universe because it permits this creative rebellion, that is, the freedom of the artist to act.

It is important to society that the artist be free to act for the very reason that the artist is the supreme type of rebel. "Civilization may be said indeed to be the creation of its outlaws," said James Joyce, but now, as my vocabulary will have suggested, I am thinking not so much of Joyce as of Albert Camus, and Camus as he writes in *L'homme révolté*. Very boldly, when he comes to talk specifically of the artist, Camus begins with Nietzsche's dogma, "No artist tolerates reality," and, qualify that remark as he does, he recognizes its primary if hyperbolical accuracy.

Camus makes importantly obvious points: the terms "realism" (suggesting a duplication of reality) and "formalism" (suggesting a total flight from reality) are meaningless: no art can duplicate reality since all art is selection from, distortion of, and an imposition of order upon reality; no art can totally reject reality since it then would have no materials—"The only real formalism is silence." Yet the very fact of his being an artist means that the man of letters must reject reality as it is in itself. Camus is writing now of the novel:

> Here we have an imaginary world . . . which was created from the rectification of the actual world—a world where suffering can, if it wishes, continue until death, where passions are never distracted, where people are prey to obsessions and are always present to each other. Man is finally able to give himself the alleviating form and limits which he pursues in vain in his own life. The novel makes destiny to measure. . . . In this way man competes with creation and, provisionally, conquers death. A detailed analysis of the most famous novels would show, in different perspectives each time, that the essence of the novel lies in this perpetual alteration, always directed towards the same end, that the artist makes in his own experience. Far from being moral or even purely formal, this alteration aims, primarily, at unity and thereby indicates a metaphysical need. It is the word *metaphysical* that is finally important.

Ezra Pound said, "A work of art need not contain any statement of a political or of a social or of a philosophical conviction, but it nearly always implies one"; Camus seems to extend that remark:

> Whatever may be the chosen point of view of an artist, one principle remains common to all creators: stylization, which supposes the simultaneous existence of reality and of the mind which gives reality its form. Through style, the creative effort reconstructs the world. . . .

Now we may add, to language and to the freedom to use it, the third responsibility, which is to the act of rebellion against that which so smugly and chaotically *is,* the universe, society itself. Rebellion, Camus tells us, is the pursuit of values, and that pursuit is the movement from *facts* to *rights*, or shall we say the imposition of rights upon facts. This is, I believe, precisely what Yeats had in mind when he said that the artist must hold "reality and justice in a single thought." Justice takes many forms in the many minds of men; and reality has no form at all. Art, coming out of dark disorder and ascending above the social order, presents the two together.

Lionel Trilling has written that "The function of literature through all the mutations has been to make us aware of the particularity of selves, and the high authority of the self in its quarrel with its society and its culture." The responsibility of the writer then is to maintain the high authority of his free self, which is to say his creative self, which is in turn to say his rebelling self. His responsibility, in short, is to excellence alone. ". . . the oak," said Ezra Pound again, "does not grow for the purpose or with the intention of being built into ships and tables, yet a wise nation will take care to preserve the forests. It is the oak's business to grow good oak."

A wise society will take care to preserve the freedom of its literary culture, of the man of letters, precisely because he has taken upon himself a necessary fight with the world and experience. His task is to force it into shape, into order. And this, the creative act itself, is the only affirmation that he must make: that the artist can and perpetually does create an order that did not exist before he made it. There may be other affirmations, but this is the imperative one, and it is, please observe, an affirmation about man: man creates what the creation does not contain. "The artist," wrote Yeats, "loves above all life at peace with itself." The function of the creative impulse is not to make peace with the world, but to bring into it, in the creation of his endlessly various forms, those shining examples of peace that are our "monuments of unageing intellect," and that comprise our civilization and our humanity. Only they can put limits on our chaotic nighttime fears and give form to our daytime hopes and dreams. Doing that, they help, with love and work, and for some, religion —they help to make reality continually tolerable. And is that not quite enough?

Berkeley, California   *Mark Schorer*
January 1967

TECHNIQUES OF FICTION WRITING

Madness and Measure

1. SCENE

What is a story? Without attempting a formal definition we may say that a story is a coherent account of a significant emotional experience, or a series of related experiences organized into a perfect whole. The fiction writer re-creates human events, which might be external or mental, imagined or real, and are emotional experiences for the people involved in them.

In more dramatic terms, a story is the imitation of an action—one action, complete in itself. By a complete action—at least in fiction—we do not necessarily mean the final answer to the emotional problem or the resolution of a conflict. But the action should be complete enough to reveal the underlying truth in the story, and what is important is this revelation.

The writer begins with the disorder of life and reduces it to some order before he can re-create it in words. He imitates then the rearrangement of life and not life itself, which is too vast, too chaotic. Life cannot be rendered in all its infinite complexity, and a picture of it in fiction, as we all know, is a selected image. Even a slight incident cannot be rendered in its entirety and would be confusing and incoherent if it were. The writer can re-create only a very small part of it, and in fiction the part stands for the whole. It is a symbolic picture, a metaphor.

The writer purifies his ore to show the shining metal in it. He removes the insignificant, the irrelevant, and preserves only that which is essential to his purpose, and it is not so much the experience itself as the significance of it that excites him. When we look upon fiction as an art of revelations we may readily admit that the real story is the meaning of the event.

The disorder of life may be part of some supreme order and in a novel or short story, and in a play or poem too, it does become order: thus the writer overcomes in a measure the imperfections and limitations of mortality. The reader imaginatively enjoys these re-created events, which may have actually happened, and in this sense a story is a history, though not necessarily in its historic order. Or they might happen, and it is a pretended history, though not an improbable one; it should be convincing. Or the story may be a mixture of the two, the actual and the possible, or the probable, as it so often is even in the most realistic fiction today. The perceptive writer searches for hidden meanings in human events and builds his stories around them. This freedom of imagination enjoyed by the writer is one of the characteristics of fiction—as distinguished from history—but in a good story imagination does no violence to reality and is based on reality. It is not reckless invention.

The writer can universalize. He is by nature a sort of universal person himself. By a long tradition now the writer acts as a spokesman of his group, his class, his nation, and indeed of the whole human race. The writer might be a seer like the prophet. The knowledge he possesses could well be beyond the grasp of the average person; it is intuitive. And through his insight into human nature and his ability to verbalize it, the writer enlarges the life experience of the reader and gives us the kind of knowledge which he alone can give. A great novel, like *Madame Bovary* or *War and Peace* or *Ulysses*, is a unique human document that re-creates a way of life. The sociologist, the psychologist, the historian could not do it. No matter how individualistic and self-bound, and even when living in an ivory tower, the writer serves a social purpose through mimesis.

When we say creative writing cannot be taught, we mean that one cannot learn how to write it from books and articles if one does not have the sensory equipment of the born writer, his unifying inner vision, his knack for mimesis, his rage for words. But much might be learnt from them. The writer has to train himself and become a lifelong student of the masters in his craft.

The purpose of this book is to make the apprenticeship of the writer a bit easier, if possible. It is addressed to the writer with imaginative and expressive gifts and is intended to be an introductory poetics of fiction. It may also prove to be of interest to the general reader and the student of literature who wants to have an understanding of modern fiction from the inside, from the writer's point of view.

The true writer has a touch of madness in his makeup. He is an ecstatic, the real enthusiast. He is inspired, we say. Such a writer does not always know what he is saying. He has a special sensitivity to language and is drunk with words. But he is scarcely a passive medium for the gods, as Plato suggested. In literature madness uncontrolled is madness, madness controlled is genius. Technique means control and measure. Madness cannot be taught, measure may be. This book deals with measure.

We might call the writer a bold traveler, a pioneer, through foggy country, who through the trajectory of his inner vision cuts through the fog in which most men are lost, and others follow in his footsteps. But even the writer cannot go very far, and all of us grope our way through the awful mist. Fiction can never be a completely lucid mimesis. We are dealing with approximations, with the creation of illusions, for reality itself is beyond our grasp when we try to express it in words.

From disorder to order (plot); from multiplicity to unity; from the particular to the general (theme); and back to the particular (through concrete correlates); from matter to form —this, briefly, seems to be the creative process in fiction. A good story represents a larger reality than itself; if it is, for instance, the struggle of a man and woman for happiness, or for sheer survival, the writer finds a universal meaning in their struggle, and the moment he does that he has a story. This meaning is an idea dramatized, structured, made concrete, visible, communicable. In fiction the idea is not an abstract concept as it might be in philosophy, but a living sensuous picture of life. The idea defines for the writer his subject and subject-matter, he knows through his idea what precisely he wishes to express, but this knowledge might remain in his subconscious and he could not, perhaps, explain it even to himself. A new idea could be our starting point in writing fiction, but it is only the beginning of a complicated process. A good idea by itself will not make a good story.

We have to accept the ancient principle (as stated by Plato and Aristotle) that art is imitation, or to use the classic term, mimesis. The writer is a mimos, or mime, on the stage of life. He is like an actor—and acting is another madness. Everyone delights in close, uncanny imitations. Children are great mimics, and the writer often remains a child at heart and sees things as though for the first time. This gives us poetry in writing.

A revealing imitation—that is the secret of writing. Is this a good mimesis, is it honest, is it convincing? That is the first question we might ask in judging a story, or in writing one. Every writer re-creates in words what *he* sees, and there are different ways of seeing. The honest writer can give only his own view of the world, and if it is truly his, there is likely to be something new and different about it. He can express his own visions and give us an imitation of his own inner reality or imaginative flights. He can be realistic, even surrealistic. He can write a New Novel, as it is called in France. He can write allegories, like Franz Kafka. He can write science fiction. An existentialist novel. Combine naturalism with symbolism. Or swear by socialist realism. In any case he has to work out his own forms, and every good novel or short story is a successful experiment in technique. The writer is engaged in a constant struggle with chaos, he is always fighting through the fog to make his meaning clear. And as Mark Schorer put it in his famous essay, "Technique As Discovery," form and content, technique and subject matter, are one. "To speak of content as such is not to speak of art at all, but of experience . . . The difference between content, or experience, and achieved content, or art, is technique."

The meaning of a story varies for each reader; it does not wholly lie in the story itself. Probably no work of fiction is exactly the same story for two readers. Each sees something different in it, what he himself is capable of seeing. These variations in reader response may be so great that a story becomes meaningless for one person, and highly significant for another.

SCENE RE-CREATES A SINGLE INCIDENT

There are two ways of writing a story: scene and summary. Scene is the dramatic and summary the narrative method. Fiction is dramatic narration, neither wholly scene nor wholly summary, but scene-and-summary. If it were all scene, it would be a play; if all summary, more of a synopsis than a story.

The scene is a specific act, a single event that occurs at a certain time and place and lasts as long as there is no change of place and no break in the continuity of time. It is an incident acted out by the characters, a single episode or situation, vivid and immediate. The scene is the dramatic or play element in fiction, and a continuous present action while it lasts. The scene reproduces the movement of life, and life is action, motion. As a moving picture the scene is a closer imitation of what happens in life than a summary of it would be. It is not a narrator's report about it, but the event, the experience itself which unfolds before the eyes of the reader, with the actors caught in the act.

The pictorial quality of a story and its authority depend partly on scene, and the reader's participation is greater in the scene. Seeing is more realistic and convincing. It shows the action. The reader can share an emotional experience more readily. We live "scenically." Life itself is dramatic in method.

Ernest Hemingway in *The Sun Also Rises* introduces Robert Cohn with a few paragraphs of summary, followed by a scene—a specific incident, that occurred one night after Jake Barnes, the narrator, had dinner with Cohn and his girl friend Frances. Later they went to the Café de Versailles for coffee, where he first became aware of the young woman's attitude toward Cohn, who after his divorce backed a review of the arts that started in Carmel, California, and finished in Provincetown, Massachusetts.

Robert Cohn was a member, through his father, of one of the richest Jewish families in New York, and through his mother of one of the oldest. At the military school where he prepped for Princeton, and played a very good end on the football team, no one had made him race-conscious. No one had ever made him feel he was a Jew, and hence any different from anybody else, until he went to Princeton. He was a nice boy, a friendly boy, and very shy, and it made him bitter. He took it out in boxing, and he came out of Princeton with painful self-consciousness and the flattened nose, and was married by the first girl who was nice to him. He was married five years, had three children, lost most of the fifty thousand dollars his father left him, the balance of the estate having gone to his mother, hardened into a rather unattractive mould under domestic unhappiness with a rich wife; and just when he had made up his mind to leave his wife she left him and went off with a miniature-painter. . . .

We had several *fines* after the coffee, and I said I must be going. Cohn had been talking about the two of us going off somewhere on a weekend trip. He wanted to get out of town and get in a good walk. I suggested we fly to Strasbourg and walk up to Saint Odile, or somewhere or other in Alsace. "I know a girl in Strasbourg who can show us the town," I said.

Somebody kicked me under the table. I thought it was accidental and went on: "She's been there two years and knows everything there is to know about the town. She's a swell girl."

I was kicked again under the table and, looking, saw Frances, Robert's lady, her chin lifting and her face hardening.

"Hell," I said, "why go to Strasbourg? We could go up to Bruges, or to the Ardennes."

Cohn looked relieved. I was not kicked again. I said goodnight and went out. Cohn said he wanted to buy a paper and would walk to the corner with me. "For God's sake," he said, "why did you say that about that girl in Strasbourg for? Didn't you see Frances?"

"No, why should I? If I know an American girl that lives in Strasbourg what the hell is it to Frances?"

"It doesn't make any difference. Any girl. I couldn't go, that would be all."

The scene carries more weight with the reader. These are presumably the exact words spoken by Jake Barnes and Robert Cohn. This is the original event as it took place in Paris. A scene of course cannot go on indefinitely; it ends when another scene begins. A story happens in a certain time sequence. Each scene, by itself, is a continuous action, but a lapse in time would be a break, and so would a change of place. These breaks are minimized in modern fiction, and an impression of continuous present action, as there is on the screen, is given by writers who know their technique.

What the reader is told by the omniscient author may be illuminating, but it cannot have the same authority for him as what he sees himself, with his own eyes. "Seeing is believing." The reader prefers the living picture; he would rather have a direct view of the event, of the characters in action, with no narrator and guide coming between him and what is happening, not be forced to see the event through the eyes of somebody else. The scene in its pure form does not need a narrator, just as the playwright does not have to be on the stage with the actors, and with the exit of the author verisimilitude is gained.

The scene then reproduces realistically the very process of living, and each individual scene gives us a close-up of a particular act. It is a single specific moment in the plot, a single dramatic picture, and these single acts together give us the movement of the whole action. The modern tendency is to write the story as a series of single acts, scene by scene, and to give a dramatic or cinematographic imitation of life.

The scene shows us the actors in action, but some narration is usually mixed up in it, and we hear the narrator's voice also as he describes the gestures of the speakers and gives other stage directions which in a play would guide and inform the actors and not form part of the dialogue. In its pure form, with no stage directions, no commentary, the scene eliminates the narrator's voice and is, as in an acted play, only character voice or voices, and this heightens the illusion of reality. In the scene the burden of narration is shifted to the characters themselves and they do the work, they carry the ball.

It is useful for the writer to think of his story as a series of scenes and to visualize the whole story as so many "shots" in a motion picture. The scene is a close-up of the action, made with the writer's imaginative camera and microphone brought close to the actors as they play their parts, and as in a film, the scene records their dialogue and every significant detail of the action. It also records, in fiction, their unspoken speech or internal monologue. The thoughts and feelings of the characters are included.

By working in scenes the writer can spot in advance the weak points in his story, he can see better the incongruities and improbabilities in it that otherwise might escape his attention. The scene makes him the first perceptive reader of his tale. The scene moreover gives us durational realism. A scene on the stage or screen would take as much time to act as it would in real life, and this could be done in fiction too. Through scene we can capture the very process of living in its own time sequence. The scene shows *how* it happens and does not merely give the result after it has happened, and when we are shown how it happens, we might also have the answer to *why*. The reader is allowed to draw his own conclusions from the action, instead of accepting the writer's interpretation of it.

In watching a motion picture, we would not be satisfied by merely reading the subtitles or hearing a narrator's voice explain what the picture is about. We want to see the actors performing their parts. Similarly, to tell the reader that a man leading a comfortable and respectable life developed a fatal disease, visited many specialists and tried to believe he was getting better and would recover, but actually got worse and progressively weaker, and his family continued to live as usual, busy with their social activities, indifferent to his sufferings and annoyed by his mysterious illness, and only an old servant nursed him and faithfully attended to his needs and showed him, a desperately sick man, simple human love and kindness until he died—such information might arouse some emotions in the reader, but his reaction would be relatively mild compared to the effect produced by actually reading *The Death of Ivan Ilyitch* by Leo Tolstoy. A synopsis of the story is not enough, and abstract plots make dull reading. Tolstoy, whose habitual method is scenic, though not to the same extent as generally practiced today, shows in this story the various stages of the disease and the physical and moral struggles of Ivan Ilyitch in such a manner that life becomes an emotional experience of our own when we read it.

In the scene the reader is taken through the process by which the result is obtained. The scene gives the story presentness or immediacy. We cannot narrate events that have not taken place, but the writer can give the impression that it is happening *now*, as though for the first time, and it is a unique event that cannot be repeated. The scene makes past *present*.

There is nothing like scene for giving life and movement to the story. The writer who wants to produce an effect of the present will avoid summary as much as he can. Dialogue by itself—or internal monologue—will give an impression of immediacy. Usually the scene is not only acted out, but talked out, and where there is dialogue there is likely to be scene. But there may be scenes without dialogue, which is talk between two or more persons, or without monologue, spoken or silent. We may have only one person in a scene with his thoughts not given, silent pantomime.

COMPONENTS OF SCENE

When the writer is organizing his material and blocking out his action, he can determine in advance the main events and choose these for scenic treatment. The three classic plot elements of discovery or recognition, reversal or peripety, and disaster or suffering may make exciting scenes. So would the climax of the story, as an obligatory scene. The scene may be an episode, in the more restricted sense of a separate incident or story within a larger story related to the main action but not an integral part of it. If such an episode is included then it is probably important enough to be dramatized. The scene may be a flashback. It may be an external or internal event; thought can be the highest action. The crucial incidents, the turning points, the climactic events, the advances or retreats in the attainment of a goal, pursuit and flight, various stratagems, crises and conflicts, the clash of human wills, arguments, quarrels, showdowns, trouble and misery, wounds, illness, death—these make good scenes.

But the scene need not be confined to the highlights of the plot. There is room also for small incidents, brief friendly meetings, a bit of conversation here and there. All kinds of significant acts, no matter how small, may make good scenes. The scenic or dramatic method can be used also for the apparently insignificant items in the story, and these, like secondary characters, can be extremely valuable in rounding out the picture and creating the necessary background for the principal actors and the main action. The scene is not always reserved for big moments.

A story need not be a series of dramatic explosions. The strength of fiction lies in depicting the slow, almost imperceptible changes, in re-creating the gradual growth and expansion of a consciousness with its consequent chaos or unity. We should not confuse method with content when we use the word scene as synonymous with drama. A dramatic subject with exciting situations may be written by the scenic method, and so may an undramatic subject. There are dramatic stories in non-dramatic form, and non-dramatic stories in dramatic form, scene throughout—as in much popular fiction. Here we are concerned with the method, and not with subject-matter or content, although content and method are by no means independent and content may well determine method. A dramatic subject naturally lends itself to scenic treatment. It is likely to have situations that can be shown and acted out. Some confusion is inevitable because of the various meanings of drama, and of scene, too.

The scene should not be cluttered with information, comment, biography, psychological analysis, description of the setting—the author intruding in third person. At its best it is somewhat stark, *demeublé*—unfurnished. Ideally and by its nature the scene is action pure and simple, and should be freed of those elements in the story that do not quite belong to it, though necessary for the total picture. Much may be smuggled into a scene, especially if it is a long one, in small doses, a little here, a little there, and the reader will take it in with the action without pausing to distinguish the narrator's voice from the character voices. There are few pure scenes in fiction, but the writer should clear the decks before he gets to the action and make it carry, if possible, the final punch. A good scene requires preparation and is the crest of the wave in the story line.

DIALOGUE

The scene then is a clear lucid image of action, revealing a life behind it. And since scene and dialogue go roughly together, and by scene we usually mean action and speech, short sharp sentences make not only for crisp dialogue, but contribute to the momentum of the scene. A staccato style accelerates the action. There is no need to describe repeatedly the gestures of the speakers (as Henry James does so often, and Hemingway does not), and usually "said" or "asked" or "answered" or some such simple word is enough. Gestures and other descriptions used for revealing character or explaining a situation bring in the author's voice and remind the reader he is being told a story. The author's voice should be heard as little as possible. In a dialogue scene the reader's attention should be drawn to what the characters are saying, and the words stand out better by themselves, as do the speakers, if the third person does not enter too often. When the speech is charged with emotional associations or significance, when it is loaded, as it should be, and requires the concentrated attention of the reader, stage directions might annoy, confuse and fatigue him, especially if more than three people are talking. The reader can supply the gesture and intonation himself.

Individualized speech in the authentic idiom of the speaker and in just the right tone makes descriptions of gestures and such third-person details unnecessary. An occasional identification of the speaker is enough, and a highly significant gesture should not be omitted, but the writer should depend on the speech rather than on stage directions in writing his dialogue, and not act like a fussy busybody determined to take the reader by the hand and guide him step by step through his scenes, underscoring the meaning of each speech. In the novels and short stories of Hemingway we have a series of staccato scenes, economically written, with all superfluities removed, and Hemingway is a scenic writer worth studying. His style supports his re-creation of the action. Technically Hemingway is always interesting, though limited in his choice of subjects. He excels in the short-story form, which requires more concentrated economical writing.

Spoken speech differs from unspoken speech and from written discourse, and the fiction writer today must have a good command of all three languages, using now one, now another, instead of writing in the same style or language throughout. The imitation of spoken speech and of interior monologue (unspoken, more incoherent and disorderly), requires a language appropriate to each, and they should be distinguished from each other in the scene, as they are, for instance, in *Ulysses.* Speech expressing emotion and character, necessarily condensed and stylized in fiction, with irrelevancies and repetitions removed, can contribute enormously to the effectiveness of a scene.

The dialogue should suggest, if not fully reproduce, the sharp, abrupt, disjointed nature of spoken English, with its stresses and slacks, its sudden bursts of explosive rhythm. English is a stress language and not a syllabic one in rhythm. A Frenchman who hears English spoken for the first time and is not used to such stresses and slacks would be impressed by its jerky up-and-down quality, by its long sustained vowels with abrupt breaks. In French the accent normally falls on the last syllable. We might say that while the story itself should be interconnected to make one whole, ideally a dramatic unity in structure, the speech of the characters should be somewhat disjointed, without too many connectives.

There are so many individual, class, regional, racial, cultural, period differences in spoken English that no statement about dialogue could apply to all of them, but our test again is mimesis—the closest imitation of actual speech, or thought-speech, expressive of character and emotion at any given moment in the action. In dialogue also the part stands for the whole.

Dialogue should be dramatic, as in a play; not written obviously for information or the history of the characters in quotation marks; not routine small talk; not too long, or a series of set speeches, but short, pointed, loaded.

NO ANTICIPATION OF FUTURE

As the scene is an event in progress, we cannot know in advance what is coming next, as we do not know in real life; we can only guess, make suppositions. This increases the suspense of the story. In the scene as it develops the result is still uncertain, and both character and reader are in a state of curiosity or anxiety about the outcome. "Paul was reading the paper in the college library when Mary came from behind him and blindfolded him with her hands" is the narrative method. "Paul was reading the paper in the college library when he felt two feminine hands blindfold him from behind, and as he pulled the hands away from his eyes and looked up over his shoulder he saw it was Mary" is the scenic method. Paul did not know it was Mary until he saw her, and the scenic method reproduces the original process with its sequence of motions and with the discovery of the girl's identity at the end. One tells us about a past action that has already occurred; it was Mary. The other is present action, scene, and we are shown how it happened.

A story like a poem may be an emotional experience recollected in tranquillity, but when written by the scenic method it is not retrospective; the unique event seems to be occurring for the first time, and this fresh impact makes the scene a more intense experience than recollections would be. The scene gives the story intensity, and intensity is a quality writers strive for. Poetry is more intense than prose. An intense imitation of life—an intense illusion of reality—this is what we want. It is gained through picture, point of view, plot, immediacy, inwardness, style, tone, etc. Intensity gives a tighter story line, drama and unity.

Scene makes for more active reading; it keeps the reader on his toes. As many events in life are mysteries until they are finally cleared up, or remain unsolved, so the element of mystery is maintained through the scene. Scene is not only dramatic in method, but itself makes for drama. It naturally increases the interest of the story in its successive stages and the reader's enjoyment of it is greater when, like the characters in the story, the reader makes the discoveries himself instead of having the author or his narrator tell him about them. (That it was Mary.) The reader is like a spectator in a theatre. In fiction the writer does not disappear completely from the scene; "he said," "she said," are in the narrator's voice; even in its pure form the fictional scene implies the presence of a narrator who has organized and arranged the scenes. No story can pretend to be an exact transcript of life; the scenes are selected events combined into an orderly movement of action; the reader feels that. The author might succeed in effacing himself but somebody wrote the story. The scene nevertheless makes us less conscious of the narrator's voice and we are not too acutely aware of the author's presence. This is an important gain.

The scene then is an episode detached from its surrounding life for emphasis or relief; an arrested moment in the flow of time, photographed and sound-recorded and thrown on the reader's imaginative screen. The reader sees the story as events happening rather than as events fixed or past, a continuously evolving process, with the end uncertain, as in life itself.

In a scene characters come to life as individuals, and they speak and act for themselves, instead of the author speaking

14

and acting for them. Since the original sequence of actions and reactions may be preserved in the scene, it seems to take place by itself, and is obviously a superior imitation. The experience cannot be re-created in any other way, and the scenic method, as old as Homer, is the basic technique in fiction, resting on a solid theoretical foundation and long practice. Non-fiction too is becoming dramatic, and today scene is freely used in "fact stories," in narrative forms of journalism (*Time,* for example), in sports pages, in television and radio commercials, in advertisements, and so on.

Yet indispensable as it is, scene cannot do everything; it would take too much space to tell everything in scene, and certain other values in fiction might be lost. A short story, as a single dramatic episode, might conceivably be all scene, with no more than "said" added by the author, but in a novel, or in the longer tale, the incidents must be tied together. Other problems also arise, by no means absent in the short form, which are best met by another method of mimesis: summary.

2. SUMMARY AND DESCRIPTION

Not everything can, or need, be shown in fiction. The writer can also *tell* a story. Summary needs a teller, and this is admittedly a weakness; it does not have the seemingly spontaneous movement of the scene; it is not something acted out before the eyes of the reader, who is listening to somebody tell him about it. But summary has its rightful place in the structure of the story and can be extremely useful.

Summary brings in the author, or his alter ego, his spokesman, unless it is summary by character, in which case it becomes dramatic. There is a change in voice from scene to summary and from summary to scene, and the reader unconsciously prefers a character voice, because it means more mimetic writing. When the writer speaks through his own voice the all-important element of mimesis is definitely less and the reader's interest decreases. Hearing is substituted for seeing, and the ear is weaker than the eye in the creation of mental images. Nevertheless, no matter how scenic, a story requires a narrator. Omniscience may be eliminated, but not the narrator's voice. We still hear it.

The narrator's voice added to character voices creates variety, even when that voice is an intrusion. A narrator's voice can unify the material, and a story told in one voice has a natural unity of tone, as in Poe's tales. If the speaker is one of the characters, as in a first-person story, and speaks in his own idiom, as does Jake Barnes in *The Sun Also Rises* or the barber in Ring Lardner's "Haircut," we do not care if it is summary; it is still a genuine mimesis, and dramatic.

"Paul's Case" by Willa Cather is nearly all summary, a succession of solid paragraphs unbroken by direct dialogue. We hear Paul speak only once, a few casual words, and we never hear him again, nor do we hear any of the other characters in the story. Yet it is a moving tale, an example of a dramatic subject in non-dramatic form. In this tragedy of a misfit, a problem boy in a high school dreams of another, a more ideal, life; he is unable to adjust himself to his commonplace environment and stands on railroad tracks with the blue Adriatic and Algerian sands flashing before his eyes until hit by the onrushing locomotive that crushes his picture-making brain and hurls him through the air "into the immense design of things." In "Paul's Case" we have an author's account of an event we remember.

The scenic method by itself will not make a story interesting. Scene is of little value in the absence of a significant emotional experience, which must always be our starting point in reading, or writing, a story. The experience in "Paul's Case," it may be argued, needs no heightening by scene, and the charm of Willa Cather's writing lies in its quiet tone. It is deliberately pitched at a lower emotional level, as most good stories are, and the picture-making ability of the author, the descriptive language, strengthens the summary method she uses throughout the story. We do not hear Paul speaking, but it is so pleasant to hear the narrator's voice that we do not mind it, and the impersonal manner of narration, with Willa Cather effacing herself as author, and being careful not to remind us of her presence by direct allusions to herself in the manner of old Victorian novelists, makes the story more dramatic. A stylist can achieve much with summary, and charmed by the language, we may insist as readers that the writer speak as often as possible in his own voice.

Summary, unlike scene, does not individualize characters through their actions and speech. It throws the whole burden of narration on the shoulders of the author or his narrator. It gives us experience secondhand. Scene is self-explanatory; in summary the narrator explains. Summary tends to be abstract, discursive, with something fanciful and "literary" clinging to it, in contrast to the concrete specific act of the scene. Scene at its best has the impact of life. In it, the characters are on their own (with an occasional assistance from the narrator); in summary they lack this independence. In scene, the reader

also is on his own, judging the action for himself and inter-
preting it in his own way; in summary, the reader is guided by
the narrator, who speaks in his own voice, whether or not the
reader is directly addressed. Something is happening in the
scene; in summary it has already happened.

Summary makes for distance. It does not give us a close-up
of the action as it occurs; it is a long shot. We no longer have
the words spoken by the characters to others or to themselves;
the narrator summarizes their speech, spoken or silent, and
he is the only speaker we hear. The dialogue or internal
monologue is indirect, in third person, and dissolves in the
general stream of the narrative. The third person itself makes
for distance. Summary may reveal the characters, describe
their actions and thoughts and feelings, but it is not a close
re-creation as in the scene. It does not have the power of
dramatic imitation, and the reader is deprived of the pleasure
of viewing the event for himself.

Summary lacks the vividness of the scene, the immediacy,
the presentness of the action acted out by the actors. There is
obviously a difference between an event shown to us while
it is taking place, and merely telling about it. Today's reader
does not care to read synopses or outlines, but demands fully
developed stories, told the way it really happened, and no
rhetorical tricks will satisfy him if the concrete event is missing. The fiction writer speaks best through pictures, and in
the imitation of life, there is no real substitute for the moving picture of the scene. Summary not only makes action
distant in space and time, but also makes it abstract, unless
written in highly visual prose, and even then some of the
basic weakness of summary remains; style is burdened with
greater responsibilities in the absence of scene, and there is a
danger of overwriting and heightening the event through language, when it should be the other way around.

In summary we do not have the give-and-take of opposing
forces that makes for lively reading. We do not have the clash
of voices, of wills in conflict, of contradictions within the
character: the drama of contrast. With all his sentimentality
and melodrama Charles Dickens continues to attract us by

the extraordinary vitality of his characters and he remains to this day a master of the scene. Summary is not the language of conflict. It tends to become description, rhetoric, exposition; instead of imitating characters in action it becomes too often a commentary upon them. Even when not addressed to the reader, the commentary is for the benefit of the reader, and reminds the reader he is being told a story; that weakens or dispels the illusion of reality. The commentary may be necessary, or an excellent thing in itself, but it does not meet the test of mimesis. It is something added by the author and no part of the original event. It changes poetic to rhetoric.

But only life is fully scenic. In fiction, the scene itself is actually a summary, a condensed action, and the art of narration would be impossible without summary. Summary is the birthright of the fiction writer, and one great advantage he enjoys over the playwright. The difference between scene and summary is one of degree rather than of kind.

We have then acknowledged the defects of summary. It lowers the mimetic quality of a story. When the author speaks, what he says is colored by his own sentiments and opinions, no matter how impersonal and objective he tries to be, even weeding out most of his adjectives and adverbs. There is inevitably some distortion of reality from the reader's point of view when he is forced to see events through someone else's eyes. The same distortion exists even when the narrator is one of the characters in the story, although the authority of an internal voice may be greater than the author's. Summary by character may be more credible, but the objection to summary is not entirely overcome; summary in character voice is still too general, not particular enough, and the specific incident is missing. Somebody in the story is describing it for us, while we are denied a direct view of the event.

Yet summary does many important things in a story. It links the scenes together and gives the story continuity and unity. If we consider scenes the main building blocks, summaries are the cement in creative construction. Summary may be reduced to the minimum, but that minimum is essential by the law of artistic economy if nothing else. Summary can span long periods of time when nothing of great importance happens, and the writer does not have to dwell at length upon them.

"And this life lasted for ten years," we read in "The Necklace" by Guy de Maupassant. "At the end of ten years everything was paid off . . . Madame Loisel looked old now." It is not necessary for Maupassant to show these ten years in detail, for the reader at this stage of the story can imagine what they were like. Through this brief summary statement Maupassant prepares us for the final scene; how one Sunday, while walking along the Champs-Élysées for a bit of rest and relaxation, Madame Loisel meets Madame Forestier from whom she had borrowed the diamond necklace she wore at the ball, and which she then lost. She and her husband ruined their lives to buy another necklace like it, paying thirty-six thousand francs for it. Madame Loisel has changed so much that the still youthful Madame Forestier does not recognize her until she says, "I am Mathilde Loisel." And Mathilde learns that the necklace she borrowed was an imitation, worth at most five hundred francs.

Summary gives the writer freedom of movement from scene to scene, from one high point of the action to another. The skill with which the writer arranges his material into scene and summary shows his knowledge of story values and his sense of form. Henry Fielding boldly explained to the reader the necessity of not telling all in a much quoted passage.

> When any extraordinary scene presents itself (as we trust will often be the case), we shall spare no pains nor paper to open it at large to our readers; but if whole years should pass without producing anything worthy his notice, we shall not be afraid of chasm in our history, but shall hasten on to matters of consequence, and leave such periods of time totally unobserved.
> . . . My reader then is not to be surprised, if, in the course of this work, he shall find some chapters very short, and others altogether as long; some that contain only the time of a single day, and others that comprise years; in a word, if my history sometimes seems to stand still, and sometimes to fly.
>
> (*Tom Jones*, Book II, I)

A story is a dramatic concentration of life and the writer skips the detail of months and years in which nothing remarkable happens and re-creates the extraordinary rather than the ordinary. He sees the uncommon in the common, the general in the particular, and every good story is something of a wonder tale. It would be boring to tell the reader everything. The gaps in the action and characterization stimulate the reader's imagination; he fills them in himself.

The action moves by fits and starts; it does not proceed at a uniform rate of speed. Scene accelerates the movement, summary slows it down, and generally the longer the scene the greater its power over the reader, although length by itself cannot be the sole criterion of its effect. Short scenes, short chapters, chop up a story; long scenes unify it, and especially in an episodic plot, long scenes or long chapters give better continuity. Since the scene is a continuous act it has a natural unity of its own and makes for an unbroken story line, as long as it lasts. Continuous action is more lifelike. Film and fiction can do without curtains. The short story particularly is a unified event, and some novels, like *Mrs. Dalloway* by Virginia Woolf, have no chapter divisions. The sustained scene heightens the illusion of reality and may be an excellent unifying and intensifying device, but what seems to be an unbroken story line is actually disconnected. Even in the cinema we do not have an uninterrupted sequence from beginning to end; scenes fade in and fade out or dissolve into the next scene, but it is done so unobtrusively we scarcely notice it (or do not mind it if we do). The same effect may be gained in fiction by short, skillful summaries carrying us from scene to scene, and the impression of one continuous movement is maintained.

The summaries that link scenes also disconnect them. Summary means a break in the action, a lapse in the continuity of time, or a change of place, but if it does not happen too often, the story keeps moving despite, and because of, these breaks. An extended summary, as when the author inserts an essay or biography or a long description in the story, would break the continuity of the action. It may be done in a novel like *War and Peace* because of the huge scale on which it is built, but the damage is evident even in *War and Peace*. Today such massive authorial intrusions are avoided by most craft-conscious writers.

VERSATILITY OF SUMMARY

The weakness of summary may be turned to advantage. Beautiful economies may be achieved through summary and it is more versatile than scene. It gives a story depth, body, vividness, variety, freedom of movement, and brings out its full meaning, the philosophy of the tale. Summary may be narrative, descriptive, expository, or all three at once. We noted earlier that summary creates distance; it is a long shot. The long shot is as necessary as the close-up. Imagine a motion picture shot entirely in close-ups. The control of distance means among other things the control of intensities, of reader attention, and this may be done through summary. The writer changes the position of his camera to get certain effects.

In the scene we are sometimes too close to the action to understand it; summary gives perspective. As readers or writers, we see the situation better by withdrawing a little, just as a painter steps back to take a good look at what he is doing on the canvas, and the viewer of the finished painting regulates his distance to see it better. Then too, by supplying the connections between the incidents, summary is an aid to a better understanding of the story. We may go from the particular, scene, to the general, through summary.

Since summary favors a more detached spectator attitude, it may be used for giving the reader emotional relief when his nerves are frayed by the scenes. When a scene arouses too much anxiety, summary allays it. The reader's emotional tension relaxes when he comes to a summary, and as he moves back he is not so intimately involved in the events and can rest for a while—until the next scene.

There are certain subjects, certain events, that should not be rendered too vividly. The Greeks, who had a taste for bloody dramas and relished the horrors of family murders, took the precaution of having them committed offstage. Horace cautioned against representing on the stage certain actions that had better be done offstage. "Do not let Medea murder her sons before the people." Greek tragic writers sought subjects in which love turns to murderous hate, friends become enemies, a man kills his brother, a son kills his father or mother, or intends to, and, as Aristotle says in his *Poetics*, such situations arouse the pity and fear of the spectators, and he calls it the tragic pleasure. Such nerve-shattering events are better narrated than brought close to the reader and acted out before his eyes. There are things that should be told and not shown. Too close identification with a character or a special milieu or situation may arouse so much anxiety in the reader that the story, halfway, leaves him in such a state of nervous exhaustion, that he cannot finish it. Then there are those who recoil from intimate contact with others, even if they are only fictional people, who do not want to touch or be touched, and summary lets them wear gloves while reading. Some stories should not be too minutely documented in their particulars.

If I may be allowed to introduce a personal note here, let me say that I did not take this precaution in writing my novel *98.6°*. I tried to give an honest picture of life in some hospital wards, and poetic intensity was my watchword. It took me four years to write the book. "A Snake Pit of Tuberculosis," one reviewer called it. "Tale Affects All Senses," was the title of another review. As I see it now, the story was not properly distanced; it was too vivid in spots. A more relaxed, ironic tone would have been better, and irony requires distance. One can be too grimly realistic and hell-bent on mimesis. There may be dramatic wisdom in offstage actions, and summary tones down the horror of dreadful events and milieus, but on the other hand a writer should not skip a scene when a scene is called for. To show it is much harder than to tell it. The difficulties of fiction begin with the picture in scene, character, setting, but there is a point of diminishing returns in showing, and the writer should switch from the eye to the ear to hold the reader's attention.

It may be worth repeating that in his famous definition of tragedy Aristotle says that tragedy is the imitation by men acting, and not through narration, of a serious, worthy and celebrated action; by having the right magnitude or length and grandeur, in pleasing language, the action is complete in itself, one perfect whole; and, through incidents that arouse pity and fear, the catharsis or purgation of these emotions is brought about. The Greeks were a highly emotional people —they still are—and while recognizing the place of the emotions in human life, they feared them. We do not know for sure what Aristotle means by catharsis, but obviously he had in mind its healing and purifying effect and considered it a salutary influence on the spectator. Art can be an antidote to sorrow and pain. We may assume the Greeks acquired a certain intellectual serenity by the release of their pent-up emotions while watching the performance of a tragedy, and what were purely personal emotions for them, became universalized through the plot of a tragedy which dramatized a story with universal implications; or these personal emotions were redirected to worthier and more impersonal aims, so that ultimately the play became a means of spiritual readjustment and re-education, a way to wisdom through suffering, pathos-mathos, carrying the spectator or reader from the personal to the universal, and restoring his inner equilibrium.

What is of especial interest to us is that Aristotle laid such stress on the importance of making the tragedy—and the epic —an emotional experience for the receptor. The play or narrative that produced a strong emotional reaction was a good play or story in his view. Mimesis comes first, catharsis comes later; though catharsis in the Aristotelian sense is too much to expect from the modern reader or theatre-goer. Whether the end result of the emotional response is purgation and conducive to virtue and happiness is another matter, and technically what we should bear in mind is the necessity of the emotional response itself. If a story stirs the emotions of the reader, the writer need not worry about entertaining

24

him. It is not insignificant that the *Poetics,* our basic text in the craft of fiction, the oldest, and still the best, is a treatise on structure. It points out the connection between emotion and structure. Structure makes possible the re-creation of the emotional experience, which will remain formless, chaotic and uncommunicated otherwise. We shall return to this topic when we discuss in more detail problems of plot.

CONTROL OF EMOTION AND
AESTHETIC DISTANCE

The writer must regulate the reader's emotional reactions. He may intensify an emotional experience through scene just so much, after which, as indicated above, he has to establish a margin of safety through summary. Sophisticated fiction tends to a lower emotional tone, and the scene, unrelieved by summary, may be too much for any reader to take. We live in an age of social distances, and summary perhaps is a psychological necessity today.

It is largely through summary that the fiction writer piles up his details, and summary can cover a lot more territory than the scene. Scene excludes; summary includes. Its reach is longer. It is not confined to one particular incident at a particular place and time. Summary can range far and wide. We need summary for the slow march of years, for the erosions of time. We need it for recollection, for retrospect, for reflection and comment. The basic method of *À la recherche du temps perdu* by Marcel Proust is summary, as is the endless monologue in *Finnegans Wake.* Henry James wrote *The Awkward Age* in scenes, like a play, but it is not a very good novel and he did not repeat the experiment. The fiction writer should not deny himself the privilege of the general survey and the freedom of movement from peak to valley and from valley to peak, between present and past, that summary gives him.

Some readers apparently cannot have enough direct dialogue, but dialogue can become monotonous after a few

25

pages, especially when nothing much happens. Like some movies, a story can be too "talky." The stage relies on dialogue more than the screen—it has to—and film and fiction are closer in method than the novel and the play. There is no summary in the stage play, except through dialogue as part of a scene, but a motion picture, through subtitles, narrator's voice, montage, locations, sets, process shots, and other devices, approaches the freedom of fiction. A lot can happen simultaneously on the screen, as in a novel. The film can also narrate, as the play did once through the Greek or Shakespearean chorus, and is attempting to do again in the epic theatre.

Scene is the foreground, summary the background, and without the background, the foreground appears thin and abstract. The scene by itself cannot give the movement of a wider life around it; that is the job of summary. The scene cuts off the immediate event from its surroundings, its tendency is to narrow it down, to detach and isolate it, just as a stage play is an isolated action, with its scenery and properties suggesting the wider life from which it is separated. On the stage the scenery and props are "summary." In fiction the writer has to supply the scenery and props himself. Sets are a later development in the theatre. The Elizabethan stage was practically bare.

Through summary the writer can give the social and geographical aspects of the story. Summary gives the action space, and even magnitude and grandeur. It is independent of time and place, and through it the writer can give the past, present and future of his characters, moving back and forth at will.

As the scene itself is summary, a condensed action, to write a story means to summarize. But there is more in summary. Scene is piecemeal imitation, act by act, speech by speech, drama; summary deals with reality on a larger scale, bringing together great masses of fact and information that cannot be given through scene and making the story a more coherent whole. The story is tied together through summaries; this would be particularly important in a loose, sprawling plot.

Summary, like the plot itself, is a synthesis. It is putting things together to make one whole, and doing this is part of the artistic rearrangement of life and reflects the unifying vision of the writer. The basic structural process in writing fiction is to form one perfect whole by the right combination of a story's various parts or elements, and above all of its incidents.

By enlarging the scale, summary makes indirectly for greater realism, gives us the whole picture, even though as a method it is not a close mimesis of the action. The modern novel, and to a lesser extent the short story, is epic in structure. As we call summary the narrative method, we evidently believe it is natural to narration, and a story is a dramatic summary. The great novels are built on a large scale; this is important for beauty, the ultimate aim of technique. When the screen is widened, summary comes in, and with it, the complexity of life. Some of the intensity of drama may be lost, but the fiction writer can well afford this loss to gain other effects: the picture of a whole society, the imitation of places and manners, of a way of life, as in *Madame Bovary*. The scale is reduced in the short story, which lends itself more readily to close scenic treatment because it is short and can be more dramatic in structure, more like a play in method. Some successful novels are written like short stories or like plays with the whole action taking place in one day, but a subject may also be ruined by overdramatization. It is difficult to make changes in a character convincing if they occur within a few hours and much may be lost for the sake of intensity or unity.

Summary makes for density in writing, packs prose with concrete details of the setting, of the characters and their actions, and the story becomes richer and more significant through summary. By enlarging the scale to lifelike proportions, the writer gets the reader off the narrow stage of drama and out into the open as it were. Summary may be a counterpoise to theatrical effects, to quick turns of fortune, sudden reversals, swift changes in character and motive, which are not too convincing even on the stage. Lost tension may be recovered through the increasing suspense. Summary may be invaluable as a delaying maneuver, postponing the blow or the climax. Intensification is not always gained through speed. When a man speaks slowly in a tense situation, the tension increases; there is more power, more drama, in his speech. If there is no talk in summary, there may well be the drama of silence in it. Note how the music stops at a highly dramatic moment in the movies and the action is played in silence or largely in silence. Silence can be a powerful dramatic device.

Summary, then, widens and deepens the scope of the story and, by supplying the connective tissues, makes it an organic interrelated whole. It breaks up the monotonous sequence of scenes, making for variety and diversion, for change of pace. With the main action concentrated in a few big scenes, the events of other years and of peripheral actions, of incidental byplays, may be summarized, and the intervals between the main events need not be shown if they can be told, but the shorter these intervals the better. If we may risk another generalization here, let us say the safe rule for the writer to follow is summary in small amounts, here and there, without making the bridges from scene to scene too long. A lengthy summary in the midst of the action, with the story well on its way, and in prosaic prose, can be deadly. The craft-conscious writer avoids full stops and keeps the story moving, unless he has good reasons for not doing so. He knows that generally interest falls off when the reader comes to a summary. Crossing the bridge can be dull business, but it has to be done, and the quicker it is done the better, if there is no reason for lingering on the bridge.

SCENE OR SUMMARY

Usually the writer can tell in advance whether the subject he has chosen is dramatic or panoramic, a scene or summary kind of story, and always the best method is that which does the most for the particular subject. A novel crowded with hundreds of characters and covering a long span of time, like

War and Peace or a family chronicle like *Buddenbrooks* by
Thomas Mann, needs a lot of summary; so does a novel without a hero like *Vanity Fair,* in which there is no strict dramatic
progression of events. Thackeray began as an essayist, and
one can see in his writing the affinity that summary has with
the essay and memoir. A story, grounded in its particular environment, which gives a picture of customs and costumes,
one that is definitely located, in Russia, in Germany, in Mayfair, in Yonville, with the action extended over many years,
cannot do without summaries.

One of the first things a writer must do in organizing his
material is to place his scenes and summaries. He has to de-
cide in advance what goes into scene and what goes into summary and work out his scene line, and summary line. The
scene line is the main line of action, supported by the summary line, and the writer weaves scenes and summaries together into a pattern that makes a well-balanced whole. During the actual writing process some scenes will emerge as
summaries and some summaries will break up into separate
scenes, but the initial planning can save the writer false motions and wasted time and effort. Is it going to be a close-up,
a medium shot, or a long panoramic shot? Essentially, the
organization of a story on dramatic principles is a problem
in distance, and not only scene and summary but point of
view also have to do with the control of distance and the
related problem of authority.

Once he has placed his scenes and summaries and integrated his two lines the writer can visualize his story as a
whole and have a fairly clear idea of what it might look like
in the end. Like a film director he can move his camera and
microphone back and forth, now coming close to the actors
on the set and now moving away from them; now recording
their speech, and now photographing a panoramic view of the
New York skyline or an island in the South Pacific. If the
writer takes care of his big scenes, the summaries in between
will probably take care of themselves. The story is built around
scenes, not summaries, important as they are in the total structure, and the writer must hold on to his main scene line, the

central action, and not get lost in summaries or secondary events. Occasionally he will leave a gap in the story, now and then omitting a summary. Summaries may be eliminated by a break on the page or by beginning a new chapter. Since scene can draw the reader into the action, it may be wise for the writer to begin with a scene and cut summary down to a minimum in the opening pages, but there can be no general rule about this. Summary should not be introduced too soon, or the momentum and illusion gained by the scene would be dispelled. It comes too soon in *Madame Bovary*, in the first chapter after the schoolroom scene.

Scene can merge into summary, summary into scene, often in the same paragraph, or even in the same sentence, and the narrator's voice can be mixed with character voices. There are medium shots in prose, with some direct dialogue in quotes in an otherwise solid paragraph of summary. It is not always possible to tell a scene from summary since the two methods overlap, but it is a good habit to watch the change from scene to summary and summary to scene when reading fiction.

As we have defined the scene as a single action acted out by the characters, one particular incident, it has to be a unique occasion that happens only once. "John said, 'I will not do it,'" is a scene. "John would say, 'I will not do it,'" is summary. *Would* means he said it more than once. "John drove to the beach" might be a scene, but "John often drove to the beach," or "used to drive to the beach" is summary. *Often, always, every now and then, usually, used to,* and such expressions make it a habitual or repetitive action. By changing a few words and eliminating *would* or *used to,* summary can be made into scene and the story given immediacy with an unbroken story line, for *would* and *used to* are author or narrator words. It is sometimes surprising how a story can improve by this simple action, but there are also legitimate occasions for *would* when it should be used.

The difference between scene and summary should be fairly clear by now. Each method has its strengths and weaknesses and they complement each other. We move in and out of scene and summary continuously when we read or write a story, and generally, as readers at least, we are not aware of it. Some people are astonished when they first learn about scene and summary and it becomes an important reading tool for them. It is the basic writing tool. Expository, or fact, writers become hardened in their habit of writing in summary and cannot write fiction until they learn to write in scene, shifting from explanation or commentary in one voice, their own, to imitation in several voices, from article or essay or editorial to moving pictures of life.

DESCRIPTION

To these two methods of narration we may add a third, description. This is a separate method although summary can be descriptive, and description, if not dramatized, is actually a kind of summary. Literary description is a reproduction of sense impressions, and in a story description is part of narration. In its pure form, description is more likely to be found in an essay or article than in fiction. Since events happen in time, narrative is time conditioned, but description is not. In a story, however, we cannot definitely say this is description and this is narration, for description also narrates and narration also describes and both serve much the same purpose in fiction.

Since the image is basic to all kinds of imaginative writing, description is artistic by its very nature. Image and imitation are related words. Sense impressions are expressed by the writer in the form of images, and imagination feeds on the memory of these earlier sense impressions. The writer depends on his power to create mental images in the reader; imagination is another word for this insight and the unifying inner vision of the artist. It is seeing more deeply and essentially in new combinations.

Description gives a sensory representation of reality. It is painting in words and adds a spatial dimension to fiction. When we look at a painting we see an arrested moment on the canvas. It may suggest movement, it may be a narrative

31

picture, but is not moving. In life the picture moves; in life there are no still pictures. But the writer, like the painter, can arrest the moment, freeze it, hold it, to gain dramatic intensity.

As news cameramen want action shots, and editors are always looking for pictures with a dramatic impact, so writers should describe life in motion. Aristotle, in his *Rhetoric* (Book III), explains some of the qualities of good description. The graphic style makes the reader *see* things, he says, and he advises the use of expressions that show things "in a state of activity." He mentions Homer's practice of giving "metaphorical life to lifeless objects." Moving objects attract more attention, as in neon lighting and advertising posters. The use of active verbs is based on the same principle. Both living and lifeless things are seen more vividly when represented in a state of activity.

If a writer wants to describe a sunrise, for instance, he would give us the closest imitation of it if he were to show the sun in motion. Sunrise is a tremendous activity in nature, a daily battle between light and darkness, a cosmic drama in an unending cycle, in which neither the sun nor the earth stand still, they are moving, they are in action forever. A static picture of the sunrise would not be realistic. The description should suggest its movement in nature, in its own time sequence, and could be integrated with the action of the characters. We might see the sunrise through a character's eyes or through the author's eyes, depending on the point of view. It could be a cumulative or impressionistic description; the details arranged in a spatial, chronological, causal or psychological order, fitting the mode of the story as a whole. It could have its own unity with one predominant impression.

It takes a poet to write really good descriptions. Description, like summary in general, should not arrest the movement of the story, unless definitely used for a break in the action, for a change of scene, or for freezing the action. A lyrical interlude, marking the end of a sequence of events, as a dividing line in the story before the beginning of another series of events, can be a beautiful pause, and highly

effective. A bombing raid followed by the picture of a peaceful countryside, the contrast between the roar of the planes
and a bumble bee, the restoration of the normal after a fire
or riot or murder—these may be good places to insert a picture. The scene itself should not be burdened with too many
descriptive details, which are more useful and appropriate between the scenes. When action lags, description can hold the
reader's interest. Description does not need an event.

Description by the author may be objective or subjective;
description by character is subjective, but objective and subjective are relative terms in fiction, and the objective author
is only less subjective. Everyone sees differently, and sees
differently at different times, and what attracts our attention
depends largely on our mood and interests at the moment. A
woman may be ravishingly beautiful to one man and plain
to another; a city may be enchanting to one person, and
hideous to another. Description is inevitably a personal comment on the object described and reveals the attitude of the
observer. There are few neutral adjectives. Images tell the
truth about a writer or his characters.

In a story written by the scenic method with the description
interwoven with the action, there is no anticipation in description, and the picture is incomplete at the beginning, and,
if it is completed at all, complete at the end. The description
of a town or a character gradually emerges from events,
but within this larger picture there may be minor pictures
completed at once, in summary form, and the method is always mixed, in varying degrees. Balzac first had to set his
stage even if it took him a hundred pages to do so. The modern writer who has Blazac's lust for significant details of a
place and can characterize his people through setting with
Balzac's skill can write block descriptions in advance and
complete the picture before the action starts. Yet we should
not overlook the advantages of dramatized pictures, description blending with the flow of action, scattered throughout the
story as the action progresses instead of given by the author
wholesale. There may be legitimate occasions for a formal
still picture, a set piece, such as the description of Yonville in

33

Madame Bovary, but in general the writer is safer with the dramatic method.

Everything we have said about summary may be applied to description. It is used for transitions, for linking scenes together, for variety, for change of pace and place, for breaking the pace, for suspense, for filling the gaps in the continuity, for street scenes, crowd scenes, panoramas, montage effects.

With all its careful economies, *Madame Bovary* is built on a larger epic scale than a strictly dramatic story would be, and its basic method is scene-and-description. In Flaubert summary is almost invariably descriptive. The charm and power of the novel lie in its word pictures, and it is not so much the acted scenes we remember as the marvelous descriptions in it. This novel could serve as a model for studying the art of description in fiction. When we read it, we are on a farm near Tostes; we are at the château of the marquis who gives a ball, the scene of Emma's introduction to high society; we are in Yonville and Rouen. The book is packed with closely observed details of people and places, and the setting is part of the theme if not the main theme, as the subtitle, *Madame Bovary, Mœurs de Provence,* indicates. Flaubert's principal concern was these provincial mores, and he gave a scientifically accurate description of the environment he knew as a native of Normandy. This is essentially a pictorial subject, the description of a society; it is not a conflict of individual wills, nor a dramatic subject, as Percy Lubbock has pointed out in *The Craft of Fiction.* Emma's own story is not as important as the account of the environment in which she lived, dreamed, and died, a victim of the romantic quest. Flaubert himself called it a biographical novel.

The action in *Madame Bovary* is continuously interrupted by descriptive paragraphs and, despite the relative absence of dialogued scenes, notably in part one, we have a sense of immediacy in reading the book. The descriptive summaries are even more vivid than the scenes. The sharply visualized closely observed detail makes everything real. Flaubert is always specific. "Under the hangar there were two large carts and four plows." "A young woman in a blue merino dress

34

adorned with three flounces." If there is a draft coming in under a door Flaubert notices and records it. This minute description adds to the documentary value of the novel and the modern reader can imaginatively reconstruct this section of Normandy a hundred years ago. *Madame Bovary* may be read and reread for its descriptions alone, and the reader will discover significant new details at each reading—a test of a good book. With Flaubert, it is *two* carts, *four* plows, *three* flounces. He lavished his attention on the physical setting and the social milieu. Though he may not have loved the French bourgeoisie, he loved the landscape. *Madame Bovary* is a basic text in the craft of fiction and we shall refer to it from time to time. It is a completely modern novel.

By the middle of the nineteenth century the influence on man of his physical and social environment was fully recognized. Realism was based, one might say, on the pots and pans of kitchen walls; the painting technique of the Dutch school applied to fiction. In older paintings, as in novels, the pots and pans are missing. There is surprisingly little description in *Robinson Crusoe;* its summaries are not strengthened by pictures, the concrete specific detail is missing. Daniel Defoe had never been on the island he described and unlike Flaubert, was no poet. Flaubert is full of objects, things.

Description, then, makes for immediacy in the absence of scene. In *The Gentleman from San Francisco* by Ivan Bunin there are only a few lines of casual dialogue, but the description of the great ocean liner is so vivid (even in translation) that we are there, with the unnamed merchant prince who is sailing to Europe with his wife and daughter to enjoy life. But it is too late, he dies in Italy of a heart attack, and his body is shipped back on the same liner. A floating Babylon with its palatial ballroom and marble baths, it has nine-course dinners, jeweled ladies and Negroes in red jackets. The ship is named *Atlantis* and given a personality against which the figure of the gentleman is vague by comparison. To Ivan Bunin the American multimillionaire was evidently an exotic, and he writes about him as if he were a Chinese mandarin from San Francisco, with "something Mongolian in his yellowish face." Bunin is a poet, and this is a parable on death and the vanity of earthly possessions. The American here is Everyman. The people dancing at the ball aboard the ship, on the return voyage with a handsome young couple playing again at being in love—they are hired for that purpose—are dancing a dance of death, though they do not know it. Death is the most important passenger on the *Atlantis* and will reduce all of them to the condition of the gentleman from San Francisco, whose body is hidden somewhere in the great cold depths of the ship plowing through the Atlantic. Dead at fifty-eight, he was a tired desiccated old man in middle age. He did not enjoy, if he still had any capacity for enjoying, the love of young Neapolitan girls, and the carnivals at Nice and Monte Carlo, the bullfights in Seville, Venice, Paris, Athens, Constantinople —one of those rich Americans who, it was said, went to Paris to die. The reader is made to feel that his body is put where it belongs after all the homage the gentleman received when he was alive.

The other characters in Bunin's story are also types rather than individuals. In a parable characters are usually personifications rather than persons. Summary here serves an artistic purpose and keeps the dead man at a distance as an allegorical figure, and the ship is brought forward for a close symbolic view. The description of the ship gives an air of reality to the tale, with the moral that death is the only reality.

SETTING A STORY BY SCENE

Since the scene is an action occurring at a particular place and time, the where and when is an integral part of it. This is the setting, which supplies the time and space dimensions of the scene. To draw a cinematic analogy again, the actors must perform on a sound stage or on location, and sets are built or locations chosen before a story is filmed. It cannot be pure action in a vacuum; without the background, the scenery and props, there is no motion picture—and similarly the modern realistic story is action and sets.

Indeed by scene, we not only mean the act but the place where it occurs; this was the original meaning of the word in Greek. We say "the scene of the crime," or a "scene painter." It is the particular place and time that makes the action a scene, and we noted that the scene ends when there is a change in time or place. Instead of calling a story action-and-sets, we might call it scene in both meanings of the word. The story then is a scene in its structure, at once action and setting, drama and picture, scene and summary.

How much of the scene in this double sense should be action and speech—speech itself is a form of action—and how much of it place and time, or setting, is an intriguing question. The proportion will vary from story to story or from writer to writer, and perhaps, from country to country, as the proportion did vary at different periods in the history of prose fiction. There is more action in modern American writing. Scene, drama, seem natural to this country. The American is a man of action. European fiction tends more to the essay form.

The setting may be the most important element in a story, as in *Madame Bovary,* and good narrative prose is first of all accurate description. In Poe's stories, we have Gothic sets for the familiar, eerie atmosphere of his tales. "The Fall of the House of Usher" is top-heavy with decaying sets; no wonder it collapses at the end. In a story like "The Killers," which is almost entirely scene, we have an example of the stark, *demeublé* technique, but there are a few sets in it, and these are described briefly by Hemingway.

> The door of Henry's lunchroom opened and two men came in. They sat down at the counter. . . . Outside it was getting dark. The street light came on outside the window. . . . The two of them went out the door. George watched them through the window, pass under the arc light and across the street. In their tight overcoats and derby hats they looked like a vaudeville team. George went back through the swinging door into the kitchen and untied Nick and the cook. . . . Outside the arc light shone through the bare branches of a tree. Nick went up the street beside the car tracks and

37

turned at the next arc light down a side street. Three houses up the street was Hirsch's rooming house. Nick walked up the two steps and pushed the bell. . . . Nick opened the door and went into the room. Ole Andresen was lying on the bed with all his clothes on. He had been a heavy prize-fighter and he was too long for the bed. He lay with his head on two pillows. He did not look at Nick.

The setting is not made too particular, this could be any lunchroom and street light and rooming house in an American small town. Even Hemingway has his limitations when it comes to sensory prose, but in this story a few flat statements are enough, and the killers in their tight overcoats and derby hats stand out the more sharply against this background. The attention of the reader is drawn to them and not to the commonplace surroundings, to the extraordinary rather than the ordinary in this small town. If cluttered up with too much scenery and props, the story would lose its bullet-like impact. What we have in effect are a few stage directions, the rest reading like a play. This is description through action, and as action.

A common mistake of beginners is to have too many descriptive details in a short story, particularly in the opening paragraphs. They scatter the reader's attention and confuse him, and he loses track of the characters. We can remember only so many facts about a place or the appearance of people. In a short action story like "The Killers" a few revealing strokes of the brush seem just right, but there is more room for descriptions in *The Old Man and the Sea*. If a story is not located, if the necessary concrete visible details of the setting, the when and where, are missing, if there is no furniture at all, the story becomes unreal. The setting itself tells a story and is an important aid in characterization. A few props can save the writer pages of character description. The setting makes the action more believable and lends a factual air to implausible tales.

Through scene and summary, then, the writer rearranges the complex chaotic events of life in an orderly manner and controls the reader's attention, choosing the right distance for various parts of the story and making it more economical and convincing.

To give form to what is formless—that is the challenge before the fiction writer, and he meets this through scene and summary, structuring his events into a unified narrative with the proper emphasis and coherence, now showing, now telling, now speaking through one voice, now speaking through several voices, and having the reader follow him through the fog, his path illumined by the word.

3. THIRD PERSON

Since a story is a coherent account of a significant emotional experience the question naturally arises, whose account is it, or who is telling the story? The writer may (1) tell the story himself, from his own point of view and on his own authority, as he sees it. He may tell it (2) from a character's point of view, as the character sees it. Or (3) he may tell it through a character in first person, making a character his narrator. These are the three main choices before him, and the form and content of the story would depend largely on which method he uses.

The choice of a narrator may well be a crucial one. If the reader gets the writer's version of the event, the account is given by someone outside the action. The writer is not in the story, and he is not writing about himself. If the reader gets a character's version of the same event, the account is given by someone in the story, by one of the actors in the action, perhaps by the leading actor himself.

One advantage the writer has over any character as narrator is that he can be omniscient in the story. He can tell what a character is thinking, know his past and future, his innermost secrets. A character cannot enter the minds of other characters, he can tell us only his own thoughts, describe only his own feelings. The character-narrator is an observer in relation to other people, as we all are in real life. He sees them from the outside only.

Omniscience, alas, is only a literary convention.

OMNISCIENT—PERSONAL

Then why not tell the story from the writer's point of view? Why speak through a character? Could we have a better narrator than the author himself? Why not make it frankly an author's report?

Many of the world's great novels are written by the omniscient method. We see the action through the author's eyes and we hear his voice, except when, as in a scene, we hear also character voices. But do we really want to be told stories by somebody who was not there, who is making it up perhaps, just to entertain us? Do we want to get an author's report of what happened, which granted, might be highly interesting and charming—or would we rather see the event for ourselves, or hear it from somebody who was there, to whom it all happened, or who saw it with his own eyes?

Many writers will insist a story should not be an author's report. A character's report, or seen through a character's eyes; but not seen through the author's eyes. Most of the older fiction classics are author's reports. This has been the established, traditional method of narration. But the modern reader is inclined to doubt the authority of an author's report and to prefer a more authentic inside view of the event, looking at it through a character's eyes. The event is drawn closer to him and made more credible and convincing.

There are two kinds of author's reports: personal and impersonal or subjective and objective. The writer who uses the personal method does not efface himself or take himself out of the story. He expresses his own opinions and feelings about the event and the people in it. If Fielding, he is frankly Fielding or some unnamed narrator whom we may take to be Fielding, or his alter-ego. The writer steps boldly into the story and does not hide his presence; although he is not one of the dramatis personae, he almost becomes one when he takes an active part as Fielding does in *Tom Jones* and Thackeray does in *Vanity Fair*. While we are getting acquainted with the characters, we are getting acquainted also with the author-narrator, and by the time we finish the story, we have a definite mental image of him also. He can be a "character." We can identify ourselves with Fielding more readily than with Tom Jones or Sophia Western.

The personal author feels free to comment on the action and to speak to the reader in his own person as author-I. His commentary, though no part of the action, may elucidate the events and the people, enhancing the value and interest of the story, but no matter how eloquent and persuasive, it is after all no part of the original event but something added by the writer. It may even be a distraction or nuisance. To one reader at least, Thackeray-as-narrator is more interesting than Becky Sharp, or any other character in *Vanity Fair,* and the charm of the book consists in the fact that it is Thackeray's, or his spokesman's, report on Mayfair rather than Mayfair itself as it was in his time. How Thackeray sees it as narrator adds today to the appeal of the book. We look at old Mayfair through his eyes and see what he sees, which is a great deal, and we hear his voice. Many readers would not have it otherwise. Yet a risk is involved in this method, that becomes painfully apparent in the concluding lines of the novel.

Ah! *Vanitas Vanitatum!* Which of us is happy in this world? Which of us has his desire, or, having it, is satisfied? Come, children, let us shut up the box and the puppets, for our play is played out.

It is just a story after all, not the real thing. We were duped. We blink our eyes. The show is over, the box is shut, with the puppets back in the box. These rhetorical questions at the end, and "come, children," rouse us from our trance. The showman picks up his belongings and departs.

When the writer addresses the reader, he underscores his presence. The event did not happen by itself, as events happen in life. Somebody stage-managed the affair, it is a puppet show. To make imitation seem true: that is the challenge in this craft. "True story" magazines prosper on this craving for the true, the real. There the accounts are written in first person, ostensibly by the characters themselves, not in third person by professional authors.

The writer's presence will not invariably destroy the illusion of reality, but some damage is always done. The closest re-creation of an event should give us the impression that it is the actual thing; with the action moving on its own momentum. The writer who makes personal references to himself, or addresses himself directly to the reader, puts himself in the same position as Thackeray speaking to his "children" after his puppet show. Exit author, exit reader, sums up the dramatic way of writing fiction. What remains? The event, and that is what the reader wants. The playwright is not on the stage with his actors and the actors speak to one another, not to the audience. No writer of course is wholly absent from his tale, but he conceals his presence as much as possible.

> Reader, I think proper, before we proceed any farther together, to acquaint thee that I intend to digress, through this whole history, as often as I see occasion, of which I am myself a better judge than any pitiful critic whatever; and here I must desire all those critics to mind their own business. . . . I have told my reader, in the preceding chapter, that Mr. Allworthy inherited a large fortune; that he had a good heart, and no family.
>
> (Henry Fielding, *Tom Jones*, Book I)

> With a single drop of ink for a mirror, the Egyptian sorcerer undertakes to reveal to any chance comer far-reaching visions of the past. This is what I undertake to do for you, reader. With this drop of ink at the end of my pen, I will show you the roomy workshop of Mr. Jonathan Burge, carpenter and builder, in the village of Hayslope, as it appeared on the eighteenth of June, in the year of our Lord 1799.
>
> (George Eliot, *Adam Bede*, Chapter I)

Today, this is not done; novelists do not get so chatty with their readers. The writer who addresses the reader as narrator may have to play up to him, try to win his good will and opinion; he has to put on an act to hold the reader's attention and to be *en rapport* with him. The reader might not like it.

In the old days, in merrie olde England, the writer was rarely a gentleman and he was in somewhat the same position as the actor; he was expected to be an entertainer, let in through the back door, as it were, for the amusement of the ladies in the house and of his lordship when that gentleman sat down with a pot of ale to enjoy himself by the fireside. This tradition of literary entertainment persists in Anglo-Saxon cultures, and even today, in America, the writer's social position is not too secure. He is not accorded the honor of being a national voice, of representing by common consent the national conscience, and consciousness, as the writer has been for many centuries on the continent of Europe and elsewhere. Somerset Maugham tried above all to be entertaining. Even Henry James was a little too anxious to be amusing. Is the writer a circus clown? We cannot say of Tolstoy or Flaubert that they wrote primarily for the entertainment of the reader, and such writers are not inclined to address the reader in person. There are many ponderous comments by Tolstoy in *War and Peace,* and the novel would be a better book without them. Whenever he cites the historians and writes an editorial on the role of history in the life of peoples and humanity, we want to get on with the story, which he tells magnificently between these personal essays. Fortunately it is in Part II, after the action is over, that Tolstoy settles down for a final exposition of his theme and there is no further interruption of the story line.

A brief comment would not break up the story line. A few words and sentences here and there giving necessary information are scarcely noticed by the reader, but a long commentary running into several paragraphs or pages might be an unwarranted interruption, and this does happen in *War and Peace,* time and again. Today the writer is more artful about his explanation; a little here, a little there. The exposition is chopped up and distributed throughout the story. Yet in *War and Peace* we have an historical novel, and the historians, the documents, the available evidence and its interpretation by Tolstoy give an air of historical truth to the chronicle and make it authentic. We finish the book with the feeling that these are true events, that neither the war scenes nor the peace scenes are invented, and they contribute to the verisimilitude

Tolstoy achieves. The historians, the archives make an author's report more authentic in this case. Tolstoy did not intend to write a novel or even a historical chronicle. In *War and Peace* he created his own form.

In his next novel, *Anna Karenina,* the essay element and comment is cut down to a few sentences or paragraphs here and there and the method is more definitely scenic than in *War and Peace.* The objective scene eliminates the author, and when we have dialogue or monologue, author words are replaced by character words. The simplest definition of drama is character words without author words, and to write dramatically means to write in character words—or at least from a character's point of view. This Tolstoy does often enough, though he is never, or almost never, wholly absent from his scenes.

Tolstoy puts the thoughts of his people, in their own words, in quotation marks.

> "But what is to be done? What can I do?" he asked himself despairingly and found no answer. . . . "How terrible, how terrible!" Oblonsky repeated to himself. . . . "She was contented and happy with the children, I did not interfere at all, I let her run them and the house in her own way. . . . Oh dear, what am I to do? . . . Well, we shall see," Oblonsky said to himself.
> She ran a swift glance over his fresh, healthy figure. "Yes," she thought, "he is happy and content, but what of me? . . . And that odious good-nature of his which makes people love and praise him so—how I hate it!"

We enter now one mind, now another; we see the event also through the eyes of the characters, so that the point of view shifts continuously from author to character and from one character to another. Over it all is the omniscient author and we see the action as a whole through his eyes. It is still his report. But when we are with Oblonsky getting up in the morning and having breakfast, we see the event through Oblonsky's eyes, we are in Oblonsky's world. The author stands over Oblonsky's shoulder, as it were, to assist with some brief comment or explanation when necessary. When we are with Oblonsky's wife and she is unwilling to forgive him for having an affair with the French governess of their children, we see the situation through her eyes; we are now in her world, and the omniscient narrator is in the scene with her, describing her once thick beautiful hair pinned in little thin braids over the nape of her neck, her large anxious eyes made more prominent by the emaciation of her pale face.

Personal in his approach to his subject and his characters, (perhaps inevitably so because Tolstoy was a moralist with strong individual convictions of his own) he is quite impersonal toward the reader and does not address him as author-I. Tolstoy's method does not impress us as being old-fashioned. This seems to be a perfectly natural way of writing in third person, with all the resources of the art at the author's command, omniscience at its best. It is a mixed, well-balanced method, and the new writer can study these two novels, generally regarded as being among the greatest in the world, and particularly *Anna Karenina,* with profit. To me they are the two greatest, though not the most artistic.

The authorial "I" or "we" of the older novelists crops up in some modern works. Thomas Mann made himself narrator in writing *The Magic Mountain* (which won the Nobel prize) and he speaks in first-person plural about himself. "The story of Hans Castorp which we would set forth . . . this story, we say . . . we shall tell it at length . . . let us get the introductions over at once." If Mann had made Hans Castorp narrator or used Castorp's point of view he would have given us a more intimate and intense picture of life in a Swiss sanatorium, but a more narrow, limited one, sacrificing a good deal of his material and the philosophy and the irony that are the outstanding features of this book. When the narrator is not in the story and stands outside the action, he can stand, if he wishes, at a considerable distance from it, and distance as we have said is necessary for irony. What is ironic to an external narrator whose fate is not at stake is not ironic to a character struggling for survival.

There is a loss of intimacy in omniscience, but this loss may be turned to advantage. Irony by nature is somewhat detached and unemotional. Self-irony is possible, and a highly engaging quality when a character as narrator can stand at some distance from himself and has a sense of humor about himself, too. Hans Castorp is a patient in a cure chair anxiously watching the rise of the mercury column in his thermometer. For an ironic and philosophic novelist like Thomas Mann, omniscience may well be the right method, and it is Mann's ironic tone above all that holds this plotless novel together.

Irony may be the crowning achievement of the writer, and in almost every good story there is an ironic situation. Life itself is paradoxical and irony is a form of resignation to the mysteries and contradictions of life. Discoveries and reversals are ironic situations. It is ironic when a man finds the true state of affairs to be contrary to what he expected: the reality behind the appearance, the myth behind the fact. Irony is not bitter like sarcasm, it wears a kindly, understanding smile and is connected with the tragic sense of life. If ripeness is all then irony perhaps is everything and the closest thing in real life to omniscience. The modern reader is so skeptical that he prefers stories with a dash of irony in them.

OMNISCIENT—IMPERSONAL

Flaubert disliked the personal tone, the editorializing author with his subjective approach to his characters, and eliminated all condemnation or approval, and all references to himself in *Madame Bovary*. There are no little essays by Flaubert in which he reflects upon his action and actors, the treatment of the subject is cool, aloof, noncommittal. Flaubert does not come out openly in favor of any person in the book, nor does he take the reader into his confidence and chat with him. He is under no obligation to win the good opinion of the reader, to be amusing or witty or moralistic. *Madame Bovary* is the first modern novel and still a model of objectivity.

But complete objectivity of course is a delusion; no writer can be neutral unless he is a hopeless cynic. Flaubert is not neutral. Neutrality is a relative term in fiction. We know what Flaubert thinks of his characters from his ironic and satirical tone. There is not a single sympathetic portrait of a major character in the whole book.

Flaubert worked out an aesthetics of fiction when he wrote this novel: the author should be felt everywhere and visible nowhere. We feel his presence through his style, his tone, his choice of subject, his treatment of it, but he does not mix his own opinions and sentiments with those of his characters and stays severely separate from them. There is no author-I in the book.

Flaubert seldom quotes directly from the minds of his characters, as does Tolstoy, and relies instead on a kind of stream-of-thought in third person, on "free indirect discourse," which we shall examine later, and on psychological analysis or description. The essay element is reduced to the minimum and there is no gross interference by an intrusive author, in striking contrast to other novels of the period. It is doubtful though if Flaubert could be so impersonal with a more sympathetic subject. He despised the mores of the provincial bourgeoisie.

There are relatively few scenes in the novel; there is much more indirect dialogue and monologue than in *Anna Karenina* and Flaubert habitually summarizes in his own polished words, sometimes mixed with the words of his characters, what his people say or think, and it is generally his voice that we hear, or the voice of the narrator who represents him. He placed a supreme value on verbal beauty and was reluctant to relinquish the action over to his characters and let them speak directly in their own imperfect words; this may be expected from a stylist who sweats over his sentences. *Anna Karenina* does not seem to be a written book. The life depicted in its nearly 1000 pages is not a separate isolated entity but contiguous with the surrounding life in Russia. *Madame Bovary* is "written," and the proportion of author words is well in excess of character words. We can admire the prose (it suffers in translation) and the craftsmanlike job, but it smells a little of the study and there is something theatrical about its end; Emma dies of poison, and soon afterwards her husband dies of grief.

Flaubert as narrator sticks to his own point of view and maintains his ironic-satirical tone, but his point of view often combines with Emma's and we see her husband, her lovers, other characters, the landscape, the streets, the houses, through her eyes too when the focus of characterization is on her. But the merging is not complete, it is not a definite shift, and after entering Emma's mind Flaubert will withdraw to view her again from a certain distance. The impersonality he cultivated is a step toward drama, but the generalized narrative, the summary method, is a movement away from it, and what Flaubert gains with one hand he loses with the other. Impersonality plus more scene, more direct dialogue and monologue, would have brought about the exit of the author which Flaubert himself so devoutly wished. If *Madame Bovary* were written scenically like *Anna Karenina*, we would have had another novel of a thousand pages perhaps. Summary saves space, and summary preserves also the personality and style of the writer.

The novel actually begins in first person and the first word in it is "We." "*Nous étions à l'étude,*" we read, when the principal of the school enters the classroom, followed by a new boy whose name was Charles Bovary.

"The principal motioned us to sit down . . . we had the habit, on entering the class, to fling our caps to the ground . . . we saw him working conscientiously, looking up all the words in the dictionary." After introducing Charles Bovary as a young schoolboy Flaubert shifts from first person to third and there is no further reference to the unruly schoolroom scene, but these opening paragraphs are enough to lend a greater air of authority to the story that follows, as though the narrator were Charles Bovary's schoolmate. The point of view is internal in the first few pages and the method seems autobiographical, although Flaubert is careful to speak in first person collectively, in the plural, to say "we" rather than "I," and the nameless narrator is part of a group. We get the impression that the narrator is there, with Charles Bovary, as his schoolmate, and so presumably has known him for many years. No further evidence is offered though, and even in first person he is quite impersonal. This shift does not seem to be arbitrary; Flaubert calculated his every move.

Flaubert had to write *Madame Bovary* with the superior knowledge of the omniscient or analytical author, Emma herself being incapable of reproducing her thought stream and analyzing her own feelings, or perceiving the nature of her situation. The clumsy good-hearted inarticulate country doctor she married was even less qualified for the role of narrator. Both lacked irony and self-irony, and neither could be sufficiently objective about these experiences that destroyed them in the end. Flaubert approached his subject as a superior artist looking down on *"l'homme moyen sensuele."* It is a pitiless portrait of a romantic young woman and of small-town life, at once local and universal, satirizing the romantic spirit, exposing it for what it is, or what it was in his time, not looking at love through rose-colored glasses. Flaubert had to make himself a romantic young woman to write it. He succeeded in completely identifying himself with Emma Bovary—one of the most astonishing feats in fiction. The novel was tried for obscenity and he was right when he said during the trial, "Madame Bovary *c'est moi même.*" And he was Madame Bovary, fighting against his own romantic tendencies while writing the book, shedding his romantic sickness in its beautifully wrought pages, and his first full-length novel remains his masterpiece.

Emma Bovary traveled the passion road from illusion to reality, and, as in the case of Anna Karenina her search ended in death. Both women destroyed themselves when they did not find what they expected, but Anna is a more tragic figure than Emma, and by far the greater woman for most readers. Tolstoy did not see her plight as a subject for satire and there is a fundamental difference in the attitude of the two novelists toward their heroines.

We might say of Flaubert, but say it reluctantly, that he failed to reach a full definition of his theme; there is more to the story of Madame Bovary than he was evidently aware of. He would see it as more of a tragedy if he were. Sensual love or love-in-the-provinces was nothing to mock. Flaubert does not strike the deeper notes and advance from the particular to the general. Foolish as she is, Emma Bovary is all women in search of an impossible ideal of love, and when we view the subject in that light, she grows in stature, she becomes a symbolic, tragic figure. One of the merits of this novel is its lack of sentimentality about what had been up to then a sentimental subject, but we feel Flaubert lacks compassion, and we wonder whether the impersonal tone he adopted is not a covering up of defects within himself, in his own attitude toward women. What many readers miss in the book is warmth, humanity. Flaubert tells the truth as he sees it, but the larger truth behind it was either beyond his grasp or no part of his design. Perhaps we should not blame Flaubert for something he did not intend to do, and he did almost perfectly what he intended, using the right point of view.

This larger truth or at least another view of woman we find in a simple short story by Anton Chekhov, "The Darling." Olenka, a young woman who cannot exist without loving someone, marries the manager of an open-air theatre. She becomes enthusiastic about the theatre, takes part in rehearsals, talks about the theatre as the most important thing in life, repeating her husband's opinions and words, and completely identifying herself with his interests. After his death she marries a lumber merchant, and forgetting all about the humanizing and cultural role of the theatre she talks and dreams lumber. Theatre? What nonsense. She can't waste her time by going to the theatre; she is too busy with lumber. Her second husband dies six years later, and she is a widow once more, unable to live alone. When a veterinary surgeon who has been separated from his wife enters her life, she stops mourning the lumberman's death. She talks of the foot-and-mouth disease, and veterinary medicine becomes now the most important thing in life for her. The veterinary surgeon goes away with his regiment, leaving her alone. She gets thinner and plainer. Without a man to attach herself to she has no opinions of any kind, a strange new experience for her, and she almost ceases to exist as a person. Her life is empty, year after year; she ages. Then the veterinary surgeon comes back, gray-haired, in civilian clothes, retired from active practice, and reconciled with his wife. Olenka insists they live in her house without paying rent. Wife and husband separate again, and Olenka, now a stout middle-aged woman, lavishes her love and attention on their son. She worries now about the boy's lessons at school, they are difficult, she sighs, as she does his homework with him and dreams of the day when he will be a doctor or engineer.

The viewpoint is omniscient, and Chekhov does not make personal references to himself, nor does he editorialize, moralize. The story speaks for itself. The treatment is warm and compassionate and not without some humor. We can almost hear Chekhov chuckling as he tells Olenka's story. He does not hesitate to say that Olenka is gentle, softhearted, kind; he gives a few summary estimates of her character which the strictly impersonal writer would not do; he would neither blame nor praise. To the American reader the treatment seems a little too sentimental, but The Darling is a sentimental woman, and the tone of the narrative reinforces the theme. An American woman can identify herself more readily with Emma than with Olenka.

In "The Peasants," Chekhov presents a memorable picture of Russian peasant life shortly after the emancipation of the serfs, with their condition getting worse, not better. We see their ignorance, poverty, filth, drunkenness. They lose their precious samovars when they cannot pay their taxes. Toward the end of the story, which is considerably longer and more scenic than "The Darling," we have the impression for a moment that Chekhov at last will pass direct judgment on the kind of life these people are living. But we soon discover that he is not speaking in his own person, giving instead the reflections of a gentle pious woman who after her husband's death is leaving the village with her little daughter, unable to put up with it any more. She is going back to Moscow to work as a maid. She feels there is no hope for these peasants, she pities them, they are lazy, grasping, greedy, dissolute, quarrelsome. They live in foul huts and their language is foul. Yet they have their joys, they are human beings with some faint aspirations to a better life. This is judgment by character, not by author.

It hits the reader harder, without author comment. Comment would be superfluous. The story throbs not only with the earthy vitality of these lusty folk whom the most insignificant government clerk treats with contempt, but with the great heart of the doctor who wrote it. Chekhov knew the value of writing emotional scenes coldly. He advised young writers to be cold and impersonal in describing painful situations. But this is another kind of aloofness from Flaubert's. It is compassionate, committed.

It is a question of method, a tactical matter. A story can be a personalized subject impersonally rendered, but it may also be a personalized subject personally rendered, and in either form, personal or impersonal, it can be a work of art. Some writers see their stories in immediate relation to themselves and are lyrical by temper. When Thomas Wolfe tried to be objective in his later novels, he stopped writing at his natural heat, and *Look Homeward, Angel* and *Of Time and the River* remain his best books. Would we want William Saroyan to write impersonally? We should not be carried away by a cult of impersonality. An author must have his own individual feelings and ideas to write personally and that in our age is no little achievement in itself. The writer who has only one story to tell, the story of his own life, which he knows best, may be read and appreciated precisely for that reason, and his excitement with himself may excite the reader also. What else did Marcel Proust write in *À la recherche du temps perdu,* one of the monumental novels of the century? But, like Proust, a writer should seek universal laws in his personal experiences and make the personal universal, make history poetry.

From the subjective to the objective, from personal to impersonal, from author to character, is a dramatic progression. But if drama loses more than it gains, we had better pause and consider its value in fiction. Scene promotes the emotional participation of the reader, but so may the personality of the writer. He cannot be a cold fish personally and expect to move the reader. Summary particularly needs sentiment. He moves others who is himself moved, he arouses the anger of others who is himself angry, Aristotle says in the *Poetics*. The intensity of feeling is so low in some young writers that they, though technically competent, cannot write fiction that excites the reader. Some ecstasy is essential for the poet. Nothing great is written without enthusiasm, without getting out of yourself and being carried away by your emotions. The writer is expected to be a highly emotional person, with both abandon and control.

The epic poet should speak in his own voice as little as possible and not take an active part in his story—that was Aristotle's advice in the *Poetics*. But Homer knew, says Aristotle, what part in the story he himself should play—very little. Character voices predominate in the *Odyssey*. Homer recreates his people largely through their own speech and actions. This impersonal method of narration is a marked feature of other national epics—*Daredevils of Sassoun,* the Armenian national epic, for instance. The dramatic method, instinctively practiced by the village poets of Armenia—unlettered peasants—for hundreds of years, and in other countries with folk epics, seems to be the natural method of telling a story. When I organized and translated the Sassoun saga into English (in the UNESCO Collection of Representative Works) and examined all existing village variants, I saw that in this pure example of oral literature, transmitted by word of mouth from one generation to another, the treatment of the story is consistently scenic, with no comments.

LIMITED OMNISCIENCE

In the two methods we have examined, the writer is at liberty to enter the minds of all his characters, great and small, and give us their thoughts and feelings. A character presented from within is seldom flat; thought individualizes people. There are almost no flat types in Tolstoy. He can bring a servant, a waiter, an old peasant to life by letting him say a few words to himself in his own idiom. A few stray thoughts in first person may reveal more about a character than a systematic psychological analysis by the author in third person, and omniscience is necessary for analysis. It is the analytical method, and for this reason has been favored in psychological fiction. By using the omniscient method, personal or impersonal, the writer can present his people from both without and within. He is under no obligation to enter every mind, he can choose. If he wants to focus the reader's attention on one character, who the story is about, he can treat him both externally and internally, he can describe him and analyze him, treating the others from the outside only and not enter their minds at all. One character is brought to the foreground; the others remain in the background. It is a versatile and flexible method.

To enter one mind only is being omniscient about one character only; toward the others the narrator assumes the position of an observer, but he does not observe them the way a character in the story would. He can see more, know more, and even though his presentation of them is external, he is still omniscient in so far as the external action is concerned. He can be everywhere with his characters and if he is not there, he can know what happened, but a character as narrator has to be personally present in every scene or some other character has to tell him about it. In limited omniscience the narrator no longer stands at an equal distance from all his characters. He is closer to one of them, the mind he enters, and so is the reader, who sees the events through two pair of eyes, the narrator's and a character's, with the narrator's superior vision and knowledge added to the character's.

In "The Kiss" by Chekhov, to return to this excellent writer once more, we read about a group of artillery officers being entertained by a local landowner at tea, and we have an external presentation of several people. It is a group story at first. Chekhov alludes to their feelings as a group and describes the landowner's estate as nineteen officers see it, through their impressions of the place,—a collective impression; and meanwhile the author also describes the estate and we see it predominantly through his eyes. Then the focus is on Ryabovich, a short officer with stooped shoulders and lynx-like whiskers, wearing glasses, who cannot dance with the ladies and has never put his arm around the waist of a respectable woman: a shy modest man, the least distinguished-looking of all the officers at this party. We see the event mainly through Ryabovich's eyes; it is no longer a collective impression. Chekhov enters his mind and gives us his thoughts. Ryabovich wanders accidentally into a dark room where he hears the rustle of a skirt and is embraced by a lady he cannot see well and who evidently mistakes him for another man. She kisses him, and then withdraws quickly with a faint shriek. He rushes out of the room, thinking she withdrew from him in disgust.

He wonders who she is. Her identity remains unknown to him. There are several girls and married women at the party. The man falls in love with the woman who kissed him by mistake and is always dreaming about her—marriage, children —as the artillery brigade moves on. The tea party changes his life, while the other officers are unaffected by it. They had a good time and that is all. Fate in the person of an unknown woman caressed him, but the lady's kiss was an accident, and he will never see her again. And the whole world, his whole life, seems to this man an unintelligible jest, a cruel joke. After that bright moment in the dark room, his life once more is drab, poor, uninteresting, and he is an angry young man, angry with his fate.

This is an example of limited omniscience, with only one mind explored by the writer. We have not only his audible speech, but also his silent thoughts, and the thoughts tell the story. They are given directly in his own words, in first person, in quotation marks, or are summarized by the author in third person. The story as a whole is told from the author's point of view, with one character in the foreground, brought close to the reader.

SINGLE CHARACTER POINT OF VIEW

When the action from beginning to end is screened through one mind and we see all the events through the eyes of a single person in the story, the shift to a character point of view is complete. Our knowledge is strictly limited to his, and we are told nothing by the writer this person could not know. We enter his mind and *stay* there, and we see all the other characters in the story through his eyes, as they appear to *him,* and not as they appear to the writer or to somebody else in the story. The author is still narrator, but it is no longer *his* report of what happened.

When the writer's vision is narrowed to a character's there is a further restriction in omniscience. The viewpoint is the character's but he is not the narrator; if he were, the story would be written in first person. This method is like writing a first-person story in third person, changing "I" to "he" or "she," and the point of view is half external, half internal, with author as narrator and character as seer. When skillfully used, it may combine the best features of both the external and internal points of view.

The moment we shift to a character viewpoint and not back to the author's viewpoint, there is no longer unlimited omniscience. The character, to repeat, cannot know everything; that is a privilege reserved only for the writer by an ancient convention. The character is a mortal person who does not dwell on the Olympian heights with the author and cannot aspire to the author's godlike knowledge. If John is our viewpoint character, we can say "John thought," or "John said to himself," but we cannot say what Mary his wife thought or said to herself. We are barred from entering Mary's mind when we are confined to a single viewpoint, John's mind. John can only speculate about Mary's thoughts and feelings. He can say "Mary *seemed* to think, she *appeared* to brood over it," and much may be done in a story through such speculations. In actual practice this method is not as rigid as it seems. Generally there is some intrusion by the author in it. It is not exactly the same as writing a story in first person, but the principle is the same. We have only one pair of eyes which belongs to someone in the story whose vision, necessarily limited, is not supplemented by the superior vision of the omniscient author. If John does not know Mary's thoughts, the author does not know them either, and he has to present Mary only as John sees her. The single character point of view eliminates the author and his viewpoint, and the break with the personal author makes the story more dramatic.

This method makes for dramatic concentration and continuity, and is an excellent device for unifying and intensifying action. Loose, fragmented, episodic material, screened through one mind and shown through one pair of eyes, develops much more definite shape than in unlimited omniscience, and the writer can get an unbroken story line from it. When there is no tight causal plot to hold a story together, the writer has to depend largely on thematic unity *and* a restricted character point of view to make it a whole. Episodic stories, if not written in first person, should be written from a single character point of view.

To get back to our hypothetical couple, let us suppose that John is the central character in the story, which is rendered from his point of view. The focus is on John, and he is the seer. But John's story may also be written from Mary's point of view, and it is now Mary who speculates about John. Mary can give only her own thoughts and has no direct access to John's mind. John is still the hero of the tale, but his mind is closed to the reader, as it is to Mary. We get Mary's estimate of John, and the story is presented through Mary's impressions, thoughts, feelings, speculations. We see him through her eyes. If Mary is highly perceptive, she may give an excellent portrait of her husband, a true likeness. If she is not and the reader is ahead of her, the story could be ironic. Unless the writer is striving for irony, he had better make the viewpoint character, major or minor, an intelligent, sensitive person. If the reader has to see the events through his eyes, they should be keen eyes.

But suppose, instead of Mary, John's eleven-year-old daughter Kathleen is the viewpoint character; then instead of getting Mary's account of John, we get Kathleen's, observing him and Mary through Kathleen's eyes. The story then is What Kathleen Knows, and not What Mary Knows, or John Knows. Let Kathleen discover that her father is suspected by her mother of having an affair with another woman, and that her mother is dishonest. She herself plays a minor role in the action, but this discovery makes her miserable and she runs away from home. Now the story is really Kathleen's, though the main characters are still her parents. These three different points of view would actually give us three different stories.

It is easier to render the workings of one mind than of several, and to write from the inside out at any depth is a difficult task. Yet this method of a single character point of view is confining and the writer who uses it may long for the free loose form used by the omniscient writer entering any mind at will. Why be shut up in one mind thereby giving up a most useful literary convention? Every art has its own conventions and fiction has the omniscient point of view.

Long before Henry James wrote *The Ambassadors* and dramatized Strether's consciousness by subtle shifts, Jane Austen was writing stories in a remarkably impersonal manner and on the whole from a single point of view. We are astonished by her craftsmanship. Her dialogue is stripped of any unnecessary details, not cluttered up with author explanations and pantomime, the words standing out clearly by themselves: it is, on the whole, better dialogue than James wrote. And there were others before Jane Austen. The single point of view has had its advocates since the beginning of the English novel. Today it is almost standard in the short story, particularly the "literary" story, and is used with increasing frequency in the novel. It does give us an intense single image of life. It may be used for this purpose in certain sections of a story written from an omniscient point of view. This method is peculiarly well fitted for the modern psychological story and this age, with its emphasis on the individual consciousness in conflict with the group, or with itself. It is the method of subjective fiction, the forerunner of interior monologue. For the withdrawn man, the alienated, the stranger, the outsider, the lone pilgrim, the philosopher, the artist, the nonconformist, those trying to preserve their individuality, integrity, and wits in a mass-produced world, the single character point of view is a natural.

Henry James perfected this method; he was a stranger in both Europe and America, an observer of the life around him rather than a participant in it. Modern psychological fiction began with the depth writing made possible by James, with the exploration of a single consciousness. Like Strether, James was caught between two civilizations and ways of life and dramatized his own conflicts in *The Ambassadors*.

Portrait of the Artist as a Young Man is another good example of this method. It is written consistently from the point of view of Stephen Dedalus, beginning with the "moocow" coming down the road and ending with Stephen's diary. This is the portrait of a rebel. Everything is filtered lyrically through the mind of a young Irish poet who felt so different and isolated in his native Dublin that he had to go live as an exile on the continent, "go back" to Europe. It would not be difficult to turn the *Portrait* into first person; in the last chapter, in the diary, it is in first person.

But what does Stephen look like? We are not sure. He is nearsighted, as was James Joyce, he wears glasses and cannot see without them, and there is more sound than sight in the prose. Other physical details about Stephen are vague. We do not see him from the outside because he does not see himself. This is the main difficulty connected with this single-view method. Often minor characters are visualized better by the reader who is looking at them through the eyes of the viewpoint character, whose image seems blurred by contrast, because the seer cannot have this same direct look at himself unless standing before a mirror. A mirror is, in fact, sometimes used to describe his physical appearance without shifting the point of view. If the viewpoint character is also the main actor and it is his story, we have no clear view of him, and the one person we should see most vividly becomes vague and shadowy. The author cannot describe him, and he cannot describe himself except in dialogue.

This difficulty is overcome to a certain extent by the objective scene. The narrator stays out of the viewpoint character's mind and does not give his thoughts. With his mind sealed off, he is no longer very close to the reader, and is kept at the same distance as the other characters in the story. Such a scene, with no mind entered and no thoughts given, conveys the impression that the character is one of the actors who are objectively presented, observed from the outside as they must be, and he is now on the same level with them. It is still impossible to get a direct view of him, but he is not so different from the others and we look at him from the same distance—another fine point made by Percy Lubbock.

The objective scene, moreover, adds variety and relief and it is a good thing now and then to shut off the seer's consciousness, reducing him to the ranks, as it were. When we are constantly in one mind, seeing everything through one pair of eyes, monotony, and with it perhaps boredom, sets in. Variety is important in this method. Occasionally as readers we want to get away from the viewpoint character and the writer may do this without shifting the point of view by simply staying out of his mind and not using his eyes. We withdraw from him. For this reason alone when writing a story from a single character point of view, particularly a long story or novel, a writer should occasionally use the method of the playwright, having objective scenes, with all characters seen from the outside and from the same distance.

But some characters should not be seen too clearly. The blur has its uses. It may make for mystery and suspense; it may arouse the reader's curiosity. The shadowy figure lurking in the background becomes more sinister and terrifying; a glamorous woman seen through a veil becomes more alluring. Glamour deceives the sight, and there is sound reasoning behind the Hollywood practice of "glamorizing" their stars by withdrawing them from public view. They make occasionally a carefully staged personal appearance. The decline of

Hollywood as a "dream factory" may be due partly to the increased visibility of the stars off the screen.

The blurring of the viewpoint character may be turned to advantage also in subjective fiction where a "transparent envelope" (Virginia Woolf) is wanted. Psychological stories do not take well to illustrations anyway. The reader's imagination paints the figure of the character who is seeing but is not seen. When the writer's primary concern is with states of mind that defy analysis, and the emotion eludes a direct statement, then oblique and symbolic writing is artistically right, and the symbol can stand for the feeling that cannot be described. Though fiction is written in visual prose, it is not possible or desirable to be clear about everything and everybody in a story. As Elizabeth Bowen says in *Notes on Writing a Novel,* some characters should be only *seen*. They should be excluded from the seeing class, to make them more magnetic.

MULTIPLE CHARACTER POINT OF VIEW

Henry James used the viewpoint of the Prince in the first half of *The Golden Bowl,* and of the Princess in the remainder, thus exploring the consciousness of "but two" of the characters, as he tells us in the preface to the novel.

In *Ulysses* the point of view is not limited to Stephen Dedalus. We are first in Stephen's mind exclusively, then we are in the mind of Leopold Bloom for the bulk of the novel, and finally follow the uninterrupted monologue of Molly Bloom in the last chapter; and for shorter periods we are in the minds of various other characters.

Similarly in *Mrs. Dalloway* there is more than one character point of view. When Mrs. Dalloway is walking along Bond Street to buy flowers for her party, we can follow her thought stream and see London through her eyes. Then we are briefly in the mind of Septimus Warren Smith and his Italian wife Lucrezia as they are watching a mysterious car with drawn curtains Mrs. Dalloway thinks belongs to the queen, but Mrs. Dalloway and the Smiths do not meet. We are for a brief interval in the mind of a Mrs. Dempster who saves bread crusts for the squirrels and often eats her lunch in Regent's Park, and of a Mr. Bentley, whom we shall not meet again. Mrs. Dalloway returns home and we are back in her mind. Peter, her former suitor, just back from India, comes to visit her, and, as they talk, we are alternately in his mind and in Mrs. Dalloway's. As the title indicates, the story is Mrs. Dalloway's, and the viewpoint is predominantly hers, but other viewpoints also are used.

The author-narrator is present in both *Ulysses* and *Mrs. Dalloway*, and there are objective descriptions. The shifts are not arbitrary as in the usual omniscient novel. There is system in the method. The multiple point of view is a favorite method of Virginia Woolf's and gives variety to her work. This is probably one reason why she is more widely read than Dorothy Richardson, who wrote all twelve volumes of *Pilgrimage* from a single point of view, Miriam's. The monotony of it palls on the reader. These were in their time extremely interesting, almost revolutionary experiments in fiction, and we shall return to them in another chapter. The multiple point of view is better for the novel than for the short story, which works best with the single point of view.

DRAMATIC OR EXTERNAL POINT OF VIEW

From the strictly subjective to the strictly objective is going from one extreme to another, and a novel stands to lose more than a short story when this method is employed. *The Awkward Age* by Henry James is warning enough. In his other books, James stressed inwardness. Most readers prefer a story in which not only the external physical action but the thoughts of the characters also are dramatized. The elimination of all thought is as unnecessary as the elimination of all objective events. Generally a mixed method, objective and subjective, action and thought, dialogue and monologue is best, although in some stories it may be necessary to emphasize, and even to eliminate, one or the other.

The pure action story might do well on the wholly objective level, with no mind entered, as in "The Killers" by Hemingway. This method speeds up the action; thought slows it down. There is more movement in the story, more of the stir of life, more color. We may get a more unbroken story line by this method, with the external action unhampered by thought or interior monologue or the personal comments of an intrusive author, for not only the minds of the characters, but the mind of the author too is sealed off, and neither the thoughts and feelings of the characters nor of the writer are given. This is poker-faced fiction and makes for hard-boiled writing.

> "I'll tell you," Max said. "We're going to kill a Swede. Do you know a big Swede named Ole Andreson?"
> . . . "What are you going to kill Ole Andreson for? What did he ever do to you?"
> "He never had a chance to do anything to us. He never seen us."
> "And he is going to see us only once," Al said from the kitchen.

In "The Killers" it is all objective scene, and the story reads like a play. The writing is severely impersonal, stripped of all sentiment, brutally effective. There is no need for Hemingway to analyze the motives of the killers, or even to tell us what Ole Andreson thinks when, after the gangsters leave the lunchroom, Nick Adams hurries over to a roominghouse and warns him against them, telling him they were going to shoot him when he came in to supper. "Ole Andreson looked at the wall and did not say anything."

Obviously a strictly external point of view would not be suitable for a psychological narrative in which the reaction may be more important than the action. It does not allow analysis by the writer, or interior monologue, or such expressions as "he thought," or "he said to himself." All speech is spoken as in a play, and all action is visible.

This method re-creates only the external drama. The writer

stays out of his characters' minds, but is omniscient about external events. He can tell what is happening anywhere to anyone and give all the information the reader needs about the past and present of the characters. He can describe his people and the setting, he can write in scenes and summaries, do everything except tell the reader what a character thinks, what he is like inside, and what he himself as a writer feels about what happens.

Generally it is through various limitations of omniscience that some of the finer effects in fiction are reached, and the more we restrict omniscience, the more dramatic the method. Omniscience is intrusive and diffuse by nature; narration at the expense of drama; author words rather than character words.

Henry James perfected the restricted third-person point of view, and to him omniscience was an irresponsible way of writing fiction. We need not make it a critical dogma. Omniscience has its place in fiction, and some writers will argue it is the best method. It can take in much more territory and give us richer segments of life than a character point of view can, and if it makes for looseness, it makes also for variety; it does not shut the action off from the wider world around it.

Authorial intrusions might be annoying, but they can also be diverting, as in *Tom Jones* and *Vanity Fair*. Omniscience does require superior knowledge on the part of the author, and it is not for the writer with severe intellectual and moral limitations. Restricted third-person can shield the opportunist and the fence-sitter in fiction; it is evidently the ideal method for the commercial writer, who does not have to commit himself to anything but platitudes. It takes a great writer, and one might say a great man, to be frankly omniscient in the manner of Tolstoy. Comment implies commitment.

4. FIRST PERSON

When the narrator is a character in the story, it is a self-contained unit, a whole within itself, and the reader's attention is not diverted constantly from a narrator outside the story to people within it, and back again. First person makes for economy of attention and for a more unified coherent structure compared to the omniscient method. When the narrator is himself a character, that by itself gives us a certain unity of character; when he is a concrete personality and not some nameless or nebulous storyteller, a new dramatic element is added to the story by dramatizing the narrator. First person automatically changes author words to character words. The progression from author to character is complete.

MAJOR CHARACTER TELLS THE STORY

A story becomes a meaningful picture of life when a particular aspect of it is selected for emphasis; it is what the writer emphasizes that makes the story. Point of view is important in the strategy of reader attention.

If the writer is not sure whose story he is telling, the reader will be searching for the character on whom to pin his attention, and flounder along with the writer. This may cause some confusion in a novel with several characters, none of whom is emphasized and brought into sharp focus, with no single figure standing out as the main one nor the one most affected by the events. When a character tells his own story, the emphasis is naturally on him, and we know he is the one most affected by what happens.

In I-as-hero the story is dramatized through the actions and reactions of the protagonist, who puts his own and limited interpretation on what happens. The reader can fill in the gaps in the hero's knowledge. This limitation of knowledge on the part of the hero may have certain advantages. He can tell only what he knows and observes himself, and if he is deprived of the author's godlike knowledge, he is also free of its burdens and responsibilities. His field is narrower, and this in itself acts as a principle of selection, creating a more unified story. By the same token the hero need not report the thoughts and feelings of other people, for he cannot enter their minds. He can only tell what he himself thought and felt, and speculate about the others. All these limitations have their advantages.

The author does not come between the reader and the hero and they are in a closer relationship, for the reader gets the information directly from the character himself and not indirectly through a narrator who was not there. First person makes for intimacy and facilitates reader identification, drawing the reader into the emotional life of the character; he shares more readily the hero's anxieties and joys. First person intensifies the narrative and adds to its emotional impact.

In his short stories Poe aimed for intensity and the single effect, and as most of them are about strange and unusual experiences, he made them more emphatically one and more believable in first person. If we were to rewrite "Eleanora," "Lygia," "The Black Cat," "The Pit and the Pendulum," "The Tell-Tale Heart," "William Wilson," "Narrative of A. Gordon Pym," "The Fall of the House of Usher," and other well-known stories by Poe in third person, they would lose some of their emotional power and might sound like incredible or absurd tales. Poe's hot breath seems to be on us when we read them. A strong emotional experience is told best by the person who had it; it can be pitched at a higher level and read like a confession torn from the heart. Poe needed the first person for his emotion-charged poetic prose. His stories would be cool tepid stuff in third person. The language is in character; this is the style of a Gothic poet in contact with another world, dwelling in his own domain of Arnheim and in the grotesque and arabesque. It would be impossible to write with such agonized intensity in third person.

Robinson Crusoe has made its way around the world as the most popular adventure story for boys. Because Crusoe himself tells it, it all seems true. In first person a story seems less fictional, more like an actual experience. The "I" personalizes events and adds to their interest and authenticity. Journeys into the far corners of the world, strange adventures, are more exciting when narrated by those who made the trip and saw it all with their own eyes. *Holiday* prefers articles in first person, encourages its contributors to write freely in the first person, and the first personal pronoun is obligatory in the *National Geographic*.

Henry James tells the ghost story in *The Turn of the Screw* in first person, narrated by the young governess who saw the ghosts. Ghost stories become more plausible in first person. Omniscience and ghosts don't go well together. James was under no obligation to prove that the young woman actually saw these ghosts. She tells the story from her own necessarily limited knowledge, the event is colored by her own feelings, and as long as the point of view is hers, we have to accept her own interpretation of her experience; if she says they were ghosts, then they were ghosts to *her*, and that is what matters; that is the story. The reader need not accept her interpretation; to the reader they may not be ghosts, and he can put his own evaluation on the event. The reader can say it is hysteria, or sexual fantasy, or explain it by some other theory. James made the story ambiguous enough to lead to different interpretations, and we can accept ambiguity as part of any good ghost story. Too much clarity would kill it. These are private ghosts, as ghosts usually are, and they should be kept private. We see the young governess on an isolated country estate struggling with her problem; she is bewildered and tries to understand what is happening, and why. Such wonder and bewilderment arising from defective knowledge are excellent story elements, best rendered in first person.

The first person gives the so-called confession magazines precisely those elements they need—immediacy and intensity of emotion, an intimate tone of narration, credibility, heated prose, reader identification. They use over and over the old familiar themes, the same situations or problems. To a more sophisticated reader these narratives are fearfully boring, but the principles behind their success are of interest. Just as the "poetics" of the pulp magazines have many elements in common with the *Poetics* of Aristotle, and the lowest and highest forms of fiction may be built on the same dramatic principles of construction, so do first-person stories of the lowest and highest rank gain their effects by almost identical means, for much the same reasons. By using the methods of literature, some writers and publications that have little or nothing to do with literature stay in business.

In I-as-hero, the minor characters gain a vivid reality through their objective presentation, and in a story with a large cast this alone might be a decisive reason for choosing the autobiographical method. We get the color and stir of actual life through secondary characters seen by the hero, who can comment on them, make guesses about their intentions and mental processes. This is comment by character, more dramatic than comment by author would be.

First person tends to summary. Like author-I, character-I is a "telling" method, and the voice of the narrator may absorb other voices. In Samuel Beckett's *Molloy,* for instance, there are no quotation marks and the story is told in one voice, that of Molloy himself. There are few paragraph divisions and it is one long monologue. There is little direct dialogue in Poe's tales, sometimes none. There is almost no dialogue in "I'm a Fool," "The Egg," "The Man Who Became a Woman," "Death in the Woods," and other first-person stories by Sherwood Anderson, and we hardly notice this fact. Even without any dialogue in it a first-person story is dramatic, for we are hearing a character voice. And when the language is in character, the speech itself continuously characterizes the speaker. Take "I'm a Fool," with its race-track setting. The language is the racy vernacular of an American boy circa 1923 from the wrong side of the tracks who meets a girl from the right side. Sherwood Anderson did not write it in correct literary English. "Such fellows don't know nothing at all. They've never had no opportunity . . . Gee whizz, it was fun . . . Gosh amighty . . . You can stick your colleges up your nose . . . she don't know any better . . . Gee, she was a peach! . . . There ain't any such guy . . . I don't care nothing for working, and earning money, and saving it for no such boob as myself."

We speak in first person, and in ordinary conversation our voice absorbs other voices and we often summarize what others say. "Thompson said he would see me the next day, but he didn't keep his promise and when I went to his office he wasn't there. His secretary told me he was out of town." This seems perfectly natural speech, and we have here the speaker's voice absorbing two other voices, Thompson's and the secretary's. We do not have to make it, "Thompson said, 'I'll see you tomorrow,' but he didn't keep his promise and when I went to his office his secretary told me, 'He is out of town.'"

The language is not always in character in many famous stories. Jim Hawkins narrates the events in *Treasure Island* in Robert Louis Stevenson's best style, in lucid rhythmic prose. Even Captain Marlow talks too much like Joseph Conrad and is as much of a poet as the great brooding Pole. Marlow's speech is difficult to distinguish from the rest of the text in *Lord Jim*, written in third person. There are vestiges of foreign English in both. If Captain Marlow stands for Captain Conrad (Teodor Jozef Konrad Korzeniowski), he is a British seaman in the novel and may be expected to speak as one. But despite this similarity in style, Conrad's first-person narrator is a dramatic device. Marlow's voice generally absorbs other voices and there is much summarized dialogue when Marlow is speaking, or we have quotations within quotations, which becomes a little confusing. Whether the novel as a whole gains much by this complicated method of narration is questionable, but certain important effects are secured by it, and it makes for greater authenticity. Generally, the simplest time-tested methods are best, and a too sophisticated use of the point of view or of any other technical device may do more harm than good. We become too conscious of the author's technique when the author underscores his presence.

It is a convention in first-person stories that Lieutenant Frederic Henry in *Farewell to Arms* can write like Hemingway, and Pip can tell a story like Dickens in *Great Expectations*. This not very realistic convention is more acceptable today. We live in an age of compulsory secondary education, of newspapers and magazines with millions of subscribers, of motion pictures, television, and radio.

First person also allows remembered dialogue. In the first draft of *I Ask You, Ladies and Gentlemen,* I eliminated all direct dialogue except for a few lines here and there that I could honestly say I remembered. I wrote nearly all of it in summary. I thought it would be dishonest to pretend I could recall what I said or what others said after the lapse of so many years and I was even reluctant to summarize conversations. Gradually I had to reconcile myself to the use of re-created dialogue, which is another convention in first person or third. I realized everything in a story is imaginatively re-created, that we cannot have a direct imitation of life. Speech is stylized in any case, whether the story is written in first person or third, and a story is a stylized segment of life.

When however the language is consistent with the character of the first-person narrator, the poet speaking like a poet as in Poe's stories, Huck Finn speaking like Huck Finn, Sherwood Anderson's race-track boy speaking like one, in short, when it is individualized speech characteristic of the speaker, the character needs no author to tell the reader what kind of person he is. He imitates himself instead of an author trying to imitate him. And he imitates himself unconsciously, effortlessly, as it were.

But not every vocabulary is capable of achieving the purpose the writer has in mind. The limitations of the hero might make his speech inadequate for the subject, and if the writer sticks to the narrator's idiom he might not be able to write the story in first person. On the other hand, as in "I'm a Fool," the inadequate self-expression of the speaker, trying hard to say what he means, how he made a fool of himself with his big talk to impress the girl, may make the story more meaningful and moving. Anderson gains his effect by working within the limited vocabulary of the boy, with his "Gee whizz" and "you know how a fellow is." The question of style in first-person stories should be carefully considered by the writer, for to-day's realism demands an authentic speech.

This is particularly important with characters who speak and think in a jargon of their own. Dialect stories with their phonetic spellings are no longer in fashion and would annoy the modern reader, whether it is western, southern, hillbilly, New York, Boston, or some other kind of speech; few regional differences are left, and standard American speech is used in all parts of the country. An exception might be made for Negro speech written by writers who are not Negroes themselves, as in William Faulkner's novels. But if we read a gangster's story in first person, we would expect him to express himself like a man of his own particular category in the underworld, with its wide variations. Not all gangsters talk alike. Obviously it is more interesting to have a gangster tell his story in his own words; what a tough delinquent boy has to say about himself is more revealing than what a social scientist says about him.

The protagonist need not be a "hero." Whenever possible, villains should be rendered in first person and from their own point of view. First person is better for the sinner than the saint. Let the scoundrel speak for himself, he can be condemned out of his own words. Jason Compson in *The Sound and the Fury* is not a bad man to himself; from his own point of view he is right. The gangster does not see himself as a criminal. The miser does not see himself as a miser. The treatment of negative characters in first person becomes ironic, and irony is more effective than condemnation. In a third-person story an effort should be made to present the bad man in first person, if possible, and let him interpret the events. I-as-hero is even better when it is I-as-villain and what we have said about the hero as narrator may be applied with greater effect to the villain. That calls for real imaginative writing, however. There is nothing like first person for a devastating portrait of an unsympathetic character; then the credibility is complete. Celine's *Journey to the End of the Night* would lose its force in third person, even though Celine did not mean to be ironic.

Character voice, with its corollary character point of view, is a dramatic norm, in either first person or third. The proportion of "I"s in a story with or without quotation marks may be a fairly accurate index of its immediacy and dramatic interest. The author's report becomes a character's report in first person. Dostoyevsky began to write *Crime and Punishment* in first person as a confession by Raskolnikov, but later decided to make it an author's report in third person, using the omniscient point of view, which as we said is the analytical method preferred in psychological fiction (e.g. *Madame Bovary*). But there is so much dialogue in the novel and there are so many lengthy quotations from Raskolnikov's mind that much of the book is still in first person.

Character comment may not be enough; a story may also need some author comment, with the author's superior knowledge supplying the interpretation the reader may need for a fuller understanding of the story. The character may not know what is really happening to him, or to others, or perhaps he is not articulate enough to be narrator.

A story is also a criticism of life. The writer chooses meaningful events, and we cannot insist upon his exit if omniscience is necessary for bringing out the full implications of the subject he has chosen. *Crime and Punishment* (which we shall use as another basic text) has a dramatic plot. It is as full of suffering as a Greek tragedy, and its underlying theme is pathos-mathos. It is scene rather than summary in method. Many parallels may be drawn—and have been drawn—between Dostoyevsky's method in *Crime and Punishment* and his other novels and Greek tragedy. It is impossible to say whether *Crime and Punishment* would have been better in first person, as a sinner's confession, but Raskolnikov, a university student and author of an article on crime published in a magazine, was perfectly capable of telling his own story. Dostoyevsky often wrote in first person: e.g., *Notes from Underground, A Raw Youth, The Devils, Memoirs of the House of the Dead.*

Since the hero-narrator cannot enter other minds, first person makes for an objective concrete presentation of secondary characters, and that is all to the good. But the same inability to penetrate the thoughts of others may also be a serious drawback, for it means that none of the other characters may be presented from the inside. The omniscient author can enter minds or stay out of them, he can be partisan or detached, he can regulate his distance from any character and be as objective and subjective about any person and in any part of the story as he likes. But the hero is personally involved in the events, his own fate is at stake, and his attitude toward the other characters will be a highly personal one and perhaps prejudiced; he cannot be neutral if they influence his fate in any way, he cannot regulate his distance from the secondary characters with the freedom enjoyed by the omniscient narrator. The hero is strictly limited to his own point of view, to his own range of vision, external and internal, and the author's knowledge cannot be added to his. A dull narrator in a first-person story would not do. He should at the very outset engage the reader's attention and be a character worth knowing. If he is a person of charm, humor, wisdom, if his eyes miss little or nothing, the autobiographical method can be very effective, but it would be fatal to the story if, no matter how heroic, the protagonist is a bore.

The gaps in the hero's knowledge may add to the suspense of the story. He can be highly selective in his choice of events. This makes for economy, intensity. Many of the things we said about the single character point of view may be applied to first-person writing.

Like the personal author who addresses himself directly to the reader and calls him "gentle reader" or "my sagacious friend" or "good folks," the first person hero is exposed to the same temptation of winning the reader's good opinion. If he speaks to the reader he is like an actor addressing the audience instead of speaking only to other actors in the play. The reader would rather overhear than hear. In Albert Camus'

The Fall, we overhear the monologue of the hero, Jean-Baptiste Clamence, as he drinks his gin in a bar and tells his story to a chance acquaintance. We overhear the husband in *The Kreutzer Sonata* by Tolstoy, as he tells in a railway compartment how and why he killed his wife. First-person can be wholly or partly a monologue, a confession.

Henry James decided not to make Strether both hero and historian and denied him the "romantic privilege" of first person. He believed first person in the long piece is "foredoomed to looseness," and he warns us against the "terrible *fluidity* of self-revelation." Strether therefore tells his story in third person. First person is a risk, especially when it is addressed directly to the reader, as in *Tristram Shandy,* but today many first-person novels by Hemingway and others are tightly written, and James himself wrote short stories and novellas in first person. Whether I-as-hero should tell the story to another character, to the reader, to himself, or to no-one in particular is another delicate point. Holden in *Catcher in the Rye* tells it to the reader, but only two years after the events he describes. He is eighteen, speaking about experiences that happened when he was sixteen. This in itself gives the story a certain immediacy; he is after all still a teen-age boy. We have the feeling that this engaging narrator from a prep-school wasteland is perhaps a little too cute, too anxious to win the good opinion of the reader. We do not have this feeling when we read Tolstoy's *Childhood, Boyhood,* and *Youth,* all written in first person.

Perhaps the most serious drawback of this method is the blur of the viewpoint character we mentioned in third-person writing. The major character who tells his own story is often less concrete than the minor characters whom we see through his eyes; he is the seer who does not see himself from the outside. What does Lieutenant Henry in *Farewell to Arms* look like? We are not sure. But we know what Catherine looks like. We know what Emma Bovary looks like. This method goes with the seeing eye and would not do for characters who should only be seen.

MINOR CHARACTER TELLS THE STORY

When the observer is a minor character in first person, he can give an objective description of the hero, which the hero cannot do for himself. He himself can remain invisible, and the damage to the story is less than when the hero is invisible, for his role is a minor one and he is writing about the hero rather than about himself. He can praise the hero or criticize him, he can freely comment on the characters and the action, and everything he says is character words, drama. I-as-observer removes nearly all the objections we might raise to I-as-hero. Writers such as Somerset Maugham, who will not use the autobiographical method but want to write in first person—it is a good "telling" method, and Maugham habitually tells—prefer to have a more or less detached observer tell the story. With Maugham it is not "Dramatize, dramatize!"

True, the observer cannot enter the mind of the hero or of any other character; nor can he even have the limited omniscience of the author-observer in the dramatic method. If he is not there himself, he does not know what happened, unless somebody who was there tells him. But this too may be turned to advantage, in detective stories, for instance. In murder mysteries it would ruin the suspense if the writer were omniscient about the murderer, and allowed the reader to enter the murderer's mind. When Dr. Watson tells the story of Sherlock Holmes, instead of Sherlock Holmes telling his own story, Dr. Watson's account gains in suspense and mystery, and Sherlock Holmes does not have to sing his own praises. Mystery can add to the interest of any plot, and is of course particularly useful in crime stories. Consider the possibilities of mysterious motives in crimes. Not only Dostoyevsky but Raskolnikov himself wanted to know *why* he killed the old woman. Though this is the most important single point in the book, the novel does not give us in fact the full answer.

Defective knowledge may have great effect in fiction, when

full knowledge would give the story away. Through a process of gradual revelations, narrator and reader learn together, now following one clue, now another, and making a series of discoveries; the story may be written around these discoveries, until the mystery is solved, or not solved. It may be convenient for the narrator not to be present at the scene, and not to know what happened at a particular time and place. He may be away when something important happens, the revelation of which should be postponed, or when a lot of unimportant things happen that need not be reported at all. He can concentrate on the crucial incidents and write in larger units of action. This method allows the writer to eliminate a good many expository summaries and move from scene to scene with abrupt transitions, to report through his witness the big moments only.

The onlooker is not under obligation to give a full definitive portrait of his hero. Not having access to his thoughts he has to make suppositions, he has to speculate, with the hero remaining perhaps something of a mystery to the end. It can be an intriguing and effective end. When we finish reading Nick Caraway's account of the life of James Gatz in *The Great Gatsby*, we know no more about this bootlegger and racketeer living in the grand style and giving lavish parties than what Nick Caraway was able to learn; we feel the mystery of the man is not completely solved after his murder and that we have only one man's interpretation of him. Some of the shadows in his personality remain.

It is worth noting that in *My Ántonia* Willa Cather told the story of Ántonia Shimerda not omnisciently, or by the autobiographical method, but through Jim Burden, Ántonia's next-door neighbor when they lived together as children on the Nebraska frontier. Willa Cather had a sympathetic interest in the early Bohemian settlers, but to her they were an alien people undergoing a process of Americanization, and it is a good guess that she did not feel she was able to write about them with the same authority as she could about American pioneers. It would have been even more difficult for her to have Ántonia tell her story in her own words, or to write it in third person from her authorial point of view. Jim Burden tells it as an observer, with his necessarily limited knowledge of Ántonia, and after the passage of many years, so that his account of her is a series of reminiscences. If there are defects in his account, that is none of Miss Cather's affair; Jim Burden can tell only what he knows and remembers. We do not have the full inside view into Ántonia's character, she is presented from the outside only. It is a moving portrait, a minor classic in its field.

If the writer does not know too much about a person or a group of people, about a way of life, a period, or a place, it might be hazardous for him to write about it omnisciently or in the form of an autobiography; he is safer with a witness. He can make the witness a detached observer, even an ignorant one, and keep out of minds he does not wish to enter. He does not have to assume the responsibility of complete knowledge which omniscience entails. The writer lets the onlooker interpret the people and the events as he sees them. He may describe them as he remembers them, years later, and thus the writer can make the story more contemporary and bring it nearer to the reader in time. A few decades might be gained by this way, as in *My Ántonia*.

In I-as-hero the events happen to the narrator and the main story lies in him. In I-as-observer the events happen *around* the narrator. But it is not always possible to make this distinction, for the onlooker may be passionately involved in the action, and not only the hero's fortune be at stake, but his own, too. He may be a major character himself, one of several principals; or he may be a minor character in one part of the story and a major one in the next, begin as an onlooker and end up as hero. The two methods are often combined in the same story, as in *David Copperfield*.

The author may make himself the observer-narrator under his own name. Somerset Maugham appears under his own name in *The Razor's Edge*, as though he were telling a true story, and we are reading fact, not fiction. This method has been used more frankly and consistently by Christopher Isherwood.

My first two novels, "All the Conspirators" and "The Memorial," were written in the third person. In both these books, I shifted the viewpoint from character to character as often as the narrative seemed to demand.

By the time I was ready to write my third novel, "The Last of Mr. Norris" (called "Mr. Norris Changes Trains" in the British edition) I had come to feel that this switching of viewpoints was unsatisfactory because it distracted the reader's attention from the scene and made him too much aware of the technical mechanism of narration. Also I disliked seeming to claim that I knew how other people felt and thought. I only knew how *I* thought and felt, I said, this viewing at second-hand lacked immediacy and I wanted to describe everything from my own point of view. So I wrote the book in the first person. I was still shy, however, of admitting that the narrator was in fact me, so I called him William Bradshaw, my two middle names (until I dropped them for the sake of brevity on becoming a U.S. citizen).

When I started to write "Goodbye to Berlin," I had decided that it was silly not to come right out and call the narrator Christopher Isherwood. But, in doing this, I now realize, I wasn't being quite frank with myself; I was more self-conscious than I would admit and this gave me inhibitions. I felt myself responsible for whatever Christopher said or did (even if it was fictitious) and so I tended, without knowing it, to hold him back from mixing too freely in the action of the story and thereby compromising me. (I would never have allowed him to become as deeply involved as William Bradshaw was in the intrigues of Mr. Norris.) I made Christopher primarily an observer (who says "I am a camera") and therefore somewhat cold-blooded in his relations with the other characters. (In this respect he differed greatly from his namesake the author!) Christopher's attitude to the reader seems always a little self-deprecatory, as though he were saying, "Don't mind me, I just work here."

In "Prater Violet" I again used Christopher to tell the story in the first person, and in this case I think I was more successful, because the chief character, Friedrich Bergmann, is so dominating and so voluble that it seems natural for Christopher to be a mere observer. He has difficulty in getting a word in edgeways.

My rule for the use of Christopher had always been that I would freely invent conversations and incidents but would never make him do or feel anything that was altogether outside the range of my own experience. In "The World in the Evening" I wanted to write a story which included some situations I hadn't personally lived through—for example, marriage to a woman novelist—so I used a first person narrator called Stephen Monk, a wealthy goodlooking bisexual Anglo-American. I knew that I wasn't Stephen and yet I kept forgetting and imputing my personal reactions to him—so he lacks conviction as a character. I now think that I should have told the story from Christopher's point of view, making him a minor observer-character. Or else I should have told it in the third person.

In "Down There on a Visit" I used Christopher for the third and, as I at present believe, the last time. Here I consciously tried to involve him more deeply in the action—but this was a little like trying to liven someone up by making him drunk, it really proved nothing. The truth is that Christopher cannot by his very nature be a character like the other characters in a novel. He is merely a kind of scanning device which is being operated at long-distance by the author. So I am forced to conclude that the whole I-Christopher experiment is a failure, in the last analysis.

In "A Single Man" I used a narrative technique which seems satisfactory to me—I mean for this particular novel. The story is told in the present tense by a non-personal seemingly disembodied narrator who never says "I" and addresses the reader with the air of a surgeon lecturing to medical students during an operation. The "patient" is the chief character, George. The narrator knows everything that George feels and thinks and is present with him at all times. But he is not a part of George. Indeed it will be possible for George to die while the narrator looks on and describes his death to the reader. This technique can of course only be used under very special conditions. A narrator of this kind can only accompany one character—or possibly two very closely-involved characters—at a time, or so it seems to me. And I doubt if he could be made to switch from one character to another in the course of the same book without losing much of his effectiveness.

The novel I have just finished "A Meeting by the River," is told entirely in documents written by the two chief characters. One writes letters, the other keeps a diary. There is no narrator to represent "the truth" and of course the statements made in the letters and diary are merely subjective, indeed they sometimes contradict each other. This may have the effect of leaving the reader bewildered and dissatisfied— as if he had been listening to a lawsuit in which both sides were possibly lying and there was no judge or jury. That remains to be seen!

(Personal communication)

STORY TOLD BY MORE THAN ONE CHARACTER

The method of telling a story in first person by several character-observers, each acting as an expert witness of some phase of the action, or in portraying the main character, is not often used in modern fiction, but has interesting possibilities, and if the story is well plotted it will hang together. A recent example is *Ada Dallas* by Wirt Williams.

When a novelist's chief problem is the problem of plausibility, his solution very often will turn out to be the selection of the first person point of view, the first person narrator providing a simple, powerful authority. This is what I did in "Ada Dallas."

The materials were, in themselves, somewhat implausible. They were quite *possible*—most of the incidents in the story (though not the characters) had their origin in the recent history of Louisiana, and in a Latin-American republic. But Louisiana is an intensely implausible state.

A call girl who puts herself through a fashionable girls' college by her labor, who maneuvers to marry a prospective governor, who subsequently ousts him so that she can have his job—this is on the face of it, an improbable situation. To make it plausible requires the use of the strongest authority, and the strongest authority is developed by the first person point of view.

I became convinced of this, but not until after I had written seventy thousand words of my novel, using the effaced narrator (as in "Madame Bovary") as my authority—the authority to which most formally trained writers tend to gravitate. The result was not convincing, not believable, I thought. I do not say the story could not have worked with the method of the effaced narrator: I only say I was not able to make it work.

Intuitively, I shifted to a first-person narrator. And to explore a wider range of experience, to see the story from as many perspectives as possible, I shifted from one first person narrator to another, three in all.

The result is a case study in the interrelationship of all fictional problems. The solving of one led here, as it so often does, to the solving of many more.

The use of the three first person narrators liberated and made visible to myself one of my esthetic thrusts: I realized

I wished to make of the novel not simply a tragic narrative, but an exercise in the formal strategies of the tragic theater. In each character, I wished to embody the existential thrust toward choice and final definition by action. Chosen at first by intuition, the three characters evolved to represent definite components of the human psyche as work on the book progressed. Together, they made one integrated personality: as representations of abstractions, they and what they did made a philosophical fable.

In the fable Ada became reality, as seen by each of them.

To put it as simply as I can, the search for the right point of view helped me find my entire novel. It started, incidentally, from nothing more than the skyscraper capitol of the state of Louisiana (which, technically, became my co-ordinating symbol). This building I saw as an incomparable concentration of motives and acts, of good and evil—Huey Long was shot on the first floor, the bullet streaks are still on the walls—and I wanted to get as much of its passion as I could into my book.

(Personal communication)

PRESENTNESS IN THE FIRST PERSON

"Here and now" is a basic principle of the dramatic method in fiction, although something may be said also for the historic or narrative method. In some stories it is necessary to emphasize the pastness of the past and to make it definitely history—and the past may be seen through the golden haze of memory. Presentness is an illusion promoted by the scene. Every story in first person is past action, it has happened already. The dramatic present is a device for bringing the action nearer to the reader in time and place to make it more immediate, as in a play. This might be done more easily in third person, but it may be done also in first.

Thomas Mann chose to tell the story of Hans Castorp as something that happened long ago, giving it a "historic mold." The novel was published only ten years after the outbreak of the First World War with which the book closes. Mann deliberately threw the story back as though into a remote past, and, indeed, in 1924 the world before 1914 seemed ancient enough. Time is an important story element in *The Magic*

Mountain, and by this treatment the sanatorium at Davos-Platz acquired a timeless mythical quality. The subject required this; the effect he sought was part of his theme. "Since histories must be written in the past, then the more past the better," he says as he begins to tell the story of young Hans Castorp, speaking in his own person, as though he were looking back into the distant past before the First World War.

But, unless it is the writer's intention to give his story this historic or legendary quality, presentness is highly desirable and is a marked feature of modern fiction. And presentness goes well with inwardness. Interior monologue is both present and inward, written in first person, present tense, and is our clue to immediacy in first person. We need monologue and dialogue for immediacy whether the story is told in first person or third, but they are more important in first person because of its tendency to throw a story backward in time. When a story is written as though the events depicted in it have only just taken place, before they become memory and while the narrator is still in the grip of the original agitation, with the outcome uncertain, it will have a quality of presentness as in a diary or letter.

There is a difference between an event in progress, currently developing and rendered as such, and an event that is over, past, finished: the difference between scene and summary, drama and narrative. In the developing action or scene, the first-person narrator is looking ahead and wondering what will happen next; in the memoir or history he is looking back after it has happened. There is more turmoil in the former; we are not dealing with ashes after passions have cooled off, the conflict perhaps is red hot, the joys are intense, and so is the pain, the anguish. The narrator is still wrestling with his problem: it is still war, not peace; the raw throbbing wound rather than a healed scar.

In "The Horla" by Maupassant, we have the diary of a man who is going mad. (Maupassant himself died insane.)

> May 8. I have spent the whole morning lying in the grass in front of my house, under the enormous plane tree that covers it completely in the shelter of its shade. I love this part

of the country and I like to live here because I am attached to it with deep roots. . . . I love my house where I grew up. From my windows I can see the Seine flowing by the side of my garden. . . . How delicious this morning has been!

May 11. I have had a slight fever for the past few days; I feel ill or rather in low spirits. Whence do these mysterious influences come that change our happiness to depression and our self-confidence to discouragement?

May 16. I am certainly ill! I was so well last month!

His situation becomes progressively worse, though there are some temporary improvements. The diarist is haunted by an elusive mysterious Being, a monster who becomes his master, and to free himself of his tormentor he burns down his house. The journal ends on September 10 with these frantic words, "No . . . no . . . without any doubt he is not dead . . . then . . . then . . . I suppose I must kill myself, myself. . . ."

An acute emotional crisis may be rendered effectively in diary form, in the words of the person going through the agony, and such diaries are often inserted in novels and short stories. The diary gives variety through change of viewpoint, whether the story as a whole is written in third person or first. In *The End of the Affair,* by Graham Greene, written in first person, the diary gives information about Sarah which the narrator, a novelist by profession, is not in position to know at the moment. Letters may serve the same purpose.

Should a whole novel be written in diary form? A diary is a pretty shapeless thing, loose, fragmentary. Since a novel needs more unity and continuity than a short story, the diary is not the ideal form in a long piece of fiction. *Nausea* by Jean-Paul Sartre, *A Hero of Our Time* by Mikhail Lermontov, *Gentlemen Prefer Blondes* by Anita Loos, and other diary novels are generally short books.

The method of the diary is what happened today or yesterday, and the event is recorded shortly after it happens. The advantages of the method are that the dialogue in a diary often sounds more authentic; it is useful if the writer needs to shorten the time between the event and its report; and the present tense of the diary makes for presentness. Within the present tense the past tense also is used, to express time distinctions.

Wuthering Heights opens with Lockwood's diary.

> 1801.—I have just returned from a visit to my landlord—the solitary neighbor that I shall be troubled with. This is certainly a beautiful country! In all England, I do not believe that I could have fixed on a situation so completely removed from the stir of society. A perfect misanthropist's Heaven—and Mr. Heathcliff and I are such a suitable pair to divide the desolation between us. A capital fellow! He little imagined how my heart warmed towards him when I beheld his black eyes withdraw so suspiciously under their brows. . . .

We do not seem to be in 1801 as we read these impressions of Lockwood. We are not looking back at some remote past on the moors. "Yesterday afternoon set in misty and cold." It seems as though this did happen yesterday; Lockwood is jotting down on the spot what happened today or yesterday.

The Stranger by Albert Camus is not a diary novel, but it uses the same method of today and yesterday. "Mother died today. Or perhaps yesterday; I can't be sure." Samuel Beckett begins *Molloy* on the same doubtful note. "I am in my mother's room. It's I who live there now. I don't know how I got there." These modern characters suffer from amnesia. No oceans divide the wastelands of the world.

The present tense contributes to presentness and slows down, prolongs, or freezes the action. "I go," or "I am going" is slower than "I went." It is present action; "I went" is already past. The present tense may be used for emphasizing critical or otherwise significant moments in the story, for a magnified close-up to bring out the salient features of the scene and increase its emotional impact, or for giving the scene a timeless dreamlike quality. It may be a retarding or an intensifying device. Japanese actors are said to commit hara-kiri in slow motion. Dream scenes on the screen are often shown by slow-motion photography. A close-up of a strangling scene will magnify the hands and slow down their movement.

"He raised his rifle and fired" is a completed act. "He raises his rifle to fire," or, even better, "he is raising his rifle to fire," is an action still in progress, and slower. It gives us the process rather than the result, and prolongs the event. We get a closer imitation of the act. A short piece in present tense will stretch out the event and may enhance its dramatic or poetic values. Though we usually need the speed-up of the past tense, some whole novels have been written in present tense, a well-known, recent example being John Updike's *Rabbit, Run*. And we have, of course, *Tristram Shandy* by Laurence Sterne, forerunner of interior monologue. Present tense is more popular in France than in this country, perhaps because we Americans live in a land of high-speed action.

One may write part of the story in present tense and part of it in past tense. It may begin and end in present tense. By ending a story in the present tense the writer can bring the story time up to the moment of its writing, closer to the reader's time, and thus make it more immediate. James Baldwin's *Giovanni's Room* begins and ends in the present tense.

Speech, too, makes the story present. *A Farewell to Arms* and *The Sun Also Rises* do not seem to be memoirs because they are written in first person. They have dramatic immediacy because of Hemingway's habit of direct dialogue in specific scene.

"I am sure," "I suppose," "I remember," "As I recall it now," "It was many years ago," and such expressions make the story reminiscence, satisfactory only if that is the writer's purpose, and diminish or destroy the illusion of story time, widening the gap between it and the writing time. If it is not moment to moment as in inner monologue and today or yesterday as in diary and letter, the time lapse between the event and its narration increases and the story is thrown farther back into the past. Let us say we are reading about an event that happened in Chicago in 1957, and the narrator has carried us mentally to Chicago in that year. "I was sure," "I supposed," "It seemed to me," will keep us with him in Chicago, or with the story time, but any reference to 1967 will jerk us out of Chicago in 1957, and when we go back to Chicago again, back to the scene where we left off, its momentum might be lost. If the writer wants to tell the story dramatically, the action is more immediate when he renders it without retrospective comment. But there is nothing wrong with restrospection if the story is a memoir.

The dramatic method does not favor the backward retrospective glance, but it may be a good practice for the writer to think a story backward even if he does not write it backward. Thinking backward means getting down to the causes of the present situation, tracing the chain of causality from the end to the beginning, and answering perhaps some crucial why's. A story written backward has its own suspense. Suspense is not always the result of what happens next; it may be what happened before, and some stories are told best through flashbacks. The flashback can be dramatized and given as scene, and within the flashback we can have a forward movement, a progressive series of incidents. Too many flashbacks however may disconnect the story line and confuse the reader. Generally a flashback should not come until the present situation is well established and the story is well on its way.

REFLECTION OF THE WRITER'S ATTITUDES AND VALUES

Point of view is more than a technical or aesthetic problem in fiction. It is not simply a question of literary optics, and both sight and insight are involved in this matter. Behind the point of view as the method of narration there is the moral point of view, and we have to use this term in both its meanings. The writer's total vision of life, or his world view, and his personal character, his worth as a human being, enter the picture, particularly in critical realism.

A story is a subject plus an attitude. Different attitudes give us different themes out of the same material, and different themes give us different stories. The author's attitude sets the tone and provides a subtle inner unity for the story he writes. The interpretation of the events is ultimately the writer's, no matter how impersonal his method, and whether he himself is the narrator or speaks through a character or from a character's point of view. The author is making a personal statement on life by writing his story. He is not just a camera or a tape recorder. Such a statement involves a moral judgment, and a writer is judged by his judgments. He cannot go beyond his own scale of values.

It may be argued that a writer's primary task is to see and not to judge, that what we expect from him is a truthful imitation of life and not a commentary upon it, which he can leave to the philosopher or the scientist. It is an attractive doctrine. But the writer cannot make his mimesis truthful if he does not understand human nature, the social system, economics, politics, and so on. He cannot be ignorant. He does not give us random camera shots; he selects his pictures, and he arranges them in a certain order to make their meaning clear. A story is more than the sum total of its parts. But the writer's judgment should be an integral part of the story, and not a sermon.

It should be clear by now that there is no one best point of view. It is good or bad, better or worse, according to the particular subject, and what may be good for one story, or writer, may be bad for another. The method of narration has to point up the meaning of the tale as well as of individual incidents in it. A well-defined point of view, consistently employed, means a well defined theme. The idea, which means "seeing" in Greek, springs from the writer's inner vision. The initial organization of the story begins in the writer's imagination. When he has an idea for a story, he has already done a good deal of seeing and rearranging. In selecting his narrator the writer has to consider not only problems of vision and degrees of knowledge but the total meaning and intention of the story he has in mind. The point of view should bring out the significance of the events, and it is the point of view in its double sense that would give his story shape and meaning. Point of view may be the difference between a well-told story and a half-told tale, or story and no story.

We saw the advantages and disadvantages of various points

of view, and others may be added to the list. We may look forward to some brilliant individual experiments. New themes, fresh subject matter, hitherto unexplored areas of experience, new values and assertions in life and literature may require new methods of narration. Various combinations are possible, third with first (*Lord Jim*), first with second (*The Fall*), and method may be combined with method.

Few readers are conscious of these differences in point of view, and even some professional writers, editors and publishers are not aware of them. They write or judge by instinct. Once we make a systematic study of point of view, we cannot write or read stories as innocently as we used to. It seems like eating from the tree of knowledge and paradise lost. But it is a discovery worth making, and will excite the experimental writer. We are far from knowing everything about point of view. It is almost beyond the power of the individual writer or critic to gain a full mastery of this subject, yet nothing is more important in fiction than the authority of the narrator and his control of distance, the mind he enters or does not enter, whether he should tell the story directly himself or indirectly through a character, from his own point of view or that of a character, and what should be his attitude and tone in order to bring out the full implications of his theme. The writer has to consider carefully the particular position from which an experience is to be re-created and evaluated, and when the reader becomes aware of such problems he develops a new respect for the writer. He realizes what a difficult and complicated thing it is to write a novel, that inspiration is not enough, and something more than imagination is needed in mimesis. That something is technique.

Flaubert had it. He would have ruined *Madame Bovary* if he had made it simply an author's report and not used Emma's eyes in crucial scenes. The story goes flat when we do not see this provincial life through Emma's eyes. We are continuously in Emma's mind after we meet her on her father's farm, until her death, and the point of view shapes the story as well as the style in this great book.

5. PLOT: THE CHALLENGE
OF CHAOS [I]

The craft of fiction is basically a study of story structure and style. The poet is a builder or maker or arranger according to the original meaning of the word, and we can draw many parallels between writing and building.

Structural problems are of great technical interest to the writer because they are part of the very essence of his craft. He needs a touch of madness to be sure, but he has to dramatize his argument through an action, whether he consciously knows his argument or not, and convert raw experience to art. Since a story is not an exact transcript from life, it does not even mirror life, but expresses it, the writer can give only his own idealized version of reality in his own language. We have to recognize the limitations of the verbal medium, but the reader's imagination comes to the writer's aid and the reader, needless to say, is willing to be deceived. Without this willingness on the part of the reader there can be no plausible plot.

The writer can start with factual events if he wishes. Just because something has happened in real life does not mean it is not good material for fiction and he has to invent his plots. What has actually happened is more probable, and the factual order of the incidents may be just right, but generally the writer takes the haphazard and disconnected facts of life and arranges them in an orderly sequence to make one significant whole. If the inner connections are missing in life, he supplies them in fiction and fills in the gaps to complete the action.

MOTIVATION OF CHARACTERS

Probably the first step in creative construction is to work out the motivation of the characters that cause the action. The writer has to know what they want even when they do not know it themselves. It has to be a purposeful action, and purpose spins plot. The story line is the wish line. All plots may be reduced to the four or five basic sociological wishes. Since the subject a fiction writer chooses is always an emotional experience he has to know the nature of the particular emotion that makes a character do certain things. He has to specify it for himself, sharpen it, make it one definite feeling. The search for a father. How a daughter rejected by her mother feels about her. The psychology of the marginal man. The joy of discovering a friend when least expected. The desire for fame and glory. The desire for communication; how a person like Walt Whitman's noiseless patient spider launches forth filaments out of himself, tirelessly unreeling them to connect with somebody. The wish for recognition, for status, for simple human dignity, for security. Romantic love. Sex.

The aim of technique is to make the story an emotional experience for the reader also, and unless this happens the story fails in its purpose. Action in fiction—as in life—is a motivated action, and the motive is part of the emotion or the emotion *is* the motive. The two words have a common origin and mean substantially the same thing in a plot. Almost everything we do in life has a motive behind it, whether we are aware of it or not. The motive is the cause of the deed, of why we do what we do.

Emotions, like instincts, are necessary for our survival. By defining the basic emotion of a character, the writer defines the main motive, what a person needs most at a particular time. The central emotional drive of a character might be necessary for his survival, be an expression of his will-to-live, a matter of life or death. But intense as emotions are, one cannot always define them exactly in a story. We cannot

91

define, for instance, our unconscious emotions. There are emotions that have no names; we do not even have words to describe them with, and so this definition is not as easy as it sounds.

We might say the modern novel, and particularly the psychological novel, is the history and anatomy of a complex emotion. The writer characterizes his people and brings them to life through a minute analysis or dramatization of their feelings and ideas. The definition of the emotion means the definition of the situation in which one or more people are involved. We know then what the problem is. It is not a purely private problem, and unless the universal is implied in the particular, we do not have a work of art. Like the scientist, the fiction writer deduces general laws from the particular cases before him.

The writer should feel that what he wants to say through pictures is of great human interest, that it is important, that he has some real news for the world, he has made a discovery about human nature, and the emotions he wants to depict are emotionally immediate for him. Most people are inarticulate about their feelings and ideas and the greatest stories have never been told; they lie under cemetery stones or have turned to dust or sand. But what is dumb experience for others becomes a passionate and luminous statement for the writer.

> Though a work of art must always include something new, yet the revelation of something new will not always be a work of art. That it should be a work of art it is necessary:
> (1) That the new idea, the content of the work, should be of importance to mankind.
> (2) That this content should be expressed so clearly that people may understand it.
> (3) That what incites the author to work at his production should be an inner need and not an external inducement.
> (Tolstoy, *What Is Art?* Translated by Aylmer Maude)

To communicate a significant emotion—that is the business of story or plot. If the emotion is lacking, then there is nothing to communicate except some facts about an event—but that is the task of the newspaper rather than of the fiction writer, who speaks another language, the language of feelings, the only universal language we have and the only language that will never be dead, or dated. By defining the basic emotion, the writer clarifies the whole concept of the story. If the emotion he has chosen is not clear to him at the beginning, he may clarify it during the writing process; it is crystallized after the first draft, or second, or third, or tenth. In life, many emotions at first are vague and undifferentiated, a confused disturbance or a state of general excitement; many good stories begin that way.

When we analyze a novel like *Madame Bovary* and find that its underlying idea is what a romantic young woman, daughter of a prosperous farmer, brought up in a convent and addicted to reading love stories, wanted out of life, and what she actually got out of it, how her emotional frustration in her humdrum environment led to her destruction, the theme of the story and her motivation are clear. This is a drama of deceptions and self-deceptions, one woman's revolt against intolerable boredom and mediocrity. Flaubert did not invent his plot. He used the story of a country doctor, Eugène Delamare, well known in his circle, without making any substantial changes in it. Delamare's wife, Delphine Couturier, who died of poison, became Emma Bovary. All the characters of the novel actually existed, Flaubert did not invent them; all he did was to select his material, rearrange it, and keep his own person out of it. Emma Bovary fell on the perilous road from illusion to reality, and we have in this novel a splendid illusion of reality.

We find that her emotions are (1) consistent with her character, (2) powerful enough to sustain the action, (3) complex —a system of related feelings, including her religious mysticism, making an integrated whole, (4) believable, (5) sincere—for both Emma and Flaubert, (6) important.

Flaubert could scarcely exaggerate the power of emotions in Emma's life, but writing is an art of concentration and intensification and has its own economy. Flaubert made her emotions even more intense than they probably were, but he underwrote. Emma's emotions are not in excess of the occasion, and this is not a sentimental novel, but she is a young woman living up to the romantic ideal. Anglo-Saxons are known for their emotional reserve and are often accused by other nations of being temperamentally cold. There are no doubt national or racial differences in emotions and their expression in literature, but it is smart to write like a cold Anglo-Saxon, provided one has some real emotions to express.

The world has changed since Flaubert's time and today most women and men are cold. We are desensitized, hardened. We do not feel. We cannot. In *The Stranger,* the narrator does not care much one way or another about anything that happens to him, not even about his forthcoming execution for killing an Arab without a discernible motive; he is a man emptied of all feelings. This short novel is deliberately underwritten because the hero is so estranged from himself and from others that his feeling tone has dwindled to a diffuse twilight stage. It has to be a short book. There is just enough feeling in it to sustain the action. We read it rather coldly. If the character does not care, we do not care either. He remains a stranger to us. We expect greater emotional involvement from a first-person narrator than we have in this novel. But today readers also are cold. We too are strangers.

COMMUNICATION OF EMOTION

The defined emotion gives the writer not only a motive, a subject, a theme, but also the action, which is emotionally charged; there is the fire of desire in it. An emotion is not a stationary force, it is a tumultuous movement, and it gives movement to the plot. It is not diffuse, aimless, ending nowhere, but is definite and channeled, canalizing the action it instigates. The emotion "insists" on realizing its end. It has a goal, but its goal, as in Emma's case, is frustrated, and if fiction is to be true to life it must depict frustrated emotions. The drama comes out of frustration.

The action in *Madame Bovary* then issues out of Emma's character and emotions. Its source lies in her disposition and her foolish heart, and Flaubert took care to connect the action with her emotions. At no time is the action independent of her emotions, or contrary to them. If there is no emotion in a situation, then there is strictly speaking no action, no story. There may be activity, but it is not an action as we understand that term in fiction. By action we mean a motivated action—there is an emotion behind it as its cause, and the writer has to know the cause.

Having chosen and defined the basic emotion, which, to repeat, is not a single feeling but a pattern of related feelings making one whole, the next problem for the writer is how to communicate it to the reader. He wants the reader to be infected with the same emotion he felt in writing the story. Unless this emotional communication takes place the story fails in its purpose. The reader should not read it coldly, even if the writer wrote it coldly. He should be emotionally stirred by it; there should be some visceral disturbance if possible.

By dramatizing an emotion through an action, the writer supplies the concrete correlates that objectify the emotion and gives them sensuous pictorial form. It is not an abstract emotion in the story, but particular and concrete, emotion-in-action. Without this dramatic presentation giving it immediacy, the emotion would lose its impact, and without embodying the emotion in concrete correlates and converting it to pictures, it would remain a general abstract feeling uncommunicated to the reader. In fiction it is not love or sorrow in general, as it might be in an essay, but a particular love or sorrow (Emma's), the emotion individualized and embodied in objectifying details—and in fiction, let us remember, it is the detail that does the trick, what Stendhal called *"le petit fait vrai."* A prose dense with authentic and significant detail, packed with concrete correlates, not abstract, but visual, sensuous, precise, scientifically accurate, rhythmic, that is what we find in *Madame Bovary*.

One is tempted to say we cannot have too many of these concrete details in a novel, that the writer should engage not only in miniature painting but write with a microscope. But much as we prize the exact, specific detail, it can be overdone, and the writer has to strike a balance between the particular and the general and not bury his theme in so much detail that the reader is fatigued and his attention wanes. The idea of the story, the universal in it, should shine out through the detail and illuminate the whole.

A successful story then is an emotion communicated, and it is communicated through the form the writer gives his story. Form objectifies and dramatizes the emotion, and without form, without giving the emotion body and shape, we would have an abstract chaos of feeling and not a complex system of pictures, as in *Madame Bovary*. This is where technique, conscious craftsmanship, comes in—and unconscious craftsmanship too, inspiration, or instinct, or madness. The writer has to bring into existence something that was shapeless and chaotic, give form to what was formless, and it is a whale of a job. When the writer knows the nature of the emotion, precisely what it is that motivates his characters, he has a story line. If he is not clear about the motives of his characters, then he is not clear about his subject and he will flounder along with his characters and get lost in irrelevant details. The story becomes a hit-or-miss affair.

From disorder to order, from multiplicity to unity, from complexity to simplicity: that is what plot does. If it is a good plot, it is never a complete order, a complete unity, a complete simplicity; some of the original disorder, multiplicity, and complexity must be preserved or there will be no life left in the plot. Plot structures and simplifies the action. It defines and dramatizes the basic emotion and makes it communicable. Plot is the final sharpening of the action. It is a story logically structured, unified, and represents a principle of artistic economy.

STORY OR PLOT

We do not as yet have an exact technical vocabulary in the theory of fiction, and a key word like plot means different things to different people, not only in ordinary conversation but in literary criticism, too. Some say plot and mean story, others say story and mean plot. There is no generally accepted definition of plot.

When the writer succeeds in reducing the complex multiplicity of experience with its seemingly irrational aspects to a clear logical pattern that makes a point, he has a story, using the word in its general meaning and not as distinguished from plot. The experience is likely to be colored by a predominant emotion. The writer reconstructs this experience, limits it, shapes it, makes it one. "Life is many, art is one."

What happens is the story, and it is surprising how often nothing of consequence happens in stories by beginners. They are character sketches, or prose poems, or vague mood pieces, or just self-expression, and the significant event is missing in them. Now the action requires actors. Which is more important, the action or the actor? Should the emphasis be on the event, or on people? Should it be a story of character or a story of action?

This is an old argument, plot or people? To some writers and even readers, story is the least important part in a story. They are more interested in dissecting characters. Should character be emphasized at the expense of the action? By the character of a character, we mean his disposition or personality, the kind of person he is, his ethos, which is an inner cause of the action. Many writers will insist that the foundation of a good plot is good characterization and nothing else. Obviously if the people in a story do not come to life, the story is dead. The creation of living characters is absolutely indispensable in this craft.

But does this mean that what matters is the actor and not the action? Is the writer going to tell the reader about his characters, describe them, explain them, analyze them, give all the pertinent facts author-to-reader? Or is he going to let these people reveal themselves through their actions and speech, both spoken and unspoken? This is better. Characters spring to life through an action. The writer can let the reader have a direct view of his characters and bring them close to him, instead of standing between his characters and the reader. This is the scenic or dramatic method in characterization. An action, the event, is necessary for giving vitality to character.

The story part in a novel may be slight, but without it we cannot call it a novel. A collection of characters, no matter how interesting, will not make a novel. It cannot be just a gallery of still portraits, with no connection among them and with nothing happening. If we are dealing with emotions we are bound to have some action, some movement. People do something when driven by desire; they are in motion in a state of emotion. And the story is what they do and why they do it. The action re-creates not only the event but the people involved in it.

"Tragedy is an imitation, not of men, but of an action and of life, and life consists in action," says Aristotle, and to him plot was the "soul" of tragedy. Generally it was a traditional story, thought to be based on a true event. Only comic writers were expected to invent their plots. The tragic poet was rather limited in his choice; there were not too many doomed families or individuals driven to murder or incest that aroused pity and fear. Greek tragedy was grim business dripping with blood, and the primacy of the plot is understandable. In the well-made plot, as that of *Oedipus the King* by Sophocles, no incident can be eliminated or transposed without leaving a gap in the story and breaking the continuity or causal chain. Every incident is necessary by the logic of the tale and is placed in the right position. The Greek plot imitates not only the action but also the actors, who have certain qualities of character and thought. Characters gain their importance through the event, which was no mere trifle, but of tremendous consequences, taken directly from the religious folklore of Greece. The Greek plot had to do with nothing less than the destiny of man, and the gods themselves were involved in these actions. If the story is vastly important, there is no reason why we cannot place story or plot, character, thought, diction in this order, as in the *Poetics*.

He who knows the rules of good drama knows also the rules of good narrative, says Aristotle. The epic, or narrative poetry, should have a dramatic plot and be one complete and perfect action with a beginning, middle, and end. Aristotle emphasizes unity of action in the epic also, but he makes some important distinctions between the two forms which some modern writers ignore. In a dramatic novel like *Crime and Punishment,* the characters are presented through a causal action and we can see how important a series of events can be—but we cannot say that the action is more important than the characterization. Dostoyevsky is a great novelist not because of his plots but because of his characterizations, because of his insights into human nature and conduct. In the play as in the novel, it has to be character-in-action and not just character. And character-in-action can be, as it is in *Crime and Punishment,* character-and-thought.

Trollope confesses in his *Autobiography* that he had little taste or ability for plotting and he plotted his novels as he went along, not always knowing in advance what the end was going to be. And Thackeray, whom he admired, also improvised his plots instead of working them out carefully in advance. So far as we know they did not prepare scenarios like Flaubert.

> The plot of *Doctor Thorne* is good, and I am led therefore to suppose that a good plot,—which, to my own feeling, is the most insignificant part of a tale,—is that which will most raise it or most condemn it in the public judgment. . . . A novel should give a picture of common life enlivened by humour and sweetened by pathos. To make that picture worthy of attention, the canvas should be crowded with real portraits. . . . To my thinking, the plot is but the vehicle for all this; and when you have the vehicle without the passengers, a story of mystery in which the agents never spring to life, you have but a wooden show. There must, however, be a story. You must provide a vehicle of some sort. . . . I have from the first felt sure that the writer, when he sits down to commence his novel, should do so, not because he has to tell a story, but because he has a story to tell.

Trollope insisted on the story, not on the plot, by which he evidently understood a complicated scheme of action with sudden turns of fortune and the paraphernalia of the theatrical novel or the mystery story worked out by Wilkie Collins. He wrote for the amusement of the young of both sexes, and so "there must be love in a novel." His specialty was the elucidation of character, the passengers in the vehicle rather than the vehicle itself, and it paid off. "I wished to make an income on which I and those belonging to me might live in comfort." At the end of his *Autobiography* he presents his impressive financial record, how much each book earned for him. An excellent bookkeeper. He staked his literary fortune on reader identification, knowing people like to read about "characters like themselves—or to which they might liken themselves," and on love, pathos, and humor. Trollope was a shrewd judge of human nature and as a postal clerk and administrator negotiating treaties with Egypt and America he met all kinds of people, whose likenesses he made passengers in his vehicle. Construction was not his forte, but in book after book he had a story to tell.

STORY DISTINGUISHED FROM PLOT

We cannot sharply distinguish story from plot; they differ in degree and not in kind, for after all the plot, too, is a story, and the story also is plotted. By plot we mean a well-made story with tight causal relationships—the dramatic plot. Life furnishes us with stories and not with plots, in the sense that life is full of irrelevancies and waste. It is up to the writer to make a plot, and to complete the action begun in life.

And herein lies the main objection to plot, that is what makes us a little cautious about it. Plotting—causal plotting—requires wisdom, and at its best it is a philosophical exercise of a high order. One has to reason it out, supply the inner connections and the correct answers. The action is inevitable by the inner logic of the events, or at least highly probable, and many a plot is wrecked on the rock of probability. If plot falsifies life, then it is not a good plot. It need not falsify it, of course, but the risk is great in fiction.

Plot is essentially a dramatic convention, arising out of the limitations of the stage: two hours' playing time on a few square yards of space. It is a highly concentrated and organized action, a causal affair. The classic unities of time and place make for unity of action—the only unity Aristotle insisted on, necessary also in the epic, he said. But a writer can ruin his story by too much order, too much unity, too much plot. The reader feels it is contrived and not true to life. The appeal of the true story is eternal and the trick lies in making fiction read like fact when fact is converted to fiction. A story seems truer when there is some disorder in it, and this disorder can be art concealing art.

Objections to plot have to do with verisimilitude. The imitation of the action (plot) cannot please us if it is not a faithful mimesis. To make it convincing—that is the main problem in plotting, that is the challenge. It is better to err on the side of too little than too much plot. Let the story be a bit shapeless if necessary. A writer can sacrifice some beautiful formal effect to gain this all-important lifelike quality we expect today in serious fiction.

The whole problem of plotting revolves around probability. As a logical structure, plot has to be logical by the laws of its own internal probability, and probable also from the reader's point of view. A plot is made more probable on the stage or on the screen, large or small, because the actors can make it lifelike; a good actor can breathe life into a dead part. We see him, we hear him, and by his own reality the actor makes the action real. There is no such direct presentation of an event in fiction; the novelist must furnish more particulars, the concrete correlates of the emotions depicted in his story. But by the same token, what is seen with the eyes, what is shown, has to be more believable than what may be conveniently summarized in a novel. A scene requires a more likely action. It is easier to camouflage through summary.

Structure a novel must have, but not necessarily a causal action, unless one is writing detective fiction. Today even some plays are plotless (*The Time of Your Life* by William Saroyan), and we have the "epic" theatre of Bertold Brecht. Life is plotless, at least while it is being lived. Later, after the perspective of many years, we may see the inner connections of the events and the pieces of the jigsaw puzzle may fall into place. Or often it is irrational to the very end, a series of accidents, absurd all the way through, and even the perspective of years cannot supply the answers to Why. Plotting raises complex philosophical questions. Time, causality, probability, chance—these are difficult words to deal with.

In *Aspects of the Novel*, E. M. Forster distinguishes story from plot in these words: "Story is a narrative of events arranged in their time sequence . . . A plot is also a narrative of events, the emphasis falling on causality. The king died and then the queen died is a story. The king died and then the queen died of grief is a plot. The time sequence is preserved, but the sense of causality overshadows it."

This is a useful distinction, but it does not tell us that the plot is a complete story, one perfect whole, with a beginning, middle, and end.

There is obviously a difference between events that follow from and events that follow merely after each other, as Aristotle has pointed out, and this is the crucial difference between plot and story. But story, too, may have causal events. Because one thing happens after another does not mean that the law of causality has ceased to operate. The mere succession in time implies a causal relationship, philosophers of time tell us. The story question is What happens next? The plot question is Why it happens? Causes are difficult to determine and can lead both writer and reader into blind alleys.

Evidently the Greeks were the first to ask Why as they contemplated the course of human events. They created plot, just as they created geometry, and geometry in turn created Europe. Plot is the geometry of fiction, a proved theorem. When we start looking for reasons and want to know why, we may find the inner connections, the causes. Plot makes for economy, intensity, excitement. It is a more sophisticated and philosophical structure. It makes a story more definitely one and more dramatic. A chronological story in simple time sequence is a relatively naive form, but it may be enough to hold the events together. "Why" keeps a writer going in the right direction, but only God knows the final answers. "No final answers" is a safe guide for mortals. As Chekhov said, the writer's duty is to put the question right, to state the problem correctly, and he need not provide the answers; he can leave the right answers or solutions to the specialist or to the individual reader. A brooding quality of wonderment may give depth and honesty to a story.

Writers who are approaching a professional level should know the principles of the well-made causal plot even if they do not intend to use it, or reject it outright. No one has expounded these principles better than Aristotle. These principles have stood the test of time, in all civilized countries. They are the only real rules on plotting we have.

Aristotle was not a poet himself, but he analyzed the existing Greek plays and epics and saw how they were put together. We may differ with him on some minor points, but the body of technical doctrine in the *Poetics* remains unassailable. When he says that those who know what makes a good play also know what makes a good narrative, which should be constructed on the same general principles as drama, a single action, whole and complete, with a beginning, middle and end, we should not get impatient, but read on. For he also says narrative is constructed on a larger scale, and its dimensions are wider than in drama, for in narrative we can have several lines of action progressing at the same time, many events that take place simultaneously, at different places, provided they have some relation to the main subject and are not irrelevant incidents. Narrative is longer, has less need for unity, has greater variety, and can have "mass and dignity" and "grandeur of effect" beyond the scope of drama. The narrative writer can deal with vaster themes and include dissimilar episodes in his story. Aristotle mentions these special advantages of narrative fiction over the dramatic, which a fiction writer would be a fool to give up, but otherwise the same basic rules of construction apply to both.

A novel may be written on dramatic principles and may be a better novel for that reason, but a novel is not a play, and even when it has a strict sequence of its own, it is a relatively free form, and this freedom, this looseness is the birthright of the novel. But no novel is worth reading that does not have some order, some arrangement and necessary inner relationships among the parts. Even when it is a naturalistic monograph, a human document, life in the raw, it is a selected, concentrated, organized piece of writing. The naturalistic monograph, the sociological representation, the slice of life without a definite beginning and end appeals to the honest writer, and if the question were put to honest writers they would probably want to abolish plot, but there is something almost instinctive in the reader's preference for plot. Plotting requires hard thinking, and skill in plotting comes after skill in characterization or the development of a personal style. Construction can be an immensely creative job in itself—we are not speaking here of mechanical, badly constructed plots.

The classic distinctions between the dramatic and narrative forms of poetry, the tragedy and the epic, are important and should be kept in mind. They are two separate forms of storytelling and we should not confuse one with the other. The "tragic pleasure" is different from "epic pleasure." There cannot be any or all kinds of pleasure for either drama or narrative; each is designed to produce a pleasure proper to itself. The play is exclusive, the novel is inclusive. As we have repeatedly indicated, a novel should suggest the rich multiplicity of life if it is to be a complex story of complex people in complex interrelationships. The play is shorter than the novel, and its unity is necessarily tighter than the novel's. It has to be more concentrated, and the causal plot concentrates.

The design of the play is on smaller scale. The novel often does best on the grand scale, and it is interesting to note that some of the greatest best sellers in fiction have been long novels. There were the Victorian three-deckers. The major novels of Dostoyevsky and Tolstoy are long, and so is *Ulysses*, or *Gone With the Wind*, *Remembrance of Things Past*, and other popular works. The pleasure we derive from reading a long novel is different and often greater than the pleasure we get from a short novel. Length can make for beauty. "The Dead," the longest story in *Dubliners*, is the finest short story James Joyce wrote. "The Short Happy Life of Francis Macomber," "The Snows of Kilamanjaro," "The Undefeated"—these are long stories and more beautiful and memorable than Hemingway's shorter pieces. A short short story often reads like an extended anecdote. The longer story allows development. "The blessed novella," Henry James called a story midway between a novel and a short story.

Story or plot? The open or closed form? The argument comes down to how much unity we need for a fictional representation of life. A novel can be a single action, complete in itself, with a beginning, middle and end, not arbitrary or careless in its design, without an airtight causal plot.

A novel should not be too tight or too loose, too exclusive or too inclusive, too causal or too casual, and the writer has to strike a happy balance between these extremes, the exact proportions varying from book to book, depending on the subject and the treatment. In one novel the action may be causal (*Crime and Punishment*), in another casual (*Portrait of the Artist as a Young Man*). If the structure is too tight and causal, one event *from* another event, too much may be left out, and incidents that do not fit this causal pattern become irrelevant. If the structure is too loose, then the novel is shapeless, just a series of episodes. In any case, the frame should be wide enough to include a lot of life and not confine the story to purely causal incidents, but a writer has to work within a frame. Freedom of form, but too much freedom leads to incoherence and chaos.

There is no one simple answer to this question, plot or story, causal or casual. Perhaps we should sum it up in this way: the substructure of the novel should be well laid out, plotted, with all the parts interdependent, but the superstructure, the visible form, what we actually read, should be loose, with plenty of room for the writer to move around in, even in a dramatic plot. Causal underneath, casual or seemingly accidental above. Plot below, story above, with the plot part hidden. The short story requires tighter writing and can be more strictly one, and often is one as a single episode. Many of Chekhov's stories may be extended at both ends, they are loose but well constructed, with the foundation carefully laid out, the main lines firmly established.

But when the action is largely or wholly internal, as in the stream-of-thought novel, both plot and story may disappear, fade away. Here mental events do not follow a chronological or a conventionally causal sequence, for thought is free of the limitations of space and time, and what we have instead is a seemingly free association of ideas, a psychological sequence. In this whimsical moment-to-moment writing the fragmentation of external experience is almost inevitable and the external continuity is broken; the story line moves capriciously forward or backward, as anticipation or memory, and another organizing principle replaces plot.

Plot does not mean that every event follows invariably from the preceding event and all the events except the last one prepare for what comes immediately next. Causality operates as a general movement toward a goal rather than a strict linear cause-and-effect progression scene by scene and chapter by chapter and blow by blow. Nothing could be more artificial than that and it is not good even in a play. Causality makes for probability, and even better, a necessary order. It means selection, relevance, composition, harmony.

Variety is so important in the novel that the strict unity of the play should not be imposed upon it. If we exclude too much of life for the sake of dramatic unity, and force the novel to renounce its birthright as it were, we are likely to get a finished product that is dead, all the life juices have been squeezed out of it, and we have an empty shell for a book. Vitality should never be sacrificed to unity. There is such a thing as too much measure, too much control. The perils of cerebral fiction lie in that direction.

Yet the beginner who takes a loose chronicle like *War and Peace* as his model can drown in it, as in a vast lake. Henry James himself sounded this warning. Here is magnificent diversity with mass and movement and grandeur of effect that somehow, in Tolstoy's hands, makes a unified impression on the reader, an impression of the totality of Russian life it embraces, and one might say of all life. Henry James described *War and Peace* as a "wonderful mass of life, an immense event, a kind of splendid accident." But he found fault with its method, preferring Turgenev's method with its "sharp" outlines and "concision." Turgenev was a "beautiful genius." Turgenev himself acknowledged Tolstoy's superiority and called him from his deathbed "great writer of the Russian land." *War and Peace* is not a perfect novel, it is too big to be perfect, but in terms of achieved content it is a tremendous work. Even Percy Lubbock's verdict, following that of James, might be questioned. There is, we suspect, much unconscious art in Tolstoy, and if he had written his novels by the method of Henry James, or of Turgenev, if he had restrained his all-inclusive vision and given up huge chunks of life for the sake of a formal unity he might have produced a few of those great unreadables James mentions in his criticism. A great novel *is* a kind of splendid accident. Talent is not enough. Technique is not enough. A writer must also have luck. Truly original works are not copies of other books, and in writing *War and Peace* Tolstoy ignored the conventional forms of the European novel, just as he said Gogol did in writing *Dead Souls*. And it came off beautifully. James considered Tolstoy and Dostoyevsky "fluid puddings, though not tasteless," and deplored their lack of composition, of architecture, economy. Formlessness was their great vice, according to James. But it was this kind of formlessness that Tolstoy prized in Gogol; in *Memoirs of a Sportsman,* which he thought the best book Turgenev ever wrote; in Dostoyevsky's *House of the Dead;* in Lermontov's *Hero of Our Time.*

Dostoyevsky acknowledged his faults: his novels are crowded with too many separate stories and episodes and lack proportion and harmony; carried away by his poetic enthusiasm he chose ideas to which his strength was not equal, he said. But it was precisely this abundance of material he was unable to fully control and his creative daring and defiance of literary conventions that made him a great new voice in fiction. He wrote as though with an ax in his hand, with a madman's gleam in his eyes, furiously writing day and night to meet publishers' deadlines and pay off his debts, with creditors clamoring at his door. There is this same overflowing abundance of material in Tolstoy, and despite the brilliant achievements of the experimental novel in the twentieth century and all the refinements of the Jamesian and post-Jamesian techniques we do not really have better novels than those written by these two Russians. The modern trend is against omniscience, the writer is expected to wear character masks, to disguise himself by oblique methods, but a dry formal beauty is a poor substitute for a thickly populated novel teeming with life.

DRAMA AND CONTRADICTION

How important is conflict? Is it the basic element in the action of a story? Aristotle makes no mention of conflict in the *Poetics*. Some writers will say there is absolutely no drama, no story, no art without conflict; others will deny its over-all importance. In most plays action and conflict are virtually synonymous. No conflict, no play. There are good short stories without any conflict in them, and individual chapters or scenes in a novel may contain no conflict. A young couple in love need not necessarily be in conflict with each other. But whether we call it crisis, tension, or something else, conflict is a highly desirable ingredient in fiction, particularly when internal, man against himself.

Man is never a permanently harmonious whole. All of us are in a state of unstable equilibrium, and the action in every story springs from this unbalance. The story line moves from one temporary equilibrium to another, for man is a restless being, always becoming, always changing. Nothing is, everything becomes, said Heraclitus. And whether the world consists only of four elements, fire, water, earth, and air continuously transmuted into one another in fixed measures as in antiquity, or of all the elements arranged according to the periodic law, as today, there is no permanence. The atoms themselves are never at rest and the astral systems whirl in space.

O! that this too too solid flesh would melt,
Thaw and resolve itself into a dew. . . .

Hamlet's lamentation echoes in every heart. The dew potentially exists in the solid flesh. We are floating in liquid
solutions.

The concept of becoming, or of the potential and the actual, was elaborated by Aristotle in his *Metaphysics,* and it
is as important as anything he says in the *Poetics.* This idea was
picked up by Hegel and made the basis of his dialectic. We
need not go into the intricacies of Hegel's logic, but it contains important suggestions for the fiction writer. Hegel found
that a concept or thought may contain its own opposite hidden within itself, and he worked out a triad of being, not-being,
becoming. Being, an affirmative category, is not a permanent
state, but the first stage of a continuous process of becoming,
and because it contains a contradiction within itself, its own
opposite, nothing or not-being, and the reason cannot rest
in this contradiction, we advance from the second, negative
category of not-being or nothing to the third stage, becoming,
and becoming resolves the contradiction between being and
not-being, the opposites are reconciled in it. In this third
stage we have a synthesis of the thesis and antithesis. Becoming is a new being, an affirmative category, and it, too, contains a contradiction within itself, it is potentially nothing or
not-being, and so the equilibrium established by becoming is
upset again, and this dialectical process of being, not-being,
becoming is endlessly repeated. We have a never-ending inner conflict in this law of internal negation and only a temporary balance or synthesis is achieved.

This idea of an unstable equilibrium may have wide applications in literature, and at the moment we need not concern
ourselves with its ultimate scientific value. It can move the
story line, create the action. No matter what the initial situation or thought or sentiment, what desire or emotion a story
starts with, it may contain a contradiction or its opposite
within itself, and out of this contradiction the writer may get
the inner dynamics of a continuously developing process, the
power that moves the story line, not to say the power that

moves the world. Hate potentially exists in love and love potentially exists in hate. Misery potentially exists in happiness and happiness in misery. Heat potentially exists in cold and cold in heat—and one may change into the other.

The equilibrium, never stable, may exist between two persons of the same or opposite sex, between self and society, between one group and another group, one idea or ideology and another, or between two sides of the same person, one emotion or desire clashing with another emotion or desire. It is this very instability that gives a writer the conflict and movement he needs in his plot. These are some of the conclusions we may derive from the Hegelian dialectic, which is in accord with Aristotle's views of the potential and the actual widely accepted by philosophers today. The higher stages contain the lower, and the lower stages the higher. Thus, to mention an old example, the oak tree contains the acorn, and the acorn contains the oak tree. The father contains the child and the child contains the father. The past and the future exist in the present. Nothing is ever lost or forgotten, and the past stays with us. Character changes in fiction, to be convincing, must be from the potential to the actual, and the writer should plant the seeds of change in advance.

A story usually involves a change or growth and is a movement from the potential to the actual, from one unstable equilibrium to another, and the succeeding changes contain the preceding ones. Every man and every community or city or state is the sum total of past changes that took place because of unstable equilibriums, and this same process is responsible for all progress and decay. We are all caught in a cycle of continuous change and incessant strife by the inner nature of things. No wonder they called Heraclitus, who first propounded this idea of constant change, "the Weeping Philosopher." The dew dripped from his eyes.

Man seeks peace, stability, security, a state of permanent harmony within himself and in his relations with others, but he is doomed to change and insecurity, and if this were not so and we had permanently fixed states, writers would have almost nothing to write about. They write stories of change, of balance and unbalance, of tension and release, of contradictions in people and the social milieu. Since there is no security for man, because he is always becoming, almost any story is a fight or flight for safety, a search for security. People long for steadfast relationships, for permanence, for a home, for a roof over one's head, for roots somewhere; we want to stand firm against the winds of the world, to survive the storm blowing about us, and to resist as long as possible the final irrevocable change, not to melt into dew.

And in the clash of opposite forces, more dramatic effects are often gained when the reader's sympathies are almost equally divided among the antagonists, and they are pretty evenly matched. The reader is not too sure whom he should root for, and both sides have some claim on his sympathies.

RIGHT VERSUS RIGHT, GOOD VERSUS GOOD

Let us examine conflict further. The true tragic or dramatic conflict is a clash of two rights and not right against wrong. Right against wrong is a relatively simple matter. We have a hero and a villain, characters drawn in black and white and no intermediary shades merging into each other. It is not very exciting, or honest.

But when in a conflict each side is justified, each side is right, but the right of each side is pushed into a wrong by insisting on its own exclusive domain over the other, when each side goes to this extreme, then catastrophe is inevitable, and the conflict becomes more dramatic and more truly tragic because it is a fight to the finish of two rights colliding. Each side completely negates the other. Each side represents a moral power or principle that is essentially a worthy one in itself, each side separately has our sympathy—and they collide.

In *Hippolytus* by Euripides the real conflict is between two goddesses, Aphrodite and Artemis. The play opens with Aphrodite asserting her power over men from Atlas's Pillars to the Pontic Sea. She says Hippolytus has blasphemed her and honors instead Artemis, the Maiden Goddess, that he is continually with Artemis, hunting in the woods and staying away from the bed of love and marriage, which Aphrodite takes as an affront to her, and declares she will punish him for it, and she does. Hippolytus pays for his purity with his life. It is right for a young man to be a hunter, but not to the exclusion of love and marriage, and the theme of the play, as of many other Greek tragedies, is the clash of these two rights, each right represented by a goddess or god. Aphrodite also destroys the passionate Phaedra for being secretly in love with Hippolytus, her stepson, and killing herself when her timid advances are repulsed by the handsome and chaste athlete, whom she accuses in a note of trying to violate her.

In *Anna Karenina* we have a beautiful society woman, married to a minister of state, falling in love with Count Vronsky, the most eligible bachelor in her social circle. She leaves her husband and goes to live with the handsome officer. Anna Karenina does not want to lose her little son Seryozha by getting a divorce; she loves the boy very much. She bears her lover an illegitimate daughter. Their affair is a great scandal, but society condemns Anna rather than Vronsky. They manage to live happily for some time. They travel through western Europe and then settle down on the count's estate. But she feels she is losing her hold over him, they have some disagreements, she is not too sure of Vronsky's love. She thinks he continues to live with her as a matter of honor and duty and not because he truly loves her, as he did at one time, and she throws herself under the wheels of a train, just as Emma Bovary commits suicide when in a crisis she is deserted by her two lovers.

What makes this novel so moving is that Anna's conflict is truly tragic, good versus good, and there are no villains in the story. Her husband is an upright man, somewhat rigid and inflexible but entitled to our sympathy. He is another tragic figure in this triangle. And we can sympathize also with Count Vronsky, who after Anna's death goes to Serbia to fight for the independence of that country from the Ottoman Empire, hoping to die quickly of a Turkish bullet. All three of them are right. We have here a mother's love for her child in conflict with her love for a man she is not married to.

Or consider this situation, a true story that is the theme of an Armenian narrative in verse. A young man joins a guerrilla band and vows to die for the freedom of Armenia. He takes the required oath with a sign of the cross. Henceforth, his life belongs to his people. All members of the band have to agree in advance that they will not marry; they have to be single and unencumbered by family duties and cares in order to devote themselves wholly to the cause. They are engaged in a desperate struggle with the Turkish Sultan, Abdul Hamid, and Kurdish tribesmen in the area are their deadly enemies. The warlike Kurds are Moslems, organized into irregular cavalry regiments by the Sultan to put down the rebellious Armenians and block a possible Russian advance southward.

The young man distinguishes himself in several encounters with the Sultan's troops. It is a hopeless insurrection, but the Armenians fight on, hoping the Christian Powers will intervene and save Armenia. They are cut off from the outside world and trapped in their towering mountains with their Kurdish neighbors, who are very glad to have this chance of killing off the men and carrying off the goods and women of the infidels. The Kurdish chiefs enjoy seignorial rights over Armenian brides.

The young man falls in love with a Kurdish girl, a wild mountain beauty, and she fully returns his love. Armenians and Kurds never intermarry; the barrier of religion is too great. He finds a priest to marry them secretly, but news of it leaks out and the young man surrenders his weapons and is tried by his comrades-in-arms. The revolutionary court sits under an oak tree and after due deliberation condemns the bride to death, and in order to be readmitted into the ranks as a revolutionary in good standing her husband has to carry out the order of execution.

The young couple are passionately in love with each other. She has been a good wife. But he has taken an oath to die for the freedom of Armenia, and every man is needed in the bloody fight. He shoots his wife to death and rejoins his band.

This situation strikes us as inherently more tragic than that of *Anna Karenina,* for here we have a family murder, and something more than purely private emotions or private aims intersecting in the same breast. He kills his wife so that his nation might live, and if this were made the subject of a play by a good playwright it could arouse pity and terror. Here the young couple gain a dramatic interest through the event, and we can place the event first, action over character. Here the story is more important, as in Greek tragedy.

An event like this might well become a fable, and note, too, that the husband must make a decision. He is caught between two opposing emotions, love for his wife against love for his country. It is because each love is extreme and leaves no room for the other, and under the circumstances coexistence is not possible between them that a catastrophe ensues.

What makes such situations dramatic is not so much the misery of the persons involved in them, for suffering by itself is not tragic, as A. C. Bradley suggests in his essay on Hegel's Theory of Tragedy in his *Oxford Lectures on Poetry,* as the conflict of two rights or two moral forces each of which, by itself, is justifiable. It is right that a man should love his country, and it is also right that he should love his wife. But when one love is incompatible with the other, with no adjustment or moderation possible, they cannot be reconciled, the conflict as in this case ends in death. In such stories then the emphasis should not be on the misery and pain but on the underlying conflict, because the real story is the conflict and not the suffering it causes.

When a person is torn between two conflicting emotions, each right, each good in itself, though not equally so perhaps, and each making exclusive demands on him, we get one of the basic human situations of modern times: self-division. And it is the oldest tragic situation.

The novelist himself is likely to be a split personality, a tragic character to begin with. The writer is like other men, only more so: more introspective, more keenly aware of anxiety and suffering, more responsive to sensory experience. In discussing plot we should remember that human actions cannot be fully described or understood. In life, as in fiction, people have to make decisive choices by using their freedom; the central problem today, more urgent than ever before, is how to live a free, authentic life. In plotting his story the young writer should not forget the essential ambiguity of the human condition in what appears to be, at least from a secular point of view, a purposeless, uncertain world. I-want-to-know-why is an excellent story line, with no final answers given, and the young writer would do well to think of himself as a philosopher of history, placing his plots in their historic context, *sub specie æternitatis*.

6. PLOT: THE CHALLENGE
OF CHAOS [II]

DISCOVERY AND REVERSAL

Plotting is another aspect of the writer's shaping vision that perceives the similarity in dissimilars, and it is essentially an imaginative act, the result of new combinations rather than of fantasy or invention. By relating one thing to another, the writer finds their inner connections and groups them around an idea, which illuminates the whole. We may call the objective part of the story plot, the subjective part idea. Plot dramatizes the idea.

At the heart of almost every good story one can think of, there is a discovery or recognition (Aristotle's "anagnorisis"). Either the entire story is a process of discovery or recognition, or there are discoveries or recognitions in it, in individual scenes or smaller units of action, that produce decisive changes in the situation and become turning points. The story line may be one discovery or recognition after another, leading to the final discovery at the end that sums up the meaning of the entire action.

From ignorance to knowledge is a basic story line. Emma Bovary discovers that adultery can be as banal as marriage, that the only man who truly loved her was her hopelessly mediocre husband, who discovers after her death that she was unfaithful to him. Eugene Gant discovers in *Of Time and the River* that Starwick, the Harvard esthete, is a homosexual, and that ends their friendship. In "Bliss," by Katherine Mansfield, Bertha Young discovers during a dinner party she is giving in her home that her special find, a cool blonde beauty who is one of her guests, is having an affair with her husband. In "Rain," by Somerset Maugham, Sadie Thompson discovers

116

that the missionary who wanted to save her soul was just another man after all. The natives find his body floating at the edge of the water, his throat cut from ear to ear, still holding his razor in his right hand, after his last visit with her. Raskolnikov discovers that his crime has separated him from society and condemned him to an unbearable solitude.

The starting point in the plot may be a state of relative ignorance or innocence. There is something the character does not know, he is not in possession of all the necessary facts, but he will find out before the story is over; he will make a discovery that will change the situation for the better or worse. There is some mystery at the beginning that will be cleared up at the end. If this gap in the character's knowledge did not exist, there would be no story.

Perhaps the character is worried about a situation he is confronted with, and drama begins with worry. Or perhaps he does not know of the danger lurking ahead of him and is due for some surprises and shocks; he will make mistakes, the wrong decisions, the wrong choices and inferences, until he sees the light, and it may be too late by then.

The revelation of a fact unknown before may bring about a complete reversal of the situation, or a peripety. We see this often enough—too often—in courtroom trials staged on the screen, and it is certainly common in everyday life. The best discoveries are those that result in a reversal, which is always good drama, if not overdone. The plot of *The Ambassadors* revolves around a peripety. Strether goes to Paris to save Chad Newman and is himself seduced by the sinful city.

The entire story may revolve around a discovery and reversal, or it may form the basis of some individual scene or scenes in it. If important enough it will bring about a change either in the external situation or within the character himself, and in psychological fiction the emphasis is on inner peripeties.

What we have here is the "come to realize" plot, and despite its endless abuses in formula fiction, in hackneyed situations, the principle itself is sound and goes back to Aristotle. A fundamental conflict in both life and fiction being the contrast between the ideal and the real, myth and fact, discoveries or recognitions—from not knowing to knowing—may be expected in any dramatic situation. What it seems and what it really is has broken many hearts besides Emma's. And it is not only in fiction that people are fooled by appearances. To the devout Hindu the world is enveloped in the veil of Maya, and Kant used his formidable logic to separate the phenomenon from the thing-in-itself, the illusion from the reality. A whole book can be shaped by it. The entire movement of the story can be toward this comprehension by the character of what he is up against, or who he is, what he is, or what has happened to him or other people. The discovery may bring about a new equilibrium of the contending forces, or it may be a new awareness of self or society, of the irrevocable passing of time, or perhaps a new joyous beginning.

Early in his youth James Joyce wrote "epiphanies," sudden revelations or manifestations of character by a few seemingly casual words, and these he placed strategically in *Stephen Hero,* which later became *Portrait of the Artist as a Young Man,* or he developed them into short stories. *Dubliners* are built around such secular epiphanies. The epiphany, which we might call a discovery or recognition, made its own point and Joyce did not underscore it or comment upon it, and it is more effective for remaining unstated or merely hinted at. Such stories require close attentive reading. In "The Dead," mentioned before, Gabriel Conroy, an Irish schoolteacher approaching middle age, discovers after a party he attends with his wife Gretta that she has been loved by a delicate gentle boy of seventeen with big dark eyes when she was young herself. A song sung at the party brings the memory of this boy back to her; he used to sing it, she says after the party. The boy may have died of consumption. "I think he died for me," she says. She had to go away and enter a convent, and their separation killed him. Conroy, who is in a fever of desire for his wife, realizes what a poor lover he has been, that she has been comparing him in her mind with this dead boy, and as he sees his wife in tears and so distant and detached, it seems to him they had never lived together as man and wife. He himself is drawn to the boy, realizing that he, too, will die, that the snow falling outside—it is snowing all over Ireland—falls upon all the living and the dead.

The epiphany is a moment of illumination in the action, and like a flash of lightning reveals character or the meaning of the whole situation, and no matter what name we give it, it is a discovery or recognition. When the writer has made such a discovery he has an idea for a story.

The uses of discovery or recognition are many. It is the plot principle in stories of initiation, for instance. The apprenticeship or educational novel, what the Germans call *Bildungsroman* (*Wilhelm Meister's Apprenticeship* by Goethe established the genre), stories of growing up, of search, are tales of discovery or recognition. A notable example is *Pilgrim's Progress*, or to give its full title, *The Pilgrim's Progress, From This World to That Which is to Come: Delivered Under the Similitude of A Dream, Wherein is Discovered, The manner of His Setting out His Dangerous Journey, And safe Arrival at the Desired Country.*

"Pilgrim," "progress," "similitude of a dream," "dangerous journey," "safe arrival," "desired country,"—these sum up not only the subject of this Christian allegory but outline the plot of any good story of discovery or recognition. John Bunyan's account is a wonder tale, as a good story should be. There are enough wonders in our wakeful life not to seek them perhaps in dreams, although life itself is a dream, and we are sleepers in the Vienna woods.

The first great romance, *The Thousand and One Nights,* spun by a master of serial fiction and the world's first woman novelist, is crowded with action and is based on the structural principle of what happens next. In its different versions—originally a Persian collection—this has been the world's most popular storybook and is full of discoveries and reversals, like all folktales.

Innocence and the impact of experience upon it is a central theme in fiction. Henry James specialized in American innocents in Europe. The novels and short stories of D. H. Lawrence were inspired by his search for innocence and for a more ideal life than industrial society has to offer. Lawrence was always dreaming of founding Utopian colonies. In *Don Quixote* we have a well-known example of this same theme, depicting the illusions or hallucinations of chivalry in a too imperfect world. In his prologue Cervantes says he was advised to publish his book under the name of an Emperor of Trebizond, his own name being too humble, and it amuses me to see that in the first chapter Cervantes has his hero imagine himself crowned at least Emperor of Trebizond. If he only knew how right was the choice, for to this day, or at least up to my boyhood in Trebizond, this region has been a natural habitat of Don Quixotes, and the country itself is as beautiful as the setting of a knight-errant's dream. Long after chivalry disappeared in the Iberian peninsula, it flourished officially in Caucasian Iberia, next door to Trebizond, and throughout Armenia, the Don Quixote of nations.

Another form of discovery is the open road or the high seas which from time immemorial have beckoned adventure seekers. The Argonauts sailed to Trebizond to find the Golden Fleece, and boys everywhere search for hidden treasure. Is there a man who has not dreamed of a Treasure Island? It is said all boys are Huck Finns at heart, sailing down the rivers of the world. In our westerns we have American knight-errants on horseback.

Illusions expand the mind and exalt man's spirit, and this would be a barren world indeed without such dreams; they are affirmations of our inmost longings and desires. We talk of "the illusions of youth"—but where would we be without them? It is an innocence we cannot do without, and these illusions are never wholly lost. Illusion rules the world.

PAIN AND SUFFERING IN PLOT

In addition to discovery and reversal, Aristotle mentions a third element in his complex plot, pathos or suffering, which does not turn on surprise, and this is the closest he comes to conflict. Drama begins with pain. Pain is a big subject in literature and a serious discussion of it would carry us far. We mention pain here in passing to stress its rightful place in plot. Pain is disillusionment, even on the instinctive level, physiologically speaking. An instinct is a biological emotion, and like any other emotion it works to an end. It is an action or a struggle to attain something. Now when the instinct does not realize its aim, there is pain. If it does reach its goal, there is pleasure. All action is instigated by pain or pleasure, and pain enters into the very structure of pleasure, and there is no pleasure without pain. We invariably suffer when reality does not come up to expectation, and an expectation unfulfilled is pain. Pain is the difference between what we expected and what we discovered, what we hoped for and what we got, the difference between illusion and reality.

The writer, like the physician, is a specialist of pain.

> Canst thou not minister to a mind diseas'd,
> Pluck from the memory a rooted sorrow,
> Raze out the written troubles of the brain,
> And with some sweet oblivious antidote
> Cleanse the stuff'd bosom of that perilous stuff
> Which weighs upon the heart?

This cry by Macbeth echoes in every heart. In life as in literature, pain is the most universal feeling, and whether physical or mental, it is the greatest evil we have, but not altogether an unmitigated evil. The appeal of pain or pathos in literature explains a great deal about its place in human life. Desire would cease to be desire without pain, and in nirvana, which extinguishes the fire of desire, oriental religions promise freedom from pain. To us in the West that is perhaps too big a price to pay and we would rather burn with the fire of desire than put out the flame of life.

Even romantic love is a painful condition. This emotion springs from the will-to-live, and the love line is the will line. Love is the principal theme in literature, for the survival of the race depends on this primary passion. It is a provision made by nature, part of the law of self-preservation. In the popular songs of the old world, love is always unrequited love: an eternal yearning. Married love, or love fulfilled, does not stir the listener. It is a torch song, full of pain and longing. And it is precisely this quality that makes a novel like *Wuthering Heights,* with all its faults, such a powerful book. It is a woman's torch song. Woman grieving over lost love—that's the plot also of *Madame Bovary, Anna Karenina,* and many other novels with a romantic theme. When love, expressing the elemental life force, runs its full course and there are no more obstacles before it, the uncertainty is over, the suspense is over, the pain is over; the story is over, too.

Pain is a necessary ingredient in suspense. The poised expectation, with the outcome in doubt, is a painful condition. The jagged line of action that generates suspense, with the fortunes of the character rising and falling, is a painful line.

The universal appeal of pain is understandable, for no one is ever free of it, and the tragic effect of fear and pity is another proof of its value in literature. Pain is as necessary in comedy as it is in tragedy. True comedy can probe the deepest layers of mental pain, and in the really comic story the characters are comic to themselves and the spectators of their own comedy, not playing up to the reader. Irony, as in *Don Quixote,* is conscious of the difference between illusion and reality and does not allow itself to grow bitter over the difference; it continually rises over the pain of disillusion, of deceptions and self-deceptions, though subject to them, and this is one reason why great writing is ironic writing.

The man who writes out of his own sufferings should maintain a detached attitude toward his personal sorrows, and the two sides of him, the sufferer and the writer, should remain separate. To himself he is just another character, and if he is an artist he views the sufferer within himself with an ironic eye. Not until he has reached such detachment is he ready to make proper use of his unspoken pains. If a writer eliminates his own painful experiences, he is probably writing several degrees below his natural heat and relying mostly on what he imagines or observes, what he picks up here and there. Such substitute material does not make for intensity, and there is a danger of sentimental and rhetorical exaggerations, or of too much technique to make good the loss.

A writer has to be these two separate people in one, and the unity of his work is derived from such creative duality. A writer can be quite impersonal toward himself, his own detached observer, at once subject and object when writing. Such objectivity lessens the pain, and this is no little blessing and compensates in some measure for the sorrows of the artist. The writer feels like other men, only more so, and his detachment saves him, both as a man and as a writer. Desire and pain go together. If we were to abolish pain, we would also abolish desire. Desire would cease to be desire without pain. And it is only after we lose them, or before we have them, that the good things of this world gain their true value. We dream of happiness, or we remember it; it is keener in anticipation than in realization.

THE DRAMATIC PLOT

It is difficult to attempt a classification of plots, for we are dealing with overlapping forms and the best we can hope to do is to make some rough distinctions. The dramatic plot is a story of intense conflict in which the outcome is in doubt until the climax, and everything builds up to that climax. Anything that does not lead to this climactic point is an irrelevant episode. The beginning is not arbitrary but definitely the beginning of the present action and points to what is coming next, and is followed by complications, and these in turn lead to the end, which is not followed by anything else; it is definitely curtain, and beginning, middle, and end are connected causally. The principal characters are introduced at the beginning, or at least are mentioned by name, and the reader looks forward to their appearance. The middle or the second act is harder to write. It is the complication, and complications can be complicated affairs. But the end is the chief thing in the dramatic plot. It cannot be an arbitrary end, but the inevitable result of all the preceding events—inevitable and unexpected. There is a long theatrical tradition behind the surprise ending.

The dramatic plot has a moral: "They have sown the wind and they shall reap the whirlwind," to quote from Hosea, 740 B.C. Or as we read in The Epistle to the Galatians, "Whatsoever a man soweth, that shall he also reap." Or "By their fruits ye shall know them" (The Gospel According to Matthew). And it is well to remember also the Buddhist maxim, "Every effect becomes a cause." And these words in Ovid's *Metamorphoses*, "*Causa latet: vis est notissima.*" (The cause is hidden, but the effect is known.)

When events are tied together strictly by causality they make one big event, a single story line from beginning to end, and this unity of action is the most important structural principle in plotting. The action is more sharply defined in the dramatic novel, and takes place on a relatively narrow stage, as in a play. In *Crime and Punishment* Dostoyevsky treats intensely only one segment of life in St. Petersburg and shuts out the rest of the city. The story gains in intensity what it loses in scope. The action in this novel springs mainly from the character and thought of the central figure, Raskolnikov. Thought is important in the dramatic novel, which needs a subjective element, reflective characters, people faced with alternatives and debating about ways and means, to avoid the deadly mechanizing effect of a tightly logical plot moving inexorably to its inevitable end. The vitality of Dostoyevsky's characters is largely the result of their thought; these intense, neurotic people are always thinking, arguing with others and with themselves. This dramatization of thought in obsessed people—and characters in the dramatic plot are obsessed extremists—adds life to the narrative. Since the story line moves according to the law of cause and effect, the writer can give it a semblance of freedom through thought. Dostoyevsky's people are wild and unusual enough not to act like puppets in the plot, but he is not above melodrama. Realism is not the principal merit of *Crime and Punishment;* there are some strange coincidences in it.

Dostoyevsky credited himself with two important contributions to the art of the novel: direct quotations from the minds of characters, giving their thoughts and feelings in their own words, which he did more extensively than was the practice in his day; and the creation of the "double" as a character type. His second novel is called *The Double*, in which Golyadkin senior, a humble government clerk, and Golyadkin junior, his ideal heroic image of himself, are at odds with each other, and a good part of the novel consists of the silent dialogue between these two, a running argument, mixed with daydreams. Golyadkin senior is hounded by Golyadkin junior and ends up in a mental hospital. The novel dramatizes the plight of a minor civil servant whose personality is crushed, and then split, by the humiliating conditions of his work, a theme first used by Gogol. As Dostoyevsky himself said, "We all came out of Gogol's Overcoat." Though there are some technical flaws in it, *The Double* is a remarkable novel on the dissociation of personality and makes fascinating reading. "Dostoyevsky is the only one who has taught me something about psychology," Nietzsche said, who preached the superman, while Dostoyevsky preached Christian humility. Dostoyevsky wrote under great pressure and had no time to revise and polish. But the disorder, the repetitions, the verbosity, with great patches of sloppy journalistic style in nearly all of his novels, make them seem more spontaneous, artless and lifelike. The chaotic language in these chaotic novels seems just right and makes for better mimesis.

In the dramatic plot the scenes are not complete in themselves; each scene prepares for what comes next. Nearly everything in *Crime and Punishment, The Double* and other novels by Dostoyevsky arises from the central conflict, and these are no-exit plots. The dramatic plot is a problem plot, with the problem finally solved at the end—or not to be solved at all. *The Double* ends with insanity. *Crime and Punishment* ends with a religious conversion in Siberia—but it is not shown, we are merely told about it in the epilogue. Summary makes it more believable, but it is a forced end, not very convincing, the weakest part of the novel, which otherwise crackles with vitality. Raskolnikov's regeneration is not dramatized because that would make another story.

As Poe says in "The Philosophy of Composition":

> Nothing is more clear than that every plot, worth the name, must be elaborated to its *dénouement* before anything be attempted with the pen. It is only with the *dénouement* constantly in view that we can give a plot its indispensable air of consequence, or causation, by making the incidents, and especially the tone at all points, tend to the development of the intention.

The dramatic plot is so well established through the long history of the drama and the epic that we might draw up its structure somewhat as follows:

1. Central character. Single star, or two stars with interlocked destinies acting as a unit.

2. His purpose or motive. Purpose single or unified and integrated. Central emotional drive.

3. Important opening event which is also beginning of complication or middle. In medias res. Starting in the middle of the plot without preliminaries.

4. Purpose blocked. Character cannot get what he wants. Barriers, external and/or internal, creating or deepening the conflict. Fortune of character falls; downward curve of story line.

5. Initial barrier overcome. Purposeful character active, not passive, struggles toward his goal. Line goes up.

6. New complications. Partway conflict may shift inward and character quarrels also with himself. Situation worse than before, line goes down again and falls to lowest point, where story may end in disaster if change is from good to bad and catastrophe final. Character defeated or dies. If change is from bad to good—

7. Turning point reached after temporary catastrophe that appeared final, and line goes up again with rising fortune and reaches the denouement.

The end may be the end of the action, the end of characterization, the end of thought, in stories in which the action or characterization or thought is predominant; or it may be the end of all three in the same plot. These alternatives offer many possibilities to the writer. The action story concludes the action, the character story does a full job of characterization, the story of ideas concludes the thought, even if the conclusion is that there is no conclusion.

A faulty sequence of events will result in an illogical and unconvincing end, which should answer the questions raised by the beginning and the middle, so that the reader knows not only what happened, and how, to whom, where, and when, but *why* it happened. The answer to *why* is supplied by the end. That is where the philosophy comes in, the honesty, the truth, the significance of the whole.

How to untie the knot? An improbable denouement will falsify and ruin the story. As Poe suggests, the ideal way to write a story (with a dramatic plot) is to write it backward, beginning at the end. But why untie the knot? If the character is trapped and cannot get out of the trap, let him continue in his misery. It may be more dramatic *not* to commit murder or suicide. Death solves the writer's problem, not the character's. Even in Greek tragedy an unhappy ending or the death of the hero is not an absolute must, and though Aristotle preferred unhappy endings, considering them more artistic, the story line can be from misery to happiness if there is enough suffering in it.

In championing the discussion play, George Bernard Shaw ridicules the idea that people go to the theatre to be amused and not to be preached at. He did not hesitate to preach and he made long speeches pay. Shaw was frankly for a doctrinaire theatre, for conflicts arising out of unsettled ideals, and for fables with morals. Shaw proved talk can be dramatic on the stage. It can be even more dramatic in fiction, and what Shaw says about discussion can be applied to the novel.

> Formerly you had in what was called a well made play an exposition in the first act, a situation in the second, and un-ravelling in the third. Now you have exposition, situation, and discussion; and the discussion is the test of the playwright.
> (G. B. Shaw, *The Quintessence of Ibsenism*)

But, as Shaw points out, there must be something to discuss. The usual commonplaces in plotting would not do. A novel can begin with discussion and end with action, or the discussion permeates the action from beginning to end. The discussion novel may be said to have begun with Dostoyevsky too, and might well be the new novel, this form being particularly suitable to situations in which it is right versus right rather than right versus wrong. We do live in an age of unsettled ideals, of ideologies conflicting on a world-wide scale. We are waiting for serious political and philosophical novels above the entertainment level, with complex characters, compulsive thinkers and talkers, as in Dostoyevsky.

THE EPISODIC OR PANORAMIC PLOT

In the novel we are emphasizing variety and complexity. Novels should not be written like short stories. The short story has been a dominant literary form in America, beginning with Hawthorne and Poe. The tale proper, Poe said in his essay on Hawthorne, "affords unquestionably the fairest field for the exercise of the loftiest talent." Poe was so convinced of the artistic importance of a certain unique or preconceived single effect that he thought this could be done only in a short prose narrative and not in the novel. He laid down the rules for the American short story, and the strict unity of effect he advocated served the purposes of mass circulation magazines. Expensive advertising space requires very tight writing, for every inch counts. Magazine stories would often be better if written more spontaneously and with less of Poe's pre-established design. If a story is used for selling goods, it tends to be a manufactured product itself, mechanically well made, perfectly designed like a gadget, with all the parts tightly fitting together, but with its hackneyed theme and improbable plot giving at best the illusion of an illusion. But writing short stories is excellent discipline for the novelist.

How can a writer get this vital variety in the novel which the short story does not need and can do without? Through a loose episodic or panoramic plot, by enlarging the fictional frame. The dramatic plot has affinities with Greek tragedy; the episodic or panoramic plot leans toward the epic. It allows the writer to work with larger segments of life, with more characters, for longer periods, at more places, with less unity. In this wider, looser form the sequence of events is only partly causal, and since one event need not always follow *from* another event and be a preparation for what comes next the writer has a larger choice of scenes and is out of the causal prison. There are exits. "Might be continued," as André Gide says in the journal of *The Counterfeiters*.

The moment we break the causal chain there is no need for one logically inevitable end, the action may be concluded without theatrical tricks, and without marriage or death. What a relief for the writer. He may have a variety of incidents to round off the action, or he may even end it with a reflection—probably a reflection by character—and what comes next would make another story. Arbitrary? Yes, more or less. And the beginning also can be arbitrary, more or less. Arbitrary, but not without rhyme or reason. The beginning is another strategic position, not to be wasted on dull unimportant details or on information that can come later through flashbacks and exposition, or through dialogue and internal monologue. The conflict is not so intense and concentrated as in the dramatic plot. Freed of the tyranny of one end and one end only, inevitable by the internal logic of the events, a syllogistic end, an episodic or panoramic plot can do nicely even without strong situations and a strong climax.

The scenes in this loose form may be episodes used for their own independent value and not because they always lead directly to what happens later, although some relationship with the rest of the story is necessary. The idea can tie the episodes together, and instead of unity of action we can have thematic unity, which is very important in the episodic plot. In the absence of a causal action the theme should be clear and definite, but not a thesis to be proven, and not clear to the point of banality. The idea can hold the episodic plot together, but the little causal connections can be a mighty help.

Of all plots the episodic are the worst, says Aristotle, meaning episodic plays, and this is understandable, for this method does violate the causal principle, the law of necessity on which he based his plot. This principle is sound also in narrative, but if the incidents do not arise directly from the central action, and they do not in *War and Peace, Sons and Lovers, The Magic Mountain,* and many other novels, they may have an illustrative value in connection with major or minor themes or further the elucidation of character. They can provide humor and variety, make for length, magnitude, or delay the action and thereby increase the suspense. Most great novels are episodic. But the new writer is safer with the plot ideal of One Causal Affair, causal at least underneath, even if it has to be casual above. No matter how loose, a novel should hang together.

The problem is how much unity and by what means. Anthony Trollope dismissed plot as of little consequence in the novel, but here is what he says in his *Autobiography:*

> There should be no episodes in a novel. Every sentence, every word, through all those pages, should tend to the telling of the story. Such episodes distract the attention of the reader, and always do so disagreeably. Though the novel which you have to write must be long, let it be all one. And this exclusion of episodes should be carried down into the smallest details. Every sentence and every word used should tend to the telling of the story.

Nevertheless the beauty of this loose form is that it does allow digressions. Even in terms of the *Poetics,* we may consider the structure of a novel a play *plus* episodes. Laurence Sterne went to the other extreme in *Tristram Shandy,* but he got back on the main track in the end.

> For in this long digression I was accidentally led into, as in all my digressions (one only excepted) there is a masterstroke of digressive skill, the merit of which has all along, I fear, been overlooked by my reader,—not for want of penetration in him,—but because 'tis an excellence seldom looked for, or expected indeed, in a digression;—and it is this: That tho' my digressions are all fair, as you observe,—and that I fly off from what I am about, as far, and as often too,

as any writer in Great Britain; yet I constantly take care to order my affairs so that my main business does not stand still in my absence. . . .

Digressions, incontestably, are the sunshine;—they are the life, the soul of reading!—take them out of this book, for instance,—you might as well take the book along with them; —one cold eternal winter would reign in every page of it; restore them to the writer;—he steps forth like a bridegroom,— bids All-hail; brings in variety, and forbids the appetite to fail.

Sterne worked out an intricate design of "two contrary motions," his "digressive" and "progressive" movements, "one wheel within another." So long as digressions do not halt the progressive movement, it is "perfectly good cookery" and whets the appetite of the reader. The digressions may be mental, and it is always possible to re-establish the connection with the main action through the thought stream of the character. The episode may seem irrelevant, but when a character reflects on its significance or values it for himself, we are back with his purpose or problem, and it is no longer a separate unassimilated incident in the larger story. This may be done even in the tight dramatic plot. When the external events are disjointed, an inner subjective continuity may be maintained through the thought stream, and thought by itself adds an element of variety to the tale. For a man's thoughts are infinitely varied and thought provides a capricious whimsical inner story line which may add charm and a more lifelike quality to the plot. If a story like that of *Madame Bovary* were stripped of its precious incidentals and Emma's thoughts, we would have only the skeleton of a book left.

The picaresque (from *picaro,* rogue, in Spanish) is a variation of the episodic. It has a single hero and is usually written in first person. The basic structural unit, as in *Don Quixote,* is the individual adventure or episode, each with its own purpose or theme, most likely some immediate task to be accomplished, each episode with a beginning, middle, and end, a little story in itself, with the action concluded. These are linked together by the central character and his over-all purpose and the underlying major theme. The sequence may or may not be causal, and these separate events, complete in themselves, are parts of a larger story and the structure is by no means as formless and accidental as it seems. The freedom of the seemingly accidental can do wonders and breathe life into the story. But it is a restricted freedom. Absolute freedom would lead to chaos.

A modern picaresque hero is Huckleberry Finn. *Confessions of Felix Krull* is in this same genre. The central character may be a woman telling her own story, a contemporary Moll Flanders, heaven help us. The picaresque hero need not always be a rogue or freebooter or social climber. This form with its traveling hero is capable of wide applications and can give us the terrestrial comedy of *Don Quixote* and *The Divine Comedy* of Dante Alighieri.

The contrapuntal plot is a further development in the direction of multiplicity, worked out on musical principles. Just as a melody is added to another melody as accompaniment and we get plural melodies, and two or more melodies, combined contrapuntally, are capable of giving more than one tone at a time and we get a multiplicity of sounds and a combination of various tones, stories and points of view may be interwoven in the contrapuntal plot, and as in polyphonic music with its related but independent melodies, we may have a blending of alternating, parallel or contrasting actions, with the repetition of a dominant idea, playing variations on the same theme.

This is an experimental form that attempts to modify the old conventional story structures and create a better method for reproducing the infinitely rich and varied pattern of life by abrupt transitions and an artful discontinuity of the story line. Counterpoint may be the answer to some modern plot problems, although the experiment is almost abandoned. Whether a musicalization of fiction is really possible and a great improvement on the old conventional methods remains to be seen. It could be effective for certain parts in a novel when the writer has to reproduce the wild tangle of life, a complex or collage of impressions, the multitudinous and ironic parallels and contrasts clustered around a central action or theme. It might provide the writer with a symphonic end. "Not completion. But the opening out," in Forster's words. It could be useful for certain camera effects, as in the early novels of John Dos Passos, but with the camera work absorbed into the narrative rather than given as separate newsreels; for montage effects through associative and dissociative techniques; for giving the peripheral and background picture in a vivid impressionistic manner, little disjointed scenes captured on the wing, as it were, before their formal and logical organization, before the intellect steps in, as in the stream-of-thought technique. In *Point Counter Point* we read a tentative formulation of this method in Philip Quarles's Notebook. The passage is worth quoting again:

> The musicalization of fiction. Not in the symbolist way, by subordinating sense to sound. (*Pleuvent les bleus baisers des astres taciturnes.* Mere glossolalia.) But on a large scale, in the construction. Meditate on Beethoven. The changes of moods, the abrupt transitions. (Majesty alternating with a joke, for example, in the first movement of the B flat major Quartet. Comedy suddenly hinting at prodigious and tragic solemnities in the scherzo of the C sharp minor Quartet.) More interesting still the modulations, not merely from one key to another, but from mood to mood. A theme is stated, then developed, put out of shape, imperceptibly deformed until, though still recognizably the same, it has become quite different. In sets of variations the process is carried a step further. Those incredible Diabelli variations, for example. The whole range of thought and feeling, yet all in organic relation to a ridiculously little waltz tune. Get this into a novel? How? The abrupt transitions are easy enough. All you need is a sufficiency of characters and parallel, contrapuntal plots. While Jones is murdering a wife, Smith is wheeling the perambulator in the park. You alternate the themes. More interesting, the modulations and variations are also more difficult. A novelist modulates by reduplicating situations and characters. He shows several people falling in love, or dying, or praying in different ways—dissimilars solving the same problem. Or, vice versa, similar people confronted with dissimilar problems. In this way you can modulate through all the aspects of your theme, you can write variations in any number of different moods.

133

DISORDER IN ORDER

The musicalization of fiction is part of a general movement against the tight causal plot and neat theatrical patterns and too much logic and too many rules and restrictions and conventions. Today we are more acutely aware of the subconscious activities of the mind and the decisive role emotions play—and emotions are disorderly by nature. We know there is little order and sequence in what we think or feel, memory is involuntary, and conscious civilized life is by no means the full story of man and society, and dreams and hidden motives may tell us more about both. Life is more mysterious and inexplicable than the logic of any plot.

We have to accept the artistic necessity of some disorder in order if fiction is to be more lifelike. The action could be slightly crazy, topsy-turvy now and then, seemingly illogical, motivated by an emotion which the writer cannot analyze or explain. He can make it appear there is no motive for this particular act, or it is obscure, irrational; it is not in sequence and cannot be incorporated into the story line. It is out of order, but—life is like that. And when life is disorderly, it is surprising. If the writer can get some surprises through a little disorder, why should he hesitate to do so? Vignettes of chaos deliberately planted in the plot will make the action seem more spontaneous and inward.

There is no complete escape from chaos anyway. If one is writing of secret lives, one cannot be satisfied with conventional behavior, for conventional behavior is deceiving, and a writer wants to tell the truth about his characters. The real story is what conventional behavior is hiding; not the mask, but the naked frightened face behind it. Yet the mask also is part of the picture. There is, needless to say, a jungle in every man, and the jungle should be indicated, if not described in detail. Certain things should be left unexplained. Shadows are necessary, dark distances no writer or reader dare explore.

There is more to life than external action and the visible

behavior of people. What really matters is the inner plot, if we may use such a term, and in the inner plot there is unavoidably a large admixture of the irrational. The inner plot has its own wild anarchic sequence and enjoys a freedom denied to the outer plot, plot per se. It operates on the principle of the dream or daydream rather than of a logically worked-out series of events. The inner plot, like thought, like sentiments, like imagination, is free of space and time, and it can definitely tell a story, just as dreams tell stories, but the incidents do not always follow from each other in a dream; transitions are abrupt and automatic associations transcend the limitations of wakeful reality.

Dream stories have been written, such as *Alice in Wonderland* and *Finnegans Wake*. We should recognize the place of non-logical structure in literature. Surely a short story can be written like a dream fugue in the manner of Thomas De Quincey. This brings to mind the possibilities of automatic writing, which can be practiced with astounding results. For some writers there may be nothing like it for fresh imagery and the happy phrase, for the first draft anyway.

A dash of disorder may be good for order. It will make room for contradictions, the prelogical, the illogical, the absurd. It will permit the purely episodic, the irrelevant, the transcendent, the inexplicable, the whimsical, the idiosyncratic, the individualistic, the ambiguous, the ambivalent—and these make for wonder, for mystery, for poetry and depth.

External events, the orderly logical arrangement of which makes plot, are not always of the essence in the novel today. They are referred to casually in the novels of Virginia Woolf and Dorothy Richardson, as relatively unimportant extraneous matter, while these authors concentrate on the stream-of-thought through a free or seemingly free association of ideas. The inner flow, the continuity of this secret life in contrast to the fragmented external action reduced to a minimum, with no dramatic issue, no strong well-defined motivation, is characteristic of such subjective works. We should recognize the danger of rigidly defined emotion and motive, valuable as they are in sharpening a story and giving the writer a sense of direction. We have to admit that an emotional experience is largely an inner experience, and much of it will be lost if rendered as a well-ordered external action. Within the character himself the experience cannot be so definite in its outlines and instead of a sharp story line we have a sort of foggy glow, a mysterious incandescence with moments of searing intensity.

If plot neglects the soul or spirit of man, then it is at best a partial plot and does not tell the full story. Neat external plot patterns are convenient for those who shy away from the spirit and thus plot in this wrong sense contributes to the dehumanization of modern fiction and becomes a refuge for the soulless, irresponsible, and escapist writer. The plot cult in America is partly an outgrowth of a naive oversimplification of life and an escape from inner realities. Subjectivism, lyricism, would be a healthy countermovement in fiction. We need stories of spiritual exploration in which there is a genuine confrontation of self, action to regain the full human dimensions of personality. The battle against dehumanization is going on all over the world. The writer should lead in this war of liberation—the liberation of the human spirit. The writer who expresses this universal longing for self-completion, for becoming fully human again, for recovering one's true self, one's lost soul, for being fully free, will be an authentic spokesman of the age. Literary fame today lies in that direction. The great issue today is simply how to stay human.

There are perhaps democratic and historic reasons why the plot cult flourishes in America and at the more popular level there is so much violent action. In "An Essay of Dramatic Poesy" (1668) John Dryden says: "We conceive nothing to be action till the players come to blows." And he observes that "French writers do not burden themselves too much with plot." In a wide open society like ours there are fewer barriers before men than there were in Dryden's society. Anything can happen in America, and does, in its fiction, too. In fifteen years the penniless immigrant becomes a millionaire. Class lines are not rigidly drawn yet and there are fewer obstacles before love; the pretty little stenographer marries the boss's son or the boss himself. Love is impetuous in America and follows a straight line of conquest. We are still an optimistic nation, devoted to the egalitarian principle, and if contradictions exist between the ideal and the real in our society we do not wish to acknowledge them. Even death loses its terror in America and becomes a seemingly casual thing, calling for no loud cries and no hair-pulling by women as in older, sadder cultures. Cemetery salesmen sell to the happy living their graves on the installment plan, and funeral homes advertise their attractions in newspapers and countless posters all over America. We lack the tragic sense of life, as Europeans say. We are still the great innocents in Christendom. Hemingway with his death-haunted plots, not hiding his tragic sense of life, became significantly our most popular novelist.

In a restless, mobile, heterogeneous society like ours, agitated by a perpetual motion, with fortunes made and lost within a few years, and everybody impatient to get to the top in the shortest possible time, to learn short-story writing in ten easy lessons, to write a novel in six weeks, to read books in digest form, the dramatic plot with fast action is favored and slow developments would not do. Plot is more pleasing to the American temper. The tendency of the American novel is to be dramatic; of the European novel to be philosophical. The former thrives on action; the latter on thought. We are an active, dynamic, dramatic rather than a meditative nation. The American novel and particularly the American short story, having gone native and no longer copying aristocratic English models—though the English, too, love plots—reflect the interests of a people absorbed in themselves and in their own private destinies, in the democratic group. When there is a paucity of ideas, of larger self-transcending themes, plot becomes paramount and severely restricts subject matter in fiction designed for popular consumption.

We are fascinated with facts, but there is in the practical American mind a longing also for the ideal, and this is a romantic nation in more ways than one. There is a widespread impulse to escape from facts into an even more pleasing wonderland, and one would hesitate to resist this tendency, for it would be like going against the national temper and depriving the people of certain satisfactions and certain affirmations they must have. Almost nothing but romance is written for these people and the realistic novel has been abandoned for them. The serious writer has to fight against the romance, the improbable plot. Romances are under no obligation to tell the truth. In former days romances were clearly distinguished from novels and in some cases they still are. Fancy is more entertaining, more romantic than truth. So why stick to the truth?

But the public is catching up with such plots. The pulps have all but disappeared from the newsstands. The empire of the mighty slicks is crashing. The short story seems to be a dying form. The market has shrunk. Commercial magazines occasionally publish an offbeat plotless story with a fresh new idea in it for prestige, or perhaps even for sound business reasons. The pot of gold is still in the improbable plot with its gimmicks, and many college courses in creative writing and writers' conferences have frankly commercial aims. They do not preach holy poverty and the holy word. The writing profession is cluttered with people who have nothing new and worthwhile to say and who are not even imaginative and offbeat enough to be good businessmen. But the sincere writer, the mad one, need not despair. His day is coming.

7. CHARACTER IN FICTION

Character is the driving force in fiction. Characterization is a complex and elusive art and cannot be reduced to exact rules or to a comprehensive statement. The more we talk about it, the more we feel has been left out, and this is necessarily so because the human personality remains a mystery, subject to obscure forces; it is a universe in itself, and we are strangers even to ourselves.

Like a talent for writing, characterization is an inborn gift. It requires self-knowledge, insight into human nature, the observing eye sharpened by the inner vision, and the mimetic faculty. No one can really tell us how characters are created in fiction, and great novelists, Henry James excepted, have said precious little about it. We have only fragmentary remarks nor are critics very helpful. Characterization is more than impersonation, though it is that, too. Like the actor, the fiction writer is king today, beggar tomorrow. He can be saint or sinner, young or old, man or woman; speak in his own voice and through the voices of others. Keats said the poet has no identity; yet no man has a stronger sense of self than the poet. The writer can get so deeply involved in the destinies of his people that he laughs or cries with them; suffers their diseases; becomes the characters he creates. Meanwhile whether he is aware of it or not he puts something of himself in all of them and the characters take after their creator.

Flaubert so completely identified himself with Emma Bovary that when he described her suicide he could taste the arsenic in his mouth. Flaubert added memories of his own to Emma's prototype, notably of his love affair with the poet Louise Colet, with whom he corresponded while working on his novel, and these letters tell us how he wrote his book. The wife of a sculptor furnished him with details he used in describing Emma's financial troubles that led to her suicide. Like plot a successful character in fiction is a synthesis made of diverse elements and the result of the same unifying inner vision that sees the like in the unlike and draws the fragments together like a magnet.

Generally the most vital and vivid characters come out of the author's experiences, particularly of his early youth, a period when the most lasting impressions are made, and may represent actual or potential aspects of his own personality. The novel that established the canon of objectivity and impersonality in fiction is actually a subjective and highly personal work, and if Flaubert, the author, has technically disappeared from its pages, Flaubert, the man, is in them. He was as much of a daydreamer, as much of a romantic, as Emma Bovary. One side of him was under the spell of the exotic East. He traveled through the Near East, he wrote *Salammbô*, a novel about ancient Carthage, and *The Temptation of St. Anthony*. He was a very personal writer and his best work is his most personal work. Tolstoy, Stendhal, Proust, Joyce, Virginia Woolf are even more autobiographical than Flaubert. But of course not all fictional characters have their originals in life. Many are invented. George Sand insisted to Flaubert she invented her characters.

Though we have previously emphasized the importance of the significant event, character is the cornerstone of the novel and we read novels primarily for their revelations of character. That is what makes fiction so fascinating and instructive. The reader expects an honest exploration of private lives.

NO STOCK CHARACTERS

We might list here some qualities an ideal character might have. First, it should be new. Most commercial stories have stock characters; the people in them are not new and individualized, we know them too well, we have met them before, we can predict their actions and reactions. Indeed many readers identify themselves more readily with stock types, or with characters that are somewhat vague and general, without markedly individual traits, not too unique, or too different from themselves. In Hollywood new actresses are given the so-called glamour treatment and emerge from the makeup department with their individual features toned down or washed out. They are made to look alike according to a certain image of erotic and mysterious femininity. Some men recoil from women with pronounced individualities, and women, and Hollywood, know this. Women particularly are stereotypes.

One way to be immortal in literature is to create a memorable new character, a new Don Quixote, a new Hamlet, a new Bazarov, a new K, even a new Babbitt. In the arts we seek what others have not done, and in literature it is the fresh new statement that matters. The writer who has something new to say and a personal way of saying it will, most likely, also have some new characters, but even a vigorously original writer whose ideas are fresh and whose style is a delight may unwittingly pattern some of his people after stock types. We are bombarded daily by the mass suggestions of the entertainment industries—which, curiously, are always looking for fresh ideas and characters, within certain limits, of course —and their character-clichés lodge themselves in our subconscious. Even writers may become conditioned to stock types.

Then too in this age of conformity the herd instinct is strong. Industry and democracy are leveling-off processes. The mass man on the treadmill of mass production, the stock types in the "lonely crowd," increased communication among classes and countries so that all of us are becoming alike and the villain need no longer be a foreigner with a black mustache—in this world-wide melting pot not many new characters are left. Even LSD addicts, like beatniks and subterraneans of the road, have become familiar types. The underground man could be a compelling new character in America, as he was in Dostoyevsky's Russia, but are we to look for him among bearded hipsters and in erotic wastelands? We have always had some genuine eccentrics in America—Thoreau,

Whitman, people who raised more hell than corn in Kansas, the men and women who lie buried in the cemetery at Spoon River, the grotesques of Sherwood Anderson. The non-conformist in any community, in any occupation, is usually a "character." The oddball is always interesting. Almost all of Dickens' characters we remember best are lively eccentrics entangled in curious or absurd situations. This entanglement and the bewilderment that often goes with it, is an excellent situation for revealing character.

A good convincing character is both individual and type, even archetype, the timeless mythic model. It has certain characteristics in common with others of its class, fits the general type it represents, and is appropriate to its own kind. We assume for instance that priests are truthful men. A priest who is an habitual drunkard and liar is not typical, and is not therefore a plausible person as priest. He may be interesting on other grounds, his very aberration makes him so different and new that he will stick in the reader's mind, but he ceases to be a man of God. Gangsters are not notably merciful and honorable men, and a gangster who is merciful and honorable is not true to the type and ceases in effect to be a gangster.

There are character patterns that make people typically lovers or non-lovers, extroverts or introverts, politicians or poets, dependent or independent, brave or cowardly. We have such well-known types as the exotic femme fatale, the girl next door, the fiery redhead, the blonde gentlemen prefer, the career girl, the glamour girl, the wallflower, the clinging vine, the lone wolf, the glad hand-shaker. They bring to mind certain images and each has a character pattern proper to its own kind which the writer can weave into the fabric of his fiction. If he takes care to individualize such people and they are not generalizations or abstractions with one predominant trait, they are not likely to be stereotypes.

But if a person is so unique as to be absolutely exceptional, a very special, perhaps pathological case, it would be difficult or impossible for the reader to identify himself with him. The writer can make poetry out of pathology, and the abnormal, the pathological has its own fascination, but a character should not be too different from other men; and with all his idiosyncrasies and obsessions the fictional person should have a broad base of humanity about him. He cannot be the only one of his kind and be convincing, unless it is fantasy fiction. In Kafka's *Metamorphosis* a man finds himself transformed into an enormous insect, loathed by his family.

Perhaps the principle at work here, besides the necessity for identification, is that of the common and the uncommon. We need both the common and uncommon traits in characterization, just as we need common and uncommon words in good style. If characters are too common, we take no interest in them; if they are too uncommon, we are puzzled. The common trait will clarify the character and the uncommon trait will give it distinction. A Buddhist monk who is the champion boxer of Thailand would interest us.

Raskolnikov is not a common criminal. He kills for a principle, to prove his theory of crime. He wants to find out if he is exceptional and superior enough to be above the moral law, beyond good and evil. He has generous impulses. He is an idealist, soft-hearted. He lives in a miserable little room, and has had to pawn his father's watch; he is too poor to continue his studies at the university. Yet he pays the expenses for Marmeladov's funeral. He is devoted to his mother and sister. And what attracts him to Sonia, a frail streetwalker, is that she is a true Christian, that she has sacrificed herself for her destitute family. If Raskolnikov were totally evil he could not love Sonia. Sonia is a romanticized figure that embodies Dostoyevsky's ideas about salvation through Christian humility and love, and she helps Raskolnikov return to humanity, his terrible isolation ends through Sonia. Meanwhile she symbolizes the misery of the insulted and humiliated in St. Petersburg. All that horror is dramatized through the Marmeladovs. They are an integral part of the action. Dostoyevsky intended to write a separate novel about the Marmeladovs. He succeeded in making one story out of two stories, and the young writer can study the structure of

Crime and Punishment to see how a novel may be unified while preserving the multitudinous diversity of life, and a subplot provide love interest as well as the necessary social background. And Dostoyevsky is the novelist to study for creating living people through inner contradictions and the violent conflicts they generate, for motivations that are obscure, for the primacy of emotions in human life, for seeing the jungle in every man. For Dostoyevsky life was stranger than fiction. He thought he chose typical rather than exceptional characters, and we see the oddity in their quiddity.

A successful character may appear more lifelike when larger than lifesize. The writer might be allowed to improve upon reality. He has to select and emphasize certain traits. He needs shadows and highlights in his portraits. The epic hero is more than lifesize, and hyperbole is a legitimate emphasis in the epic. Characters become more vivid, clearer and more convincing through an intensification of their leading traits. They are imaginatively re-created and are not direct reproductions from life even when drawn from life. A photographic copy would not be truer and would lack both the particular and the universal in the character. We cannot really have photographic copies of people in fiction, although photographs of actual people can be useful to a writer when he tries to visualize and define a character. He has to "see" his characters before he can use them.

The anarchy of character, like the chaos of reality in general, needs some form, some principle of order and selection and formalization. Fictional persons are not completely realistic. They are stylized, idealized likenesses, and seem more lifelike for that reason. The writer abstracts them out of reality and fills in the concrete details. If he stopped at the abstraction he would have allegorical figures, personifications of one predominant trait rather than persons with a complex and perhaps contradictory bundle of traits. Kafka's fiction is allegorical and he does not give even a name to his central character and calls him just K. We suspect K is probably Kafka himself, and symbolic of modern man with no particular identity, frustrated at every turn, tried for crimes he is not aware of, confused, mystified, attempting in vain to reach his goal. K in *The Castle* and *The Trial* is a displaced person with nowhere to go, confronted by mysterious authorities in an indefinite nightmare world as terrifying as the extermination camps of the Nazis that followed a few years after Kafka's death and the posthumous publication of his novels. Kafka has given us an uncanny mimesis of the bewilderment of a character entangled in the bureaucratic web of police states in an age of mass murders and genocide.

CONSISTENT CHARACTERS

Characters would not be convincing if not consistent with themselves, or if inconsistent, consistently inconsistent. The inconsistency is a habit, like the caprices of some charming women; or reveals contradictions within the character. Does the *character* of the character change? Not much, if at all. There is a certain constancy of character in an eternally changing universe, and that is why we may say with Heraclitus that character is destiny. We are trapped by our characters. Every man is fated to be himself by a mysterious law of his own, and when we examine a life we shall probably find a basic continuity in it. Whether character is what a man does, or what a man is, an aggregate of his past acts and a sort of conditioned reflex or habit, or an intrinsic quality, independent of actions, not a legacy of the past, it has this self-consistent quality but is complex enough to surprise us on occasion. Actually no one is consistently consistent.

A man will grow and possibly change in various directions, according to his original bent, such change being from the potential to actual. The writer has to develop these changes by careful, gradual, logical transitions to make them plausible. A character that does not grow or change is "flat," not "round," to use E. M. Forster's terminology, and roundness is a good test of a living, individualized character. The round character is capable of surprising us, Forster says. The flat character is a type, always the same, and somewhat comic for that reason. But flat or round, there is a consistency of character that should be preserved. A character is not capable of all kinds of action, but only of those acts which are necessary or probable and are consistent with its nature.

Change as growth is more consistent with the principle of consistence, and excludes radical alterations of character. Since the novel is a story of slow developments and deals with the accumulative detail (and in the stream-of-thought novel like *Mrs. Dalloway* or *Ulysses* the emphasis is on minor incidents and the external story line is broken and discontinuous), growth is more artistic and more proper to the medium. A playwright needs more dramatic changes, he practices a more spectacular art than the novelist; he deals with decisive moments, with sudden turns of fortune, with strong conflicts or crises—the climactic points of the action. And so does, on a lesser scale, the short-story writer. What is a gradual growth in the novel becomes an explosive change in the play. Such explosive changes do not come off well in fiction, and their value may be questioned even in drama. What is good theatre is not good fiction—or perhaps even good drama. The novel derives much of its strength from what happens between the high points and the seemingly random detail.

The search for identity, the recovery of one's own self, is a common enough anxiety nowadays, and the problem seems especially acute in America, with its vast social distances and conformities, with a mixed mobile population, lacking a common origin and racial memories, with millions of uprooted or rootless, and with the soil not exercising the same influence on the soul as in older, more settled communities. Who am I? What am I? are questions most of us have asked sometime in our lives. Most of us are "other-oriented," and we are subject to other confusions of our age.

But if the character is confused, the writer should not be. He cannot grope in the dark with his character, unless he is another Sherwood Anderson, whose groping manner, as though he were trying to find the meaning of the story for

himself, is part of the story's charm. If the writer does not
know what attitude to take toward his people, the story will
be confusing and lack unity of tone.

COMPLEX CHARACTERS

Characters in a novel obviously are more complex than in
a short story. The novelist's chief job is the creation of complex characters. In the short story there is no room for the
gradual development of character and the writer portrays his
people by a few quick strokes. They are necessarily carica-
tures, and caricature is an art. But a short story, too, is better
for suggesting complexity, through contradictions within the
hero or heroine and man versus himself, man versus society
conflicts.

No novel can—or should—tell everything about a person.
A good fictional character is like an iceberg; nine-tenths of it
is below the surface, in the depths, as Hemingway once said
in an interview. There is no art without economy, and the
reader is bored when nothing is left to his imagination.
Good characters represent more than themselves. They can
be economic, social, religious, national, and racial types; they
can be landscape figures caught in the drama of soil-and-
soul, as in Thomas Hardy's fiction. A character needs symbolic
overtones, and like a good idea it should remain perhaps a
little abstract.

Unless the writer deliberately intends to create a zombie,
he should see to it that his people move on their own power
after he sets them in motion, that they are not puppets,
mechanical figures, with himself pulling the wires, or wooden
illustrations of his theme. It is a good thing now and then to
shake characters loose of the idea. Nor should a character be
the author's mouthpiece without the complexities, contradictions, self-division, eccentricities, tragic flaw, or error of the
author. It is dangerous to have a character prove something
instead of being a living picture. The writer is in trouble
when he veers away from the picture and starts writing

rhetorical arguments for his characters, or judges them in the manner of Fielding, George Eliot, and Thackeray. Today the responsible writer is less sure of his arguments, of his characters, and of himself.

A writer knows when his characters come to life. Living characters display an astounding freedom and the author feels the continuous pull of their independence. They are irascible scene-stealers and threaten to run away with the show. Often they are secondary characters, not wearing the thematic strait jacket imposed on the hero, not obliged to prove anything. A writer is often more successful with his minor characters drawn directly from life and not burdened with the thematic responsibilities of the hero, and we usually remember these minor characters better than we remember the hero, especially if they are comical people.

A writer does best with characters he loves or hates, but some cannot write about people they are not fond of in some way. Enthusiasm is important. Without enthusiasm it is difficult to bring people to life, and the story goes dead. A completely negative person would be as difficult to make convincing as the saint who never sins. When the bad man is presented from his own point of view and rendered as a complex person his portrait cannot be all black. He has his own contradictions and is driven perhaps by the same insecurity that plagues the good man.

It is part of the writer's job to endow his characters with enough freedom to turn them loose and let them kick over the traces. This freedom can do wonders in characterization and be a corrective to rigid author-imposed behavior. Good or bad, characters have to be spontaneous enough to improvise their own dialogue as it were.

Successful characters are people-in-tension, if not always people-in-action. Tension is a form of conflict. The vitality of Dostoyevsky's characters may be explained partly by the fact that they are in a state of extreme tension. And he keeps them tense and restless to the end.

Generally, the first step in characterization is naming the person. We need not dwell upon the psychology of names, but it is of some importance in fiction. An elementary precaution is not to use in the same story names that sound alike. Names should do their part in individualizing and typing people. They are labels, they identify. Henry James listed in his Notebooks hundreds of names that caught his fancy. Anything that contributes to identification is a useful device, especially in the opening pages of the story, when the characters are being introduced. Props like a cigar or a cane actors use have their uses also in fiction. Backgrounds are important. If a writer does not intend to characterize a person, he had better not name him, but it is no crime if he does. As in motion pictures, extras and bit players are not named in the cast. They are background types—hotel clerk, nurse, switchboard operator, taxi driver.

THE IMPORTANCE OF ACTION IN CHARACTERIZATION

When characters reveal themselves through a developing action, they require little or no elucidation by the author, for plot proves character. The reader is allowed to form his own opinions about them, judging them by what they do and say and think and feel, or by what others do or say or think about them. In *Crime and Punishment* Dostoyevsky lets Razumikhin sum up Raskolnikov's character, and Marmeladov introduce his daughter Sonia in a long alcoholic confession. Action, we know, is vital in characterization because it reveals and individualizes people, but action of course is not wholly a means to an end, the end being character; it has its own value. That the story is an imitation of the action rather than of the people in it is an extremely important principle for the writer to keep in mind even when he does not wholly agree with it. We cannot always separate character from action, one becomes the other. Since drama is derived from the word "doing," it means doers, active agents are necessary for drama and the instinct of much current commercial fiction may be sounder in this respect than it appears on the surface. The mass magazines, the bosomy best-sellers, want active doers, not passive people. Action alone can keep some of these implausible stories going in the absence of character and thought. In biographical, picaresque, and loose episodic novels a strong active self-conscious character will hold the separate parts of the story together and keep it moving. Without such a character at the center, these stories have a tendency to fall apart. Thematic unity may not be enough to hold the parts together. And in the absence of plot—though not of action—character becomes doubly important and needs the support of thought.

To be a doer, a character must have plenty to do. The writer has to keep him busy. Bad men are more active than good men. For most readers, characters are better understood and remembered through their vices. The gossip industry thrives on this human weakness, and fiction has been rightly called a form of gossip. The man who keeps himself unspotted from the world would be unusual enough to be new, but he does not arouse our curiosity as much as does the man who is spotted and thinks it is the smart thing to be, and only saps are saints.

People in St. Petersburg laughed at Prince Myshkin and called him an idiot. Dostoyevsky proposed to create a completely good character in this young man with a pointed blond beard and make him a Christ-like person, who like Don Quixote wanted to set things right in the world and carried its burdens on his shoulders. Myshkin in *The Idiot* represented Dostoyevsky's ideal of the Russian Christ rising against the corrupt materialistic West dominated by the Catholic Church. Myshkin is a naive, innocent, trusting fellow of angelic sweetness, radiating a spiritual charm and possessing deep intuitive insights into human nature with its private hells. Dostoyevsky contrasted him with the wild brutal merchant, Rogozhin, and all the other calculating, selfish people Myshkin met in St. Petersburg after his return from a sanatorium in Switzerland. Even Rogozhin falls under Myshkin's spell. Myshkin wanted to save Nastasya Filippovna, beautiful and damned, from Rogozhin's clutches by marrying

her himself; she in turn wanted to save him from herself. She
thought too much of him to accept his proposal; he was the
only good man she met. Myshkin loses his mind and does
actually become an idiot when Rogozhin murders Nastasya,
as she knew he would when she went to Rogozhin's house.

In *The Idiot* we do not have an active, fighting saint.
Myshkin is an epileptic (as was Dostoyevsky) and impresses
us as a strange sickly figure. He is the pale copy of a man,
not a flesh-and-blood character, not torn by contradictions,
not quite human, we feel—and this is the main weakness of
this novel. Goodness is not dramatic unless it is active goodness. The good man has to be a doer, on the offensive, a lib-
erator. Myshkin is almost a stock character in Christian goodness, while the bad man, Rogozhin, Nastasya, and other
characters are individualized.

Similarly "pretty boys" with nothing much to do play
heroes on the screen, and the villain is only a "character
actor." He does have character compared to the insipid romantic lead. In Hollywood a "lady" is—or was—a nice girl
put on a pedestal of ice: the puritanic ideal. She may be
kissed, lightly, in the last reel, registering the required surprise
if not indignation, while her rival, the bad girl, not half as
pretty perhaps, gives her lips freely to virile men. The bad
girl steals the picture. She is much more active.

This is not the occasion to explore the question why some
men love the bad woman and why some women love a heel,
but the hussy, like the heel, does what the lady and the gentleman would not do or dare not; the former are active doers.
So a beautiful wicked heroine makes a popular novel a best-
seller, and the Confessions thrive on stereotyped active sinners, with God thrown in at the end. For some readers the
most compelling character in *Crime and Punishment* is
Svidrigaylov, a complex, spectacular bad man, who has no
moral scruples, a criminal type interested only in his own
pleasures, who gives Raskolnikov an inkling of what he himself might be like a few years later. Svidrigaylov is not wholly
evil, he is a self-divided soul and has his good side; he is inconsistent.

Surface activity in itself is of course no criterion of power or vitality. Prometheus, it will be remembered, was chained to Mount Caucasus and a vulture tore his heart. He could not move—but he did not stop fighting back. He was kept chained. He was not passive. The first intellectual rebel struggling against the gods was too dangerous to be turned loose. The saint should be dangerous—more dangerous than the sinner. He should live dangerously, as in the past. The saint should not be a weakling or some spectral straw man. He should not be morally perfect. Myshkin is too perfect, too consistent. Imperfection is a necessary condition for both virtue and drama.

Long after the conventional hero and heroine are forgotten, their bold bad active rivals linger in the memory of the reader. And it is the villain who, imperfect, makes the tragic mistake that leads to his downfall. The villain becomes the tragic hero and people sympathize with him. When the end comes, he is not hated and arouses the pity and fear which provide the tragic pleasure in the poetics of movie plots and their counterparts in magazines and books, and which by right belongs to the hero. Identification is easier with the sinner, for most people are sinners.

The fakir sitting immobile in his cave or at a street corner year after year subscribes perhaps to an older wisdom than we possess and few of us would want to condemn such a sitdown strike against man's inscrutable fate, but here in the West happiness is an active pursuit, doing, and having, rather than being, and the fakir repels us. With us character is action, as it was in ancient Greece. The freedom to choose between alternative possibilities of action puts man under a tremendous moral responsibility, but it is a creative responsibility, both in life and fiction. The action a Christian chooses is not wholly predetermined and man is, within certain limits, master of his own destiny, and this is the dramatic way of living. Alternatives make for conflict, for drama, for complexity. Free will results in anxiety as well as in activity. It has meant progress and civilization, doing and having. It is not merely being. The pious Mohammedan still bows his head with his fate written on his forehead before he was born (Kismet) and submits to Allah's will. Islam means submission and he is reconciled with his lot. Islam could never produce a Shakespeare with his free and independent characters struggling against themselves and against fate—free and independent within limits. Driven by irrational forces man is never wholly free.

EXPOSITION

A writer can give background information about his characters in categorical statements on his own authority without showing them through an action. He can write little essays about them when he introduces them, tell us about their past and present, and he can halt his narrative at any point for additional comments. This information is not dramatized and may be given wholesale in advance. The character is virtually complete when first introduced. The author deals with it in summary fashion. The following is an author's report: old-fashioned.

But as we are to see a great deal of Amelia, there is no harm in saying, at the outset of our acquaintance, that she was a dear little creature; and a great mercy it is, both in life and in novels, which (and the latter especially) abound in villains of the most sombre sort, that we are to have for a constant companion, so guileless and goodnatured a person. As she is not a heroine, there is no need to describe her person; indeed I am afraid that her nose was rather short than otherwise, and her cheeks a great deal too round and red for a heroine; but her face, blushed with rosy health, and her lips with the freshest of smiles, and she had a pair of eyes, which sparkled with the brightest and honestest good humour, except indeed when they filled with tears, and that was a great deal too often; for the silly thing would cry over a dead canary bird; or over a mouse, that the cat haply had seized upon; or over the end of a novel, were it ever so stupid; and as for saying an unkind word to her, were any persons hardhearted enough to do so—why, so much the worse for them. Even Miss Pinkerton, the austere and godlike woman, ceased scolding her after the first time, and though she no more comprehended sensibility than she did algebra, gave all

masters and teachers particular orders to treat Miss Sedley
with the utmost gentleness, as harsh treatment was injurious
to her.

So now we know what to think of Miss Sedley, and we wonder if she will live up to this chatty description of her in
Vanity Fair, but the suspense is less. We know too little about
her to be really interested. In *The Razor's Edge* Somerset
Maugham starts by saying that he has never begun a novel
with more misgivings, that the story he has to tell ends neither
with death nor marriage. He says he did not keep notes of
what was said on this or that occasion and does not pretend
to reproduce the conversations of his people verbatim.
Maugham is in his favorite role of a detached observer or
witness. He wants the reader to think it is a true story. In
1919 he happened to be in Chicago on his way to the Far
East, when Elliott Templeton called him and invited him to
lunch. After a brief conversation on the telephone Maugham
tells us about this man before we meet him, and here the
narrator's authority is greater. He is a member of the cast,
not disguised under another name.

> I had known Elliott Templeton for fifteen years. He was at
> this time in his late fifties, a tall, elegant man with good fea-
> tures and thick waving dark hair only sufficiently graying to
> add to the distinction of his appearance. He was always beau-
> tifully dressed. He got his haberdashery at Charvet's, but his
> suits, his shoes and his hats in London. He had an apartment
> in Paris on the Rive Gauche in the fashionable Rue St.
> Guillaume. People who did not like him said he was a dealer,
> but this was a charge that he resented with indignation. He
> had taste and knowledge, and he did not mind admitting
> that in bygone years, when he first settled in Paris, he had
> given rich collectors who wanted to buy pictures the benefit
> of his advice; and when through his social connection he
> heard that some impoverished nobleman, English or French,
> was disposed to sell a picture of first rate quality he was
> glad to put him in touch with the directors of American
> museums who, he happened to know, were on the lookout for
> a fine example of such and such a master. . . . One would
> naturally suppose that Elliott profited by the transactions, but
> one was too well bred to mention it. Unkind people asserted
> that everything in his apartment was for sale and that after

he had invited a wealthy American to an excellent lunch, with vintage wines, one or two of his valuable drawings would disappear or a marquetry commode would be replaced by one in lacquer. . . .

(W. Somerset Maugham, *The Razor's Edge*)

The description of Elliott Templeton continues in this ironic, slightly malicious tone for a few thousand words, until the man shows up at the hotel and takes him to his sister's brownstone house in a street off Lake Shore Drive for lunch. Templeton is not the central character in the novel, and for secondary characters this method avoids unnecessary dramatization and is economical. Maugham does not have to write too many scenes in first person.

When a character is waiting for someone the writer can tell a good deal about him or the person he is waiting for, and insert if necessary a biographical sketch. In *Fathers and Sons* the novel opens with a few lines of dialogue between Kirsanov and his servant while that country gentleman is waiting for the coach that will bring his son back from the University of St. Petersburg, and Turgenev uses this occasion to introduce Kirsanov and tell us about his past.

Such summary characterizations by the author or his narrator, if done in the opening pages of a novel, before the action proper starts, will not halt the narrative. We have an example of this in *The Devils* (also known as *The Possessed*), in which there is a long introductory chapter, which is the biography of one of the principal characters in the novel, Verkhovensky. Some preliminaries may be disposed of in this manner and the decks cleared for the subsequent action. Today most writers chop up the exposition and scatter it throughout the story; a bit here, a bit there, and this enables them to cut down summaries to a minimum and speed up the action through scene. This is the dramatic way.

With the emphasis on psychological processes, the inward action, the physical description of characters is not as important as it used to be, and many readers like to form their own mental images of what the characters look like, but a brief description—in movement—is always helpful. There is probably some correlation between physical appearance and character. Surely the eyes reveal a great deal about a person and are the "windows of the soul." We do judge people by their appearance. There is also psychological description or analysis, not much in favor today, and one of the main arguments against omniscience, what Henry James himself called irresponsible authorship.

> Isabel Archer was a young person of many theories; her imagination was remarkably active. It had been her fortune to possess a finer mind than most of the persons among whom her lot was cast; to have a larger perception of surrounding facts and to care for knowledge that was tinged with the unfamiliar. It is true that among her contemporaries she passed for a young woman of extraordinary profundity. . . . It may be affirmed without delay that Isabel was probably very liable to the sin of self-esteem; she often surveyed with complacency the field of her own nature; she was in the habit of taking for granted, on scanty evidence, that she was right; she treated herself to occasions of homage. . . . Her thoughts were a tangle of vague outlines which had never been corrected by the judgment of people speaking with authority. In matters of opinion she had had her own way and it had led her into a thousand ridiculous zigzags. At moments she discovered she was grotesquely wrong, and then she treated herself to a week of passionate humility. After this she held her head higher than ever again, for it was of no use, she had an unquenchable desire to think well of herself. She had a theory it was only under this provision life was worth living. . . .
>
> (Henry James, *The Portrait of a Lady*)

This is not according to James's rule of "unrolling" a character, its gradual emergence through the action—although there is much of that too in the novel. We look at Isabel through the author's eyes, and James is a little too fond of psychological analysis in solid blocks of exposition.

THOUGHT AND CHARACTER

As Emerson said, "The key to every man is his thought." Thought and disposition or temperament go together, and thought gives us an inside view of character.

Character in Fiction

Thought is a large department in fiction, and so far the European novel has excelled in it (Dostoyevsky, Marcel Proust, Thomas Mann, André Gide, Albert Camus, Jean-Paul Sartre, James Joyce, Aldous Huxley). Evidently we Americans are too busy living to do much thinking, and we respond more readily to moral than to intellectual ideas. Many of us fear intellectual ideas; there is something alien about them, they are "foreign isms." We go for facts, not theories, we say proudly. There are relatively few abstract intellectual words in Saxon English. The abstract words for thinking come from the French, or through French from Latin and Greek, as Taine observed. Thus in a sense thinking words are alien words, foreign to the native idiom.

Greedy for experience, rich in sensations, but poor in ideas, in thought, characters in the American novel do not often reach the fuller human dimensions. Generally our writers gain their most striking effects with primitive unthinking people, which is so strange and new to Europeans, so American in their view. Even Henry James remained singularly indifferent to ideas, to the larger philosophical, political, and social problems of his time. Christopher Newman in *The American* and some of his other Americans who followed him on the international scene are primitives by European standards, or intellectual innocents. There is little evidence in his Notebooks that James perceived with his acute story sense what exciting, dramatic things ideas are in both life and fiction.

We have had in our fiction plenty of surface action, but not enough ideas as motives. Thought and character together should perform their natural function as the twin internal sources of action, but in dramatizing thought James left out ideas one would expect from a writer of his stature. Look at what Dostoyevsky did with ideas! A novel of ideas should not be an abstract story or an intellectual exercise. Ideas should be dramatized through compelling characters who act on them, and what is even more important perhaps the language should furnish the sensory proofs. Aldous Huxley wrote the finest English essays of our time and was a man of brilliant original ideas, but in his fiction he did not speak through living pictures and its mimetic quality, despite the lucid style, is low compared to its intellectual content. And it was probably for this same reason—lack of a sensuous pictorial language—that George Bernard Shaw, master of exposition, failed as a novelist and succeeded as a playwright.

When a reader cannot visualize a character, it does not come to life. James's people seem to melt into his smooth fluid landscapes, and his houses, gardens, streets are often given as states of mind, as reflected in the consciousness of a character, which doubtless is a subtle form of description and characterization, and beautiful effects may be gained by this method. James occasionally strikes lovely notes through the reactions of his people to their surroundings: Venice in *The Aspern Papers,* Paris in *The Ambassadors.* He was intimately familiar with these two cities. His subjective prose bordering on the abstract acquires a delicate golden sheen in these and other stories he wrote. We seem to be looking at old stereopticon slides while a music box plays in the room. The misty style is turned to advantage and adds to the impression by giving the setting the enchantment of dreamlike distance. The master sought a "prodigious delicacy of touch" in his fiction, as we read in his Notebooks, and he had that touch, but too often his fiction is wanting in actuality, which he sought with equal zeal but with less success.

When we read James Joyce we find that he is not misty. Joyce can be obscure, but writes in concrete images and is a wonderful mimic. The sonorous prose is matched by the rich imagery and a wealth of ideas, and his style is so suggestive, so fully documented with detailed observation, that he does not dissolve his characters in a subjective void, and on the contrary makes the reality more real. They are sharply individualized through their speech, spoken and unspoken. The environment in *Portrait of the Artist as a Young Man* and in *Ulysses* through exactly observed or remembered details becomes even more truly expressive of character than in Henry James. And Joyce does not neglect the social and political milieus of Ireland in his time. He was, or claimed to be, a socialist, and his principal characters belong to the lower middle class. They have to work for a living. We know their occupations.

The secret private self has come to the fore in fiction, and today the writer is technically equipped to tell about his people what "their best friends don't know," and to dramatize character as a process rather than a fixed state. But new characters, representative of our age, are not emerging, and such an important type as the modern American woman, for instance, has not been depicted yet in our fiction. We are painfully aware, as readers or writers, of the dilemma of the thinking man, the spiritual man, surveying the rat race and perhaps caught in it himself. We are doubles, many of us doubly double, but where is the American double in our fiction? There is a growing disparity between the inner man and the outer, the private and public self, the naked face and the mask, but such conflicts remain largely unexplored.

Thirty-five million immigrants have come to this country and America is no longer an Anglo-Saxon nation, but no American novelist has told us yet what it really means for a man to burn all the bridges behind him and change his nationality; the confusion, the agony, the anxiety along with the euphoria of the new world which millions of our citizens have been through in their search for a new, American identity; how in countless cases the inner breach never heals and a protective smile hides secret wounds. This has not been told. A great American story remains unknown and it would take courage to tell it. There are "Dostoyevskian" themes, yes-and-no, love-and-hate situations in this traumatic experience; remembrance of things past, good versus good tragedies, *Fathers and Sons,* Golyadkins senior and junior, grandeur and misery. This is a vast as yet unexplored sector of American life. The sociologist cannot give us this kind of knowledge. That is the novelist's task. What Henry James could have done with it if he were a sensitive transplanted European in America! Nor do we have authentic realistic portraits of the American business tycoon in the second half of the twentieth century, surely a new type of disciplined empire builder, who might be as imaginative as an artist, and who should be presented from the inside, and by an insider if possible—an insider with the necessary distance and self-distance, and with absolute sincerity and conviction. There is romance in big business. Big business as a theme can be a global affair. It can have historic overtones. We had the proletarian novel. Let us now have the capitalistic novel. Some will say this is the greatest untold story in America.

In his search for fresh new characters, the writer has to catch people in their inner turmoil. It is particularly the secret inner strife that reveals character. The writer has to become subjective and attack new themes. Men differ in their feelings and thoughts, in their secret lives, in their intellectual and spiritual needs, and can be surprisingly original behind the mask, because freer. When we reach the level of sincerity in a man, we are likely to find a fresh human being; but there must be some sincerity left, or all is lost.

If the novel is dying, as some say it is, it is dying of stock characters, dying through irresponsibility and the "entertainment" novel, of a lack of fresh new ideas and seriousness. It is dying of taboos, of playing safe and the fear of being involved—and the economics of publishing. Its end seems inevitable if it is to compete with journalism, with television, with Broadway and Hollywood, with glossy magazines. The novel is dying perhaps because the hero is dead. Is it not time to bring the epic back into fiction?

Let us not forget that drama developed independently in Greece, India, China, from primitive religious festivals. The theatre has been an institution like the church and the school (itself an offshoot of the church) and this idea persists in many countries to this day. Literature may not be a substitute for religion, but it has been historically connected with it. Not until the novel assumes its responsibility as the successor of the classic tragedy and epic, though a relatively new form of poetry and still in an experimental stage, will there be a real revival of interest in fiction. Art is new, personal and earnest. And art will keep us human.

The American novel needs more magnitude, and more significant action. It needs more intellectual and spiritual elements in its plot. (We might say the same thing about the British, French, or the Soviet novel.) The American novel needs beauty. It needs guts. We shall not get anywhere without an ethical conception of this craft. Art for art's sake is an alluring philosophy, but is it not an escape from reality, or a reflection of it? Does it not show the dichotomy between the artist and his environment? When the writer does not want to be a part of his society he seeks refuge in art. When he rejects the values of his society he lives in bitter rebellion, an exile in his own country. (James Joyce in Ireland, Henry James in America, to cite two well-known examples.) The ivory tower is a retreat from life. To those who are serious about this craft fiction is poetry, and writing poetry is a spiritual exercise—has been for ages. This is at bottom a religious art. Not in a dogmatic sense but in the broad historic meaning of the word religion as a high human cause, as a system of faith, of commonly-held beliefs and aspirations, as exaltation, as a drive to the sublime.

Is this too much to expect? Will the underworld of pimps, perverts, drug addicts, cesspool supermen, these initiates of a new kind, take over, and William S. Burroughs emerge a prophet? The fascination of his characters is undeniable. *Naked Lunch, The Soft Machine,* and Burroughs' other books enjoy the prestige of experimental writing. They are the saddest books I have read. Burroughs is a stylist; his work, shocking as it is, should be distinguished from commercial pornography. There is that famed offbeat writer of France, Jean Genet, with his confessions and erotic visions of a thief and male prostitute. *Saint Genet, Actor and Martyr,* by Jean-Paul Sartre, is an impressive examination of Genet's life and writings.

We cannot overlook such books. They do tell us about the age we live in. And again, only the fiction writer can give us this kind of knowledge. These are disturbing works that shed new light on the lowest depths of human nature among the damned—but they make us pause and ponder. Their novelty will wear, they will be absorbed perhaps into the mainstream of Western fiction and have to be judged strictly on their literary merits. For the present at least there can be no general agreement about their worth. But such daring sincerity and originality can breathe new life into the novel—and that is what interests us here.

8. STREAM OF THOUGHT
AND INTERNAL MONOLOGUE

The dominant trend in the novel today is psychological realism, with the emphasis on individual consciousness. We are not satisfied with mere surface realism. The objective event is still necessary, to be sure, but we ask of a serious novel a little more than that; we want some good slices of the interior life to complete the picture. We want to dig below the surface as readers or writers. It is fiction in depth now, the external experience blending with the internal.

The modern novelist can render the dark tumult of emotions also through unspoken speech; he can show a mind at work with an intrapsychic problem; he can capture sensations, memories, fugitive ideas and thoughts as they occur, dramatically. He can reveal the secret inner world of man by reproducing the uninterrupted flow of the thought stream.

When we open *Crime and Punishment* we see that Dostoyevsky gives Raskolnikov's thoughts while he is thinking them, and in the words of the character himself, putting them in quotation marks. To kill or not to kill: that is his problem in the opening pages. His chaotic thinking revolves around that idea, and Raskolnikov is startled by his criminal thoughts.

"God!" he exclaimed, "is it possible, is it possible, that I really shall take an axe and strike her on the head, smash open her skull . . . that my feet will slip in warm, sticky blood, and that I shall break the lock, and steal, and tremble, and hide, all covered in blood . . . with the axe . . . ? God, is it possible?"

He was shaking like a leaf.

"But why am I saying this?" he went on, leaning back again as if amazed at himself. "I must have realized that I should never carry it out, so why have I gone on tormenting myself until now? Yesterday again, yesterday, when I went for that

163

> . . . *rehearsal,* I must certainly have been quite sure yester-
> day that I should never do it. . . . Then why am I talking
> about it now? Why do I still go on harbouring doubts? Yes-
> terday, as I came downstairs, didn't I tell myself that it was
> vile, disgusting, base, base . . . didn't I turn sick at the very
> thought of it, *when I was not dreaming,* and run away in
> terror . . . ?"
>
> (Dostoyevsky, *Crime and Punishment*)

This is narration from the author's point of view, "as if
by an invisible but omniscient person," as Dostoyevsky himself observed in his notebook. He was not satisfied with the
first draft, in first person, and burned it. He preferred to write
in third person, focusing the story on Raskolnikov, and telling much of the story from Raskolnikov's point of view,
impersonally. Dostoyevsky is our guide when we read the
novel. He comments, he explains, he describes, when necessary, while standing outside the action. He felt he had to do
this for the clarification of his subject. He held out to the
reader a member of the new generation in Russia and he
wanted to be sure the reader understood all he wanted to
say, adding his own superior knowledge to Raskolnikov's.

Now let us take a look at Dostoyevsky's short novel, *Notes
from Underground,* which is one long monologue by a forty-
year-old man living in a hole who is writhing in self-contempt
and is tormented by his own malice. This is the new underground man, torn by conflicting emotions, a sadist-masochist,
in the turmoil of irrational forces, making a bizarre confession. This man can enjoy his own degradation, there is
pleasure even in a toothache, he says, and he is equally greedy
for pleasures derived from inflicting pain on others. Plagued
by self-consciousness, this paradoxical fellow must relieve
himself of his evil memories.

"I am a sick man. I am a spiteful man. I am an unattractive
man." That is how the novel begins. The tone is feverish,
polemical. It is not internal monologue. This is not a mental
soliloquy. The underground man is not speaking to himself,
but to the reader; he addresses himself to an invisible audience while writing his story. We find in the book such expressions as, "But do you know, gentlemen, what was the

chief point about my spite?" "No doubt, gentlemen, you imagine that I wish to amuse you. You are mistaken in that, too." "And now gentlemen, whether you care to hear it or not, I want to tell you why I could not become even an insect."

Or let us take the opening paragraph of "The Tell-Tale Heart" by Edgar Allan Poe:

> True!—nervous—very, very dreadfully nervous I had been and am; but why *will* you say that I am mad? The disease had sharpened my senses—not destroyed—not dulled them. Above all was the sense of hearing acute. I heard all things in the heaven and in the earth. I heard many things in hell. How, then, am I mad? Hearken! and observe how healthy—how calmly I can tell you the whole story. . . .
>
> Now, this is the point. You fancy me mad. Madmen know nothing. But you should have seen me. You should have seen how wisely I proceeded—with what caution—with what foresight—with what dissimulation I went to work!

This is "You" writing in first person, not true internal monologue, which, to repeat, is not addressed to the reader, though naturally meant to be read. Interior monologue in fiction is a direct descendant of the dramatic soliloquy in the Elizabethan theatre.

Exeunt Rosencrantz and Guildenstern

HAMLET. Ay, so, God be we' ye! Now I am alone.
O! What a rogue and peasant slave am I. . . .
Yet I,
A dull and muddy-mettled rascal, speak
Like John-a-dreams, unpregnant of my cause.
And can say nothing; no, not for a king,
Upon whose property and most dear life
A damn'd defeat was made. Am I a coward?
Who calls me villain? breaks my pate across?
Plucks off my beard and blows it in my face?
Tweaks me by the nose? gives me the lie i' the
throat,
As deep as to the lungs? Who does me this?
Ha!
Swounds, I should take it, for it cannot be
But I am pigeon-liver'd, and lack gall
To make oppression bitter, or ere this
I should have fatted all the region kites

With this slave's offal. Bloody, bawdy villain!
O! vengeance!
Why, what an ass am I!

During his soliloquies Hamlet is alone on the stage. He is not speaking to another character in the play, or to the audience; he is speaking to himself; he is meditating. Only by the convention of the theatre are these monologues audible. They are meant to be silent. And since they are audible they are organized, structured speech, and indeed they are written in a more elevated and passionate tone, they are emotional outbursts when the action reaches a pitch of intensity, and some of Shakespeare's most memorable passages are soliloquies.

In fiction it is not necessary for the character to be alone in the scene, but he is not heard; it is silent talk in the secrecy of his own mind. Like the dramatic soliloquy, and like dialogue, internal monologue is written in first person. It gives this secret unspoken speech direct to the reader, with no narrator coming between character and reader. By this method the reader is allowed to have direct access to the most intimate thoughts of a person and overhear what he is saying to himself. It is not a summary or paraphrase by a narrator, but the unedited, uncensored silent speech in a character's mind.

Actually, internal monologue is not as free and spontaneous as it seems. There is unavoidably some editing, some control; it cannot be a tape recording of inner speech. There is in *Ulysses*, for instance, careful selection, condensation, stylization as in spoken dialogue, but the arranging hand of the author is concealed and the reader is given the illusion that nothing has been censored; the monologue otherwise would be incoherent. The writer who uses this method follows a thin line between coherence and incoherence, especially when he gives the thoughts that lie closest to the unconscious. An exact transcript of the monologue is impossible, and even if it were possible would be as undesirable as the exact transcript of spoken speech.

Internal monologue then has these three characteristics: 1) It is written in first person, with author eliminated. 2) It is not addressed to the reader. 3) It is caught as it takes place, it is speech in the original raw stage before its rhetorical organization by a writer.

Internal monologue gives immediacy to the story, and this is one of its most useful functions. Like dialogue it makes was *is*. It need not be confined to the conscious speech level, as in traditional monologue; it can go deep into the subconscious. Being thought in process of formation, it may lie close to the subconscious; hence, it is bound to be somewhat incoherent. Dostoyevsky certainly could give a character's most intimate thoughts, and there are in his novels snatches of incoherent repetitive monologue. And Gogol before him used monologue in much the same manner. We find internal monologue in both its direct and indirect forms or reported speech very close to it in *Madame Bovary*. Knut Hamsun used internal monologue in *Hunger* (1890) and he was still using it when James Joyce wrote *Ulysses* in 1914–21. There are bits of internal monologue in *Daredevils of Sassoun,* and we can trace the method as far back as Homer. It started earlier in poetry, and Walt Whitman's free verse may be said to be a forerunner of modern internal monologue.

The difference between traditional monologue and internal monologue is not so much of intimacy as of direct penetration into the character's mind, without apparent author intervention, and without a logical or intellectual organization of the thought stream, with an element of incoherence being inherent in the method. There is nevertheless order in the seeming disorder. We have something like the psychoanalyst's couch as the mind of the patient is allowed to wander off in any direction, but this free association is actually controlled by the writer, as it must be. Interior monologue should be distinguished from automatic writing, although both methods developed in modern fiction at about the same time during or shortly after the First World War, when many writers were in open revolt against conventional morality and conventional forms of writing, and the underground man, as the typical man of the twentieth century, came to the fore. The Dada movement began in a Zurich café in about 1916, when James Joyce was working on *Ulysses* in the same city, and a few years later, in 1924, the Dadaists were followed by the surrealists.

Is there any difference between internal monologue and the stream of consciousness technique? The latter is used as the more general, inclusive term. The stream of consciousness technique includes, let us say, internal monologue, in first person, indirect internal monologue, in third person, and some varieties and combinations of these; there is as yet no exact classification and nomenclature, and some confusion is inevitable. Stream of consciousness is both a technique and a genre. We have stream of consciousness novels as we have adventure, Gothic, detective, or historical novels, and they employ a variety of techniques, as these other novels do. The action takes place wholly or predominantly in the consciousness, or in the mind, in the broadest sense of the word. It is a highly subjective novel stressing the inner reaction to the external action, and the subjectivity is maintained from beginning to end. It dramatizes the interior life. Its characters are acutely self-conscious people. Our interest here is more in the technique than in the genre, and as a technique stream of consciousness means substantially the same thing as interior monologue in both its direct and indirect forms. Interior monologue is the older continental term, used in France, Germany, Russia, and other European countries.

As is well known, stream of consciousness was first used by William James in his *Principles of Psychology* as an attempt to describe the nature of consciousness. "Consciousness, then, does not appear to itself chopped up in bits. Such words as 'chain' or 'train' do not describe it fitly . . . it is nothing jointed; it flows. A 'river' or a 'stream' are the metaphors by which it is most naturally described. In talking of it hereafter, let us call it the stream of thought, of consciousness, or of the subjective life." It began to come into general use in England and America after the First World War. Stream of thought expresses the idea just as well and is simpler, more concrete. They are interchangeable terms. All these three metaphors cited by William James are noteworthy and together they do explain what stream of consciousness means from a psychologist's point of view. Consciousness as we know includes sensations and emotions as well as thought and various states of awareness. There is magic and mystery in stream of consciousness, but as a technique it is, we must admit, something of a chimera. It can be expressed only partly in words. Granted that certain thoughts, emotions, sensations, or states of awareness are non-verbal and cannot be communicated, fiction nevertheless is a verbal art and in a novel or story a writer can express only that which does not elude language. As a workable technique stream of consciousness is no better or worse than internal monologue in its direct and indirect forms. Interior monologue is a term more directly applicable to literature, and is more precise, less vague and confusing, though not as suggestive and beautiful as stream of consciousness. William James, Henri Bergson, Pierre Janet, Freud, Jung, Levy-Bruhl, and other psychologists could not fail to influence the structure of the novel by their discoveries, and laid the groundwork for this new type of fiction.

This technique permits the writer to travel in the consciousness, and its real business perhaps is with subconscious thoughts. The silent monologue can be also perfectly coherent conscious speech in its original state. There are degrees and varieties of interior monologue and of stream of consciousness in general, and it is not necessary to engage in hairsplitting definitions or distinctions. Literary criticism is not dogmatic theology, at least not yet, thank heaven, though in certain quarters it does have its hierarchy in academic vestments. This is a writer's talk on writing, not a critic's, and necessarily informal; casual above, causal underneath.

EXAMPLES OF INTERIOR MONOLOGUE

Ulysses

We may take this novel as our textbook if we want to learn the intricacies of this technique in just about all its forms. As Stephen Dedalus is walking along the beach in Dublin at

eleven o'clock in the morning we can follow his meditations.
There is almost nothing of external action in this episode.
Objective description is mixed with the monologue and transitions from one to the other are not indicated by the author.
Joyce uses a strictly dramatic method and has refined himself
out of existence. Quotation marks would indicate the presence
of an author arranging the material for the reader. Guideposts would remind us of the narrator's presence. It is confusing at first; we wonder what is happening, where are we,
what is it all about, but once we catch on we realize this is
a highly mimetic and sophisticated art.

Leopold Bloom, who "ate with relish the inner organs of
beasts and fowls," gets up to prepare breakfast for his wife,
Molly, who likes to have her breakfast served in bed. He has
kidneys on his mind. He puts the tea kettle on the fire, talks
to the cat in the kitchen. Italics are mine, to show the interior
monologue.

> The cat mewed in answer and stalked again stiffly round a
> leg of the table, mewing. *Just how she stalks over my writing
> table. Prr. Scratch my head. Prr.*
> Mr. Bloom watched curiously, kindly, the lithe black form.
> *Clean to see: the gloss of her sleek hide, the white button
> under the butt of her tail, the green flashing eyes.* He bent
> down to her, his hands on his knees. . . .
> He watched the bristles shining wirily in the weak light
> as she tipped three times and licked lightly. *Wonder is it true
> if you clip them they can't mouse after. Why? They shine in
> the dark, perhaps, the tips. Or kind of feelers in the dark,
> perhaps.*
> He listened to her licking lap. *Ham and eggs, no. No good
> eggs with this drouth. Want pure fresh water. Thursday:
> not a good day either for a mutton kidney at Buckley's. Fried
> with butter, a shake of pepper. Better a pork kidney at
> Dlugacz's. While the kettle is boiling.* She lapped slower, then
> licking the saucer clean. *Why are their tongues so rough? To
> lap better, all porous holes. Nothing she can eat?* He glanced
> round him. *No.*
> On quietly creaky boots he went up the staircase to the hall,
> paused by the bedroom door. *She might like something tasty.
> Thin bread and butter she likes in the morning. Still perhaps;
> once in a way.*

Stream of Thought and Internal Monologue

He said softly in the bare hall:
—I am going round the corner. Be back in a minute. . . .

On his way to the butcher shop Leopold Bloom thinks about a Zionist settlement in Palestine. It has no connection with buying kidneys, but he has been reading Zionist literature and the sun in Dublin reminds him of the sun in that far-off dreamland of his Jewish ancestors. Much of the novel is built on such free associations. Brief descriptive passages in third person are interspersed with the silent monologue in first person.

> The sun was nearing the steeple of George's church. *Be a warm day I fancy. Specially in these black clothes feel it more. Black conducts, (refracts is it?), the heat . . . Somewhere in the east: set off at dawn, travel round in front of the sun, steal a day's march on him. Keep it up forever never grow a day older technically. Walk along a strand, strange land, come to a city gate, sentry there, old ranker too, old Tweedy's big mustaches leaning on a long kind of spear. Wander through awned streets. Turbaned faces going by. Dark caves of carpet shops, big man, Turko the terrible, seated crosslegged smoking a coiled pipe . . . Might meet a robber or two . . . The shadows of the mosques along the pillars: priests with a scroll rolled up . . . Fading gold sky. A mother watches from the doorway. She calls her children home in their dark language. High wall: beyond strings twanged. Night sky moon, violet, colour of Molly's new garters . . . Probably not a bit like it really. Kind of stuff you read: in the track of the sun. Sunburst on the title page.* He smiled.

In the last chapter of the novel, Molly Bloom's celebrated monologue, all description in third person, paragraphing and punctuation have been removed, though there are a few breaks in the 25,000 word meditation written as a single sentence.

> . . . and the Spanish girls laughing in their shawls and their tall combs and the auctions in the morning the Greeks and the jews and the Arabs and the devil knows who else from all the ends of Europe and Duke street and the fowl market all clucking outside Larby Sharon's and the poor donkeys slipping half asleep and the vague fellows in the cloaks asleep in the shade on the steps and the big wheels of the

171

carts of the bulls and the old castle thousands of years old and those handsome Moors all in white and turbans like kings asking you to sit down in their little bit of a shop . . . and when I put the rose in my hair like the Andalusian girls used or shall I wear a red yes and how he kissed me under the Moorish wall and I thought well as well him as another and then I asked him with my eyes to ask again yes and then he asked me would I yes to say yes my mountain flower and first I put my arms around him yes and drew him down to me so he could feel my breasts all perfume yes and his heart was going like mad and yes I said yes I will Yes.

So ends the monologue, with Yes, as Molly remembers how Leopold proposed to her. She is a sensuous, earthy woman, a concert singer, born in Gibraltar, whose manager and latest lover, Blazes Boylan, has paid her another visit, wearing his straw hat and flashy clothes. We do not have Boylan's monologue, he is presented from the outside as a moneyed swell, but we can imagine the vulgarities of his mind. Her husband knows she is unfaithful to him but can do nothing about it, and Blazes Boylan despises him as a cuckold. Molly wakes up when Leopold comes home from a brothel with Stephen Dedalus, and both men are drunk. She represents in the structure of the novel Calypso and Penelope, and appears as the receptive, female principle in life, with mythological overtones.

It is doubtful if any novelist can carry the method farther than Joyce did in *Ulysses,* but he did not invent interior monologue. He gave the credit to Édouard Dujardin (1861–1949), whose short novel, *Les Lauriers sont coupés,* first published in 1887, is written entirely in interior monologue. *Les Lauriers sont coupés* (English translation by Stuart Gilbert, *We'll to the Woods No More*) was first published in 420 numbered copies, twenty on special paper, and very few copies were sold. It attracted little attention in France and was soon forgotten. As Dujardin says sadly in his little book, *"Le Monologue Intérieur. Son apparition. Ses origines. Sa place dans l'oeuvre de James Joyce,"* one of his biographers writing in 1923 did not even mention this novel. It does not amount to much as literature. But Mallarmé, the leader of symbolist poets, saw "the immense possibilities" of interior monologue . . . "I remember his expression," says Dujardin, *"l'instant pris à la gorge."* (the moment seized by the throat.)

Dujardin himself named Theodor de Wyzewa (1863–1917) as the man who originally conceived the idea of writing a novel in interior monologue, but this does not lessen the value of his contribution, and he is not only the originator of this new method of telling a story but its French theoretician. His informative little book about it was based on a few lectures he gave in various universities after his "resurrection" by James Joyce. Dujardin dedicated the book to Joyce, calling him the greatest writer of the age.

No one before Dujardin had written an entire novel in interior monologue. *Les Lauriers* is a slight but charming story about a Parisian boulevardier who has dinner with a young actress he is enamored with. Their relationship seems to be more platonic than romantic. The entire action is a silent soliloquy by a single character, Daniel Prince, and the mind of this passive hero reflects the external world about him like a mirror, so that the narrative thread, such as it is, consists of nothing but a fragmented thought stream caught at the source in its original raw state that startles us occasionally by its freshness. Sometimes this meditation, as when he is falling asleep after taking the girl back to her apartment, descends to the subconscious level and is reproduced seemingly in its free automatic flow in a disjointed language bordering on incoherence. Evidently no attempt is made to fill in the gaps in the monologue, remove the contradictions, and make it rhetorically organized speech; yet it does make sense and we can follow the flow of images on the screen of the hero's mind and get to know him as a definite personality with his dreams, hopes, and memories. As Joyce said, the reader enters the mind of the character with the first line and it is the uninterrupted flow of his monologue that completely replaces the usual form of the *récit.*

These thoughts, feelings, sensations, impressions are presented in such a fresh naive manner that they make delightful reading. They are "seized by the throat" and not developed as retrospective reflections. Reflection lacks immediacy, it is looking back upon the event after it happens. Dujardin uses short phrases divided by dots and dashes—a sort of chopped-up diary or telegraphic style that sometimes reads like free verse or a series of mental jottings, as if his hero were making mental notes for a novel he wanted to write. There is no objective description of any kind, the third person is never used; everything is subjectively presented, we stay in the dandy's mind. If Dujardin has to describe a restaurant or a street, he has Daniel Prince describe it to himself, as though making mental notes of the place, incorporating these momentary impressions in the monologue. The boulevardier is an amiable young Parisian who sees and thinks like a symbolist poet. Without this poetic touch the book would lose much of its interest for most readers. Dujardin belonged to Mallarmé's charmed circle in Paris as a friend and disciple of the famous poet; he was a dramatist of some standing, a musicologist and historian of religions, and was a colorful figure of the symbolist movement in France. He is remembered today by a bold literary experiment that caught on in Europe and America and became a valuable new tool in psychological fiction.

The impressionistic style of *Les Lauriers* records moments of feeling and thought, and in this kind of writing we stay close to the stream of experience recorded by the stream of thought.

> The street, black, and the double line of gas lamps rising, falling; the street without passers-by; the pavement sonorous, white under the whiteness of the clear sky and the moon; in the background, the moon, in the sky; the elongated quarter, white, of the white moon; and on all sides the eternal houses; mute, imposing, with high blackened windows, iron-bolted doors, the houses; in these houses, people? no, silence; I walk alone, along the houses, silently. . . .

The prose is in present tense with, notably, some of the conjunctions and verbs missing. Many words are repeated. We have a tableau in this description of a street in Paris and the picture seems static, which emphasizes the stillness of the scene in the white moonlight. There are no long complex sentences and coordinate clauses in this simple poetic style; some of the phrases consist of one or two words only. This is a more primitive language than French readers were accustomed to reading in novels. The prose becomes more fragmented and elliptical when the monologue gets closer to the subconscious, as in a scene in which Daniel Prince is falling asleep.

The first object of internal monologue is to suppress author intervention, says Dujardin in *Le Monologue Intérieur*. He lets Daniel Prince reveal himself through his unspoken speech and tell the story to himself, not to a reader. This inner voice is the voice of consciousness, and a good deal of the monologue reads like words spoken as in a dream state. It is well to keep the idea of reverie and meditation in mind in connection with internal monologue.

Daydreams, like nocturnal dreams, may be wish fulfillments, and dream, fantasy, is a natural activity of the human mind. The interior monologue then can reveal among other things the character's secret longings, what he would be ashamed to confess, perhaps, or even admit to himself; what he hides from others behind the mask he wears, and may not even be conscious of. It should be in some way an expression of his deepest, unsatisfied wishes, and the hopes and fears and memories they generate. And so we might say that the stream of thought novel using silent monologue has a dream line in it interwoven with the stream of experience, and this dream line, or wish line runs like a unifying thread through the monologue and ties the novel together.

Critics, says Dujardin, have compared interior monologue to all sorts of things, to the cinema, the X-ray, the diving bell, but not to musical motifs as found in Wagner, short successive phrases, in contrast to the long phrases of melodies or operatic arias, and these short phrases are not developed, and each expresses equally a movement of the mind, each is a moment. These moments are not linked together in a logical or intellectual but in a purely emotional or psychological order. Dujardin confesses he was fool enough to try this method for writing a novel, on the same Wagnerian principle of composition (he was an admirer of Wagner's music and acted as his interpreter in France), in "little short phrases" reduced to a syntactical minimum.

There is no plot, no unity of action in *Ulysses;* it is episodic in structure. Besides the Homeric framework it has an intricate web of other unities carefully worked out by the author to hold its parts together. It is not just an immense eruption of the irrational in man as it may seem to some on first reading it. Its underlying theme may be said to be the search for a father and the search for a son, although many other themes are woven into it. The title indicates its connection with the *Odyssey.* Leopold Bloom is Ulysses. Stephen Dedalus is Telemachus, the only son of Ulysses and Penelope. In the novel he is a young Irish poet (whom we first meet in *Portrait of the Artist*) back from Paris and brooding over his mother's death. He refused his mother's last request to kneel and pray by her bedside, and this troubles him. He is estranged from the Catholic Church, from Ireland, and from his own father. Gerty MacDowell is Nausicaa. Bella Cohen in the phantasmagoric brothel scene of night-town is Circe, and so on. The monologue itself is a most important unifying device, and so is the complex symbolism.

Silent thoughts tell more than spoken words and "as a man thinketh in his heart so is he." Characters in *Ulysses* come to life through their monologue. It is however an additional tool at the writer's command, not a substitute for traditional methods of characterization. The fascination of *Ulysses* does not lie solely in interior monologue or in its startling technique. It is a monumental human comedy, farcical in spots; a combination of modern realism and surrealism; it is myth, drama, epic, history, reportage, sonata, symphony, opera; a picture of western civilization at the beginning of the twentieth century.

THE SOUND AND THE FURY

In this novel by William Faulkner about a degenerate once-aristocratic southern family, Quentin is a gallant tragic figure whose monologue reveals the storm raging in his soul before his suicide. This novel is not written entirely in internal monologue; of its four chapters the first three are monologues, the fourth is objective narrative in third person and from a single point of view. It has also an appendix as a foreword by the author. This is, like *Ulysses,* a complex and difficult book and is confusing in its chronology. The appendix-foreword clears up some of the mystery. It contains the author's comments on his characters, which significantly he found necessary to make in *The Portable Faulkner,* edited by Malcolm Cowley. Quentin is obsessed with incestuous thoughts about his beautiful, promiscuous sister, Candace, or Caddy, but, as Faulkner tells us in the foreword, he loved not his sister's body but some concept of the family honor.

> Who loved not the idea of the incest which he would not commit, but some presbyterian concept of its eternal punishment: he, not God, could by that means cast himself and his sister both into hell, where he could guard her forever and keep her forevermore intact amid the eternal fires. But who loved death above all, who loved only death, loved and lived in a deliberate and almost perverted anticipation of death . . . Committed suicide in Cambridge, Massachusetts, June, 1910, two months after his sister's wedding, waiting first to complete the current academic year and so get the full value of his paid-in-advance tuition . . .

Reading Quentin's monologue before he drowned himself is a moving experience and the heart and power of this book lies in it. But here we do not have Dujardin's short undeveloped phrases, the diary style. These are not brief, fragmentary mental jottings, this is conventional literary prose. The sentences often are long, elaborate, co-ordinated, complex—not a simple primitive language in its syntax but brilliant formal rhetoric in Faulkner's best manner. Quentin has gone to Harvard for a year, he represents the good blood in the Compson clan, he is intelligent, sensitive, proud, a southern gentleman, but it is unlikely that even a Harvard freshman in 1910 would talk to himself in this kind of finished economical prose. The monologue being in first person excludes the author, true, but we feel Faulkner's continuous presence through the style. The monologue is largely in the past tense. Quentin is remembering his past. Faulkner gives the incoherence and discontinuity, the disorder and confusion of the more emotional, obsessed sections of the monologue, those that have to do more directly with Candace, by leaving some sentences unfinished, by dropping one train of thought and picking up another, by eliminating punctuation partly or wholly but preserving paragraph structure, by using italics, private symbols, and by various other devices. Memories that are highly charged with emotion or rise from the deeper or suppressed levels of consciousness are given in a markedly different, breathless prose which reproduces the thought stream in its feverish flow. Quentin recalls that he wanted to kill a young man who seduced his sister.

> did he make you then he made you do it let him he was stronger than you and he tomorrow Ill kill him I swear I will father neednt know until afterward and then you and I nobody need ever know we can take my school money we can cancel my matriculation Caddy you hate him dont you dont you
> she held my hand against her chest her heart thudding I turned and caught her arm
> Caddy you hate him dont you
> she moved my hand up against her throat her heart was hammering there poor Quentin

He has removed the hands of his watch to be out of time, but he hears the clock in Cambridge striking.

> A quarter hour yet. And then I'll not be. The peacefullest words. Peacefullest words. . . . Somewhere I heard bells once. Mississippi or Massachusetts. I was. I am not. Massachusetts or Mississippi. Shreve has a bottle in his trunk. *Aren't you even going to open it* Mr. and Mrs. Jason Richmond Compson announce the *Three times. Days. Aren't you even going*

to open it marriage of their daughter Candace *that liquor teaches you to confuse the means with the end.* I am. Drink. I was not. Let us sell Benjy's pasture so that Quentin may go to Harvard and I may knock my bones together. I will be dead in. Was it one year Caddy said. Shreve has a bottle in his trunk. Sir I will not need Shreve's I have sold Benjy's pasture and I can be dead in Harvard Caddy said in the caverns and the grottoes of the sea bumbling peacefully to the wavering tides because Harvard is such a fine sound we will swap Benjy's pasture for a fine sound forty acres is no high price for a fine sound.

Benjy is his idiot brother, who cannot talk; he just whimpers or moans. Benjy's pasture was sold to send Quentin, the youngest son, to Harvard, and that thought comes back again and again. Faulkner gives an impression of simultaneity by having the quarter hour strike, by the thought about the bottle in Shreve's trunk, by having Quentin remember the painful announcement of his sister's wedding and his alcoholic father's words about liquor, and again his thoughts about the pasture. This juxtaposition and conflict of different thoughts, interspersed, produces an effect of montage.

In this same monologue we read sentences like these: "I stood in the belly of my shadow and listened to the strokes spaced and tranquil along the sunlight, among the thin, still little leaves. Spaced and peaceful and serene, with that quality of autumn always in bells even in the month of brides." Trees leaned over the wall, sprayed with sunlight. The stone was cool. Walking near it you could feel the coolness. Only our country was not like this country. There was something about just walking through it. A kind of still and violent fecundity that satisfied ever bread-hunger like. Flowing around you, not brooding and nursing every niggard stone." "The trout hung, delicate and motionless among the wavering shadows."

This sounds more like Faulkner's language than Quentin's monologue. And the discrepancy is even more evident in the first chapter, Benjy's monologue. It is too economical, sophisticated and literary for a man who at the age of thirty-three has the mentality of a three-year-old child and who

cannot even talk. Yet we do follow the idiot's mental processe
through his monologue. The monologue gives the *though*
and does not report the words: this is the principle followe
in the book. What we have in this strange novel, which
probably Faulkner's masterpiece, is internal monologue wit
the author still present through the style, the method ap
proaching indirect monologue, though written in first persor

STREAM OF THOUGHT IN THE THIRD PERSON

The indirect method was perfected by Virginia Woolf, al
though in *The Waves* she did use direct monologue, so highl
stylized that it is like indirect monologue in first person—si
people who as children lived in the same house by the se
getting together and talking in the same fluid lyrical languag
devised by the author. There is no action and no dialogue i
this novel. We follow the careers of these six people at dif
ferent periods in their lives, from childhood to middle age
through formalized monologues. Each chapter opens with
brief description of the waves, which acquire a symboli
meaning in this highly poetic work. It is one of the most in
teresting experiments in fiction, a unique work of its kind
rich in imagery, difficult, and unlikely to be repeated.

Mrs. Dalloway is a lovely novel, beautifully designed an
balanced. We see in its construction the hand of a master o
feminine sensibility. It is written like a musical composition
This is a model of indirect internal monologue in the author'
formal language absorbed into the narrative. When Clariss
Dalloway is talking and thinking and doing something at th
same time we get a montage of consciousness, and this seem
a closer mimesis of how we live in real life. There is a stor
here, but no plot. The flow of narration from one mind t
another gives us a pattern of theme and variations, as i
music. Septimus Warren Smith, shell-shocked in World War
is symbolically Mrs. Dalloway's double. When Septimus jump
out of a window and commits suicide and she hears about i
at the party she is giving in honor of the Prime Ministe

that same evening in her home, she is deeply affected by the news. The spiritual identity between them is beautifully suggested, although it seems somewhat contrived. Mrs. Dalloway is the main theme, Septimus the restatement of that theme. Mrs. Woolf originally intended to have Mrs. Dalloway die or commit suicide at the end of her party, thus joining Septimus in death. That might have been a more dramatic end for a novel permeated by a deep melancholy, but not a very artistic one. The structure of the novel is so delicate and the action so subdued that stronger effects might spoil it.

There is very little dialogue and direct monologue in the book. The author gains her ends by indirections. As Mrs. Dalloway goes out to buy flowers for her party we learn a great deal about her past through her thought stream, and much of the book is memory. The basic pattern is memory and expectation, looking back to her past and looking forward to the party. The party is the main event, the ex-soldier's suicide a kind of subplot. Mrs. Woolf lets us know who is thinking, when, and where. We come to know these people through their thoughts and the thoughts of others about them, but there is no real communication among them. Mrs. Woolf does not hesitate to say "she thought" or "she felt" or "she asked" or "she wondered" or "she said to herself" several times on the same page, and we need these guideposts or we shall be lost in the lyric stream. The setting is given, actual streets are named, the flower shop, London at dusk and other details are vividly described, and Big Ben lets us know what time it is. Big Ben allows Mrs. Woolf to move from the mind of one character to another as the sound reaches them, and we explore another consciousness.

> There! Out it boomed. First a warning, musical; then the hour, irrevocable. The leaden circles dissolved in the air. Such fools we are, she thought, crossing Victoria Street . . . She had reached the Park gates. She stood for a moment, looking at the omnibuses in Piccadilly . . .

Then we are in the mind of someone else hearing Big Ben. This same thing happens when people in the street wonder who is in the black motor car with its blinds down. The

Queen? Or watch an aeroplane advertising toffee. It would b
stifling for most readers to stay continuously in one con
sciousness and the shifting point of view provides variety in
novel in which all the characters speak and think alike, an
like the author herself.

> She felt very young; at the same time unspeakably aged. She
> sliced like a knife through everything; at the same time was
> outside, looking on. She had a perpetual sense, as she
> watched the taxicabs, of being out, out, far out to sea and
> alone . . . She knew nothing; no language, no history; she
> scarcely read a book now, except memoirs in bed; and yet to
> her it was absolutely absorbing; all this; the cabs passing; and
> she would not say of Peter, she would not say of herself, I am
> this, I am that.
> Her only gift was knowing people almost by instinct, she
> thought, walking on. If you put her in a room with some one,
> up went her back like a cat's, or she purred . . .

Mrs. Dalloway loves life, but she feels like an outsider, she i
alone among millions of people swarming through the stree
of London. Her hair has turned gray at fifty-two and she i
haunted by thoughts of death. She married for security, bu
in her youth she read Plato in bed before breakfast, sh
read Morris, Shelley by the hour, and with Sally Seton sh
meant to found a society to abolish private property. No
she is a perfect hostess. The tragedy of middle age. We ar
not always sure whether we are hearing the narrator's voic
or following Mrs. Dalloway's stream of thought flowing alon
with the traffic on her way to the flower shop and back be
cause of the third person point of view. We have a luminou
blur of sense impressions and evanescent thoughts.

In her next novel, *To the Lighthouse,* which many con
sider her best, Virginia Woolf uses this same method of indi
rect monologue in her own poetic language. There is, again
very little quoted dialogue and direct monologue. She delib
erately avoids the sharp, precise image and gives us instea
the impression of various states of awareness. The characters
a professor of philosophy, his wife, a beautiful woman o
fifty with gray hair, their children and their guests, are lik
moving shadows, never wholly alive, ghostly beings in an un

182

worldly setting in the Hebrides, on the west coast of Scotland. As we almost never hear these people talking in their own words, or see them from the outside, we never get a clear direct view of them, and they are nebulous entities: yet everything in the novel is so beautifully orchestrated that this is more like music expressing the spiritual essence and mystery of life in all its mortal sadness than a conventional story. The years pass, Mrs. Ramsay dies, the house is abandoned, but there is no dramatic development of these events. One day ten years later the professor comes back with two of his sons and finds everything changed, the house virtually in ruins, and only the lighthouse still standing, as though a symbol of Mrs. Ramsay's luminous spirit. They finally make the trip to the lighthouse they had planned years before and could not make it because of bad weather, but for James, the youngest son, it is no longer the lighthouse he dreamed of as a small boy of six, when his mother was alive. Virginia Woolf put a good deal of herself into Mrs. Ramsay, as she did into Mrs. Dalloway, and she remains, like them, a haunting figure.

This indirect monologue becomes for the reader an exercise in detection. The method is not unlike Flaubert's "free indirect discourse," although Mrs. Woolf persistently does it in her own language. But this is not the usual type of narrative novel. *Mrs. Dalloway* and *To the Lighthouse,* though artistically controlled, have the flow of fantasy thinking and the action in them is predominantly meditative and internal, located in the consciousness of various characters; they deal almost exclusively with the subjective life, the objective event being incidental to it. These are elusive works, as elusive as the essence of life itself, and much of their mysterious appeal lies in Mrs. Woolf's ability to perfect her art to the condition of music.

In *Mrs. Dalloway* the story takes place in about twelve hours; in *Ulysses,* sixteen hours; in *Les Lauriers sont coupés,* six hours. When there is little or no unity of action, unity of time (a short time) and of place (one place) become important unifying devices. London, Paris, Dublin—these are the locales. More particularly it is a section of the city. Time is slower in novels that dramatize moments, that give us close-ups or film strips of moments. This slowing down of time results in a kind of static drama. Many of the scenes in these novels are like *tableaux vivants* and we seem to be looking at intensely self-conscious people who are silent and motionless in appropriate postures as time passes. When we have a close-up of the moment, we have a slowing up, too. The emphasis is on psychological time.

Virginia Woolf sought "the essential thing" in human life and was not interested in plot, or comedy, or tragedy, or love, denying life is like these. She tried to reach the deeper levels, to explore the submarine life of human consciousness, as it were, and we have an impression of seeing her fictional world through a glass-bottomed boat. She wanted to catch the myriad impressions, no matter how trivial or evanescent, "the incessant shower of innumerable atoms" as she put it, falling on the mind, each a moment of being or feeling perhaps, invested with a "luminous halo," but they do not combine to make a coherent statement on the human condition in terms of story, or plot or an ordered sequence of events, which she rejected as not being true to life. She distrusted "reality." She sought to convey a truer reality. There are exquisite things in her books, in the murky light glow clusters of her atoms, and we are carried off on her thought stream, or her characters'—we are not always sure which. Characters become by design so insubstantial in her work that they tend to disappear.

One wonders whether the fact that Virginia Woolf suffered a serious nervous breakdown while writing these novels and in 1941 drowned herself in a canal for fear she was going mad has something to do with the kind of fiction she produced, her failure to combine the atoms and create some real, compelling characters in significant actions. It may be that the lights were dimming in her own mind, some of the vagueness in the prose has its origin in an internal obscurity and disorder; a painful thought. One must speak tenderly of Virginia Woolf. She had no great themes of wide appeal, she indulged occasionally in pretentious purple prose (as the description of the waves in *The Waves*), but she left behind her brilliant experiments full of sight and insight and the record of her dedication to the cause of poetry, of beauty, and to her own private version of truth. But we can see that her method cannot solve all the problems of the novel, though it does add a new dimension to it.

MEMORY

In *Ulysses,* James Joyce's characters do not talk and think alike; they are sharply individualized in a setting of precise, realistic images. We may not always see them clearly, but we hear them and we get to know them as we never see or hear or know the characters in *To the Lighthouse* or *The Waves*. When Joyce uses indirect monologue, as in the Nausicaa episode at the beach, we have a marvelous parody of Gerty MacDowell's thought speech, and Gerty, lame, love-hungry, exhibitionistic, silently flirting with Leopold Bloom, and getting him sexually excited, comes to life with him. Her reverie is not given in the author's style; the flavor of her own idiom in her daydreaming language with all its clichés is preserved through an imitation of the cheap romantic fiction the Gerties of Dublin were reading at the time. Joyce's method is consistently more realistic than Virginia Woolf's, and the monologue is less controlled even in third person.

> If she saw that magic lure in his eyes there would be no holding back for her. Love laughs at locksmiths. She would make the great sacrifice. Her every effort would be to share his thoughts. Dearer than the whole world would she be to him and gild his days with happiness. There was the all important question and she was dying to know was he a married man or a widower who had lost his wife or some tragedy like the nobleman with the foreign name from the land of song had to have her put into a madhouse, cruel only to be kind. But even if—what then? Would it make a very great difference? From everything in the least indelicate her fine-bred nature instinctively recoiled . . . They would be just good friends like a big brother and sister without all that other in spite of the conventions of Society with a big ess. Perhaps it

was an old flame he was in mourning for from the days beyond recall. She thought she understood. She would try to
understand him because men were so different . . . She
would follow her dream of love, the dictates of her heart
that told her he was her all in all, the only man in all the
world for her for love was the master guide. Nothing else
mattered. Come what might she would be wild, untrammelled,
free.

(James Joyce, *Ulysses*)

"Speak, so that I may see you," said the Greeks. In *Ulysses*
we see. Joyce does not have his equal in acoustical mimesis.
There is a vast pattern of sound images in the novel.

Internal monologue is a step forward in dramatization, and
in this kind of writing we have a perpetual present. Since the
emphasis is on this internal, individual life it is a more rigorous
and authentic form of realism, with a large autobiographical
element in it. Joyce wrote the story of his own life, but he
identified himself so closely with Leopold Bloom, an exile like
himself, that Bloom is a more concrete and complete character than Stephen Dedalus in *Ulysses*. Bloom, the Wandering
Jew in the streets of Dublin, emerges as an archetype of the
twentieth-century man.

As modern metropolitan man withdraws more and more
into himself in his flight from his environment, feeling uprooted, homeless, a wanderer upon the face of the earth, and
dreaming of another and better life, he is engaged, like Stephen
Dedalus, like Leopold Bloom, like most of us, in a perpetual
monologue. He is driven by inner compulsions to reassert
himself, he clings to his own identity, he does not want to
dissolve and disappear in the city, the state, the church, the
crowd—yet there is in him that tendency too, to relinquish his
personality, to lay down its burdens, to become a cipher in
city streets, a statistic. The purpose of internal monologue is
to give the reader some significant spurts of this secret conflict and soliloquy in the routine of everyday living, while
life goes on as usual. A few snatches of "the soul's dialogue
with itself" will give a new lifelike quality to a story.

The writer need not become metaphysical with this method.
It can be used effectively in little details of everyday actions,

and this use has become indeed so conventional that if we read a passage like the following, in which there is a switch from third person to first and second and back to third again, without quotation marks, we see nothing unusual in it.

> He sat on the park bench, watching the pigeons. I wonder who that girl is, he thought. Very pretty. Can't be over eighteen. I think I will follow her. I will speak to her and let's see what happens. Don't scare her off, though. Make it very casual. You are going to make a fool of yourself. At your age. Silly. Lovely girl. Well, why not? I'm not too old for her. She is alone. A nature lover like me? Okay, go ahead, and make a fool of yourself. The young man got up and walked slowly in her direction, as though admiring the bright spring scene in the park.

Bits of direct internal monologue inserted in a third-person narrative can give the story added immediacy. While this man is walking toward the girl talking with himself, the writer can give the reader a lot of information about him, information coming not from the author, as exposition, but as part of the man's thought stream, which is the more dramatic and authentic way, and the continuity of the story line is not broken. And the writer can give this information irrespective of the external action; he is not bound by it: one of the most useful functions of internal monologue.

Memory is so much a part of our personalities and figures so prominently in the stream of thought that characterization would be almost impossible without it. Give a character memories and you individualize him and bring him to life. We can tell people by their memories. Man lives largely in memory, and memory is the mother of imagination. No memory, no imagination, no story.

The old novels gave blocks of memory, but as described or reported by the author. We get it secondhand in these books. Interior monologue can do this beautifully and economically as an integral part of the dramatic present, without breaking the continuity of the story line. Through memory, thus rendered, the inner world of experience can blossom out as in the works briefly examined in this chapter. To employ the stream of consciousness technique means to use meaningful associations, and use them in such a way that there is both order and disorder in the structure of inner life, which does not follow the causal sequence of objective events that makes plot. There must be some disorder, consciously worked out by the writer, to give the illusion of true memory in its original anarchic form in the thought stream. And in the mind there is neither past nor future; all is present time.

We say fiction is a temporal art, it takes place in time, and the stream of thought novel particularly takes place in time— in significant moments, selected by the writer in a seemingly continuous and spontaneous flow. It is the pattern of these arrested moments that, by a process of accretion, as in *Ulysses*, gives us the fictional portrait, and the setting is more authentic and alive than in other, conventional novels. *Ulysses* has a spatial dimension. The action in this kind of fiction is a continuous becoming, a continuous change, but not to the point of complete alteration: the hard core of the character remains, and it is that hard core that determines the course of the change and acts as a regulative controlling factor in the flux. It channels the stream of thought. Otherwise, the character would lose his identity and would be a totally different person at the end of the story. There is change and/or growth but it is not total change, not a sudden break with the past, but with an essential continuity in it. Without this continuity we would not know who we are, what we are.

Memory preserves this continuity. And if it is destroyed, the sense of identity is lost. The inner channels between present and past have to be kept open if we are to stay sane. The great tyrants of history have tried to deny the right of memory to their victims, and the suppression of memories is the most awful tyranny of all, for it destroys the self and kills the soul of man. Mass amnesia, brain washings on a gigantic scale, emptying the minds of millions of their memories is a massacre of souls, and stream of thought fiction cannot flourish in societies in which there is no freedom of thought. A man is what he remembers. And he is free by virtue of what he remembers. We may say the same thing about nations.

The individual feels isolated in the modern city; the old primal societies of village and town with their direct face-to-face relationships have all but disappeared. In *Ulysses* we have the epic of the city. No writer before James Joyce has given such a complete picture of a city. Stephen Dedalus has cut himself off from God and from other men and like Leopold Bloom he is a man without a country, but he is not cut off from himself. With all its satire, this is a positive novel bursting with the stream of life. We have a feeling of wonder and exaltation when we read it. It celebrates the ordinary and makes it extraordinary. We are astonished by miracles of the commonplace, fascinated by an "average" man, Leopold Bloom, an advertising solicitor completely revealed from within through his thought stream, and meanwhile we see not only Ireland on June 16, 1904, but all of western Europe. Indeed this is a merciless exposure of western civilization by a mocking, witty poet given to puns and parody, the most expert, audacious mimic in the history of realism, whose contempt for the bourgeois surpasses that of Flaubert; yet he is fond of him, too, with a sort of noblesse oblige. This is a sad spectacle of the city man, but what a wonderful show, a seething world of sights and sounds, the twentieth century roaring in our ears.

The more consciousness, the more life, the total absence of consciousness is death, and this novel is full of life. Self-consciousness is increased when we become more acutely aware of the moment, and stream of consciousness fiction thrives on this awareness. To capture the moment as it is passing in the unending flow is an elusive business and this is the problem the writer is facing: how to express and reveal the inner world, this ceaseless internal action. The stream of thought method can do it. It can bring to light the reality of spirit, which together with the reality of matter, the objective world, gives us a fuller, more authentic picture of life.

To grasp the reality of spirit we have to understand the nature of memory. A discussion of memory is beyond the scope of this book, and we must leave it to psychologists and philosophers. Memory occupies a large part in the stream of thought, and memory consists of mental images. The past comes back to us in images. We dream and daydream in images. Stream of thought fiction with its large component of memory is rich in imagery, and this is the kind of memory writing in which prose poets excel, those who habitually think in images. It is not rhetorical literature.

The stream of thought novel is the poetic novel and the time novel. It is likely to be autobiographical fiction; it cannot be reportage, for it has to be written from the inside out, and mere factual documentation would not do. The peculiarity of this method lies in capturing the nascent thought, in dramatizing the inner life while it is being lived, so that we have "a continuity of becoming, which is the living reality," in Bergson's words. It concentrates on the present moment, and the present moment is not a fixed entity, but is a continuous passing from past to future; time never stops. What *is* is already partly *was* when we perceive it, and it is already becoming memory, and the present moment always contains an element of the past in it; it is the transition from past to future. So memory-writing and associating the past with the present is natural for this kind of fiction, and to record sensations and memory images requires a poetic talent.

The stream of thought technique has been absorbed into conventional methods of narrative. Whether a whole novel should be written by this method is perhaps debatable; many objections can be raised against it. But the technique is here to stay. A few lines or paragraphs of internal monologue or stream of thought in third person, vivid little vignettes dramatizing the undercurrent of emotions, the inner compulsions and divisions, moments of self-analysis and self-scrutiny, moments of self-identification, the outpourings of a mind in distress, the inward cry, as well as mental notations of the objective scene and sensory impressions—these gleaming spurts of the inner atomic flow can give a rich poetic complexity and a new psychological dimension to serious fiction. This is how life is; this is the living reality and mystery and wonder of it.

It is better in first person, as direct monologue, but the third person has its uses, although in a way it goes against the logic of internal monologue by bringing in the author when he should be eliminated. The value of indirect monologue, as of indirect dialogue, diminishes when no attempt is made to reproduce the quality of the character's thought stream in his own idiom and when we get instead the author's language and are constantly reminded of his presence. The author's language may charm us, like Virginia Woolf's, or William Faulkner's, but the objection to the indirect method in the author's style remains. In certain stories, for certain scenes, we can accept the author, and are satisfied with the fluidity of the thought stream and a suggestion of its free associations and disorder without insisting that the author do it in the character's own idiom. It is an improvement over the old conventional description by the author of a character's thoughts in formalized discourse, with all incoherence removed.

The two methods, direct and indirect, in first person and third, can be used in the same story, even in the same paragraph, like direct and indirect dialogue. Direct monologue moreover can be used in stories written in first person. The narrator can have some silent thoughts and indulge in reveries and engage in meditations, or have hallucinations, or argue with himself. The writer should make clear that these are not the narrator's present thoughts and feelings but those he had when the action of the story took place. His silent speech need not be markedly different from his style in general, and through slight variations, by shorter chopped-up sentences, perhaps by foreign words and private symbols, by repetitions of words charged with emotion and acting as motifs, by quotations from songs and poems, by unfinished phrases and words, by removal of punctuation, by using italics, the silent speech or monologue can be made more anarchic and incoherent and distinguished from the rest of the text.

The great experiments in this technique took place during and after the First World War. Dorothy Richardson published *Pointed Roofs* in 1915; *Ulysses* appeared in book form in 1922; *Mrs. Dalloway* in 1925. It would be too much perhaps to expect another Joyce, but a woman writer could make herself immortal by writing a woman's *Ulysses*. The literary challenge of the age is for women writers to reveal the feminine consciousness and not leave Molly Blooms and other types to men.

Fiction is not an exact science, despite Flaubert's, and Zola's efforts. The stream of thought technique cannot be defended perhaps on any scientific ground, but it is an advance over older methods, and we have to accept it as another convention. The tendency today is to use it without free association, with greater control; but with or without free association it gives us an added illusion of reality, whatever the ultimate nature of reality might be. It does away with psychological analysis, laborious explanation of motive and other author business on shaky assumptions of authority.

Many questions remain unanswered for the writer. It is unlikely that we shall ever get completely out of the fog. Depth psychology yesterday, physics and chemistry today, have not shed much light on the enigma of man and the world he inhabits. If anything, the mystery is growing deeper. But if mimesis is instinctive with man, and there is evidence it is, we shall continue to imitate experience no matter how ambiguous, and to struggle against chaos in our slow progress from not knowing to knowing. No matter what the merits of this or that method of narration the basic ingredients of fiction remain the same, and what was a good story three thousand years ago is still a good story; the essential principles have not changed. There have been in more recent times tendencies in this or that direction: classicism, romanticism, realism, naturalism, surrealism; omniscient narration and the oblique view; the episodic, the dramatic; the objective, the subjective. The modern American novel differs from the Henry James novel, and the so-called New Novel in France, the work of Alain Robbe-Grillet, Nathalie Sarraute, Michel Butor, Marguerite Duras, Claude Simon, and others differs from the classic French novel. The novel is a relatively new form in the long history of mimesis and it has not reached yet its final form; it may never reach it; it might even change to something else. But it is likely to remain poetry, to beguile and enlighten man as an art of revelation, to be meaningful as the re-creation of experience. This continuity of mimesis through the ages will keep a good story, no matter what its particular form and the prevailing fashion, forever fresh and new.

Every great novel is a new novel. *Madame Bovary, Crime and Punishment, War and Peace, Remembrance of Things Past, Ulysses*—these were all new novels in their time, and still are. Writers will continue to seek new forms for the novel. Theories of the novel may change, and we are likely to have some barren forms of experimentation, but what is important is experimentation itself, exploration into the nature of reality and of significant experience, searching for a form that will best express the human situation today. There is no emphasis on character or on conventional verisimilitude in the *nouveau roman*, a highly subjective form of fiction that favors the first person and present tense. Take, for example, *A Change of Heart* by Michel Butor, the story of a man's train ride from Paris to Rome, a man divided between his wife and mistress who decides to stay with his wife. It is written entirely in the form of interior monologue in the second person; while remembering and carrying on his mental debate he addresses himself as "you." Michel Butor is a gifted writer; like other members of his group, he has a passion for description—the perception of objects and people by one character in the story, objective description of things subjectively seen. As M. Robbe-Grillet says in one of his essays on fiction (in *For a New Novel*) "The New Novel aims only at total subjectivity." He is against anthropomorphic associations. Some of these New Novels are difficult, and unfortunately M. Robbe-Grillet himself is sometimes unreadable, but all bear watching.

9. NARRATIVE PROSE [I]

It is not enough for the writer to know what to say, he must also know how to say it: this is an old rule. And if style is the man himself, as Buffon said, then much depends on what kind of person the writer is. Probably the most interesting and persuasive thing about narrative prose is the personality of the writer reflected through it, and it would be futile to discuss other aspects of style if we ignore this personal factor. "Good moral character," said Aristotle (*Rhetoric,* II–1), induces us to believe something irrespective of any proof offered for it. And character thus is important for the novel also in the sense of the writer's own ethos, as revealed through his style.

Narrative prose is personal prose, and all great writers have a personal style, an individual language that expresses a strong, unique personality. Theodore Dreiser had no fine ear for the nuances of English speech and wrote in a clumsy style, but he wrote personal prose, his language is distinctly his own, stamped with his own character. Most of us would prefer it with all its faults to a good common style, to a more finished characterless depersonalized smooth language. When we read *Sister Carrie* or *An American Tragedy* we feel Dreiser is determined to tell the bitter truth. We seem to be reading actual case histories, as indeed they were. His honesty is the most compelling thing about his fiction. There is no narrative style worthy of the name without truth behind it, for nothing is as persuasive as truth.

A writer has to be personal, definitely himself, to be original and new. The suppression of personality might be necessary in other kinds of writing, but not in fiction, and narrative prose begins with the writer's character and his personal freedom in expression. This freedom is the most precious thing to the writer. And loss of self would be fatal.

The creative writer speaks in a language of his own making, and he will even coin new words to make his meaning clear, as Joyce does in *Ulysses* and *Finnegans Wake*. Words, of course, acquire new meanings through new emotional associations, through new combinations and new arrangements, and this is the kind of language we deal with in fiction. In a collection of essays on style that was probably a standard anthology forty years ago and may still be in wide use, the editor says in his introduction, "He who cultivates his individuality is lost." A curious statement. Not to cultivate his individuality means literary suicide to the writer, and indeed he cannot suppress his individuality even if he tries. He is not writing a textbook on geometry or physics. Individuality is essential in literary prose, which is fresh and surprising language, and ultimately that is what any creative writer has to offer: himself, his own unique personality, his own way of seeing the world. There is really no escape from personality in any original work of fiction. Writers are intensely personal people anyway, acutely conscious of their own feelings and responsive to the feelings of others. Every writer worth reading speaks in his own distinctive voice, and his voice is his style.

Style is an ambiguous word. By style here we simply mean expressive language, not to be confused with manner or with form in general. What makes a writer's language expressive? That is the question we have to ask in analyzing literary styles. Our approach to the problem is necessarily an aesthetic one, and in narrative prose we answer this question by saying, the more mimetic a writer's language the more expressive it is. So we are back with a mimesis.

A personal style is the trademark of the writer in fiction and non-fiction alike. We can recognize markedly individual styles without the author's name. Hemingway's, for instance, or H. L. Mencken's. Hemingway wrote his impersonal prose for newspapers, although in human interest stories or feature articles under his own by-line his language became quite personal and he used dialogue and other fictional devices to make them more vivid and interesting than straight news dispatches. He was not a run-of-the-mill reporter and we can see the beginnings of his famous style in his early newspaper pieces. But it was only when he put his own feelings and thoughts into his writing and became personal, and began asking "Why," that he became a novelist.

The self-respecting writer insists on himself. Art is *I*. The development of a personal style is no little achievement in itself. It might take years. It means reading for style, reading poetry, studying favorite masters, and ultimately falling back on oneself, with a richer "I." The first characteristics of personal prose often appear early and spontaneously, and a writer is born with the style he writes, it is part of him. The young writer who takes his craft seriously will not hesitate to be personal, peculiar, unique: there is no style without this self-assertion. He will give full play to his idiosyncrasies if need be and have the courage to be himself and tell the truth. Even newspapers are becoming personal. The better ones feature more and more personal styles and by-lines in their pages.

We expect a newspaper account of a court trial to be fairly impersonal, not colored by the reporter's emotions and opinions, and usually the name of the reporter is not given, but if the same trial is reported in more personal prose, under a by-line, with the writer expressing his own feelings and convictions about it, the first step toward fictional prose is taken. It is likely to be a more readable and interesting piece than the impersonal report. A news magazine like *Time* has worked out its own style, which gives it a certain collective personality. What strikes an American on first reading an English newspaper like *The Observer* is its distinctive personality. It has an identity of its own; there is something new and different about it, it is "London," it is "British." *The Observer* is full of by-lines. *The Times Literary Supplement,* to mention another British publication, has a personality different from that of *The Observer*. Its tone is less lively perhaps, but more urbane. The King's English at its current best is often found in its unsigned articles, maintaining a vigorous tradition in British prose. The essay is still a flourishing genre in Britain.

PERSONAL PROSE IMPERSONALLY WRITTEN

Flaubert wrote *Madame Bovary* and James Joyce wrote *Ulysses* impersonally in personal prose. A writer can be personal and impersonal at once. That is what sets him off from most men. By personal prose we do not mean a subjective treatment of the story. A good narrative style is necessarily personal language because it springs from the individual sense-perceptions and memories of the writer, it is alive with his imaginative insights and reflects his own temperament. What determines a writer's choice of subject determines also his language and the same fundamental motives, conscious and unconscious, are at work in both.

Exposition or information prose, such as a business contract, instructions for building a bridge or operating a machine, an engineering or technical paper, a medical or financial report, and in general the vast amount of printed matter we might call fact writing, and without which our civilization could not function, is not personal prose, and need not be. The personal feelings of the writers are irrelevant, and the information is given in established stable words without emotional associations blurring their meaning. Nor is it necessary for such prose to be pictorial. But the creative writer has another kind of information to give; he has to convey a special knowledge which is his own unique possession, and the emotional associations of the words he uses are highly relevant to the matter at hand and he is very largely dependent upon them for making his meaning clear.

Much of the confusion about style—and it goes back to ancient times—results from a failure to make a distinction between rhetoric and poetic. Aristotle wrote his *Rhetoric* and *Poetics* as separate books and did not confuse one with the other. By rhetoric he meant persuasive speech—good argument—and he considered it the counterpart of dialectic. By poetic he meant mimesis, though mimesis also must be persuasive. Rhetoric tells, poetic shows. All good writing, we know, is good argumentation, but fiction argues best through the picture; a story is a complex system of pictures; and information prose differs in its vocabulary and syntax from narrative prose. With the growing emphasis on scene and picture, narrative prose has undergone a change for the better and become more mimetic than it was at the time of Defoe and Richardson. The older novels contain more exposition and tell much more than they show.

The function of narrative prose is the pictorial re-creation of life, and the true creative writer thinks in pictures, but this does not mean that every word he writes must be a picture word. A scene is a picture, and it might be written without a markedly pictorial language and without a single qualifying adjective or figure of speech. But it would have to be in concrete language if we are going to see it. We have to distinguish between the scene picture or character picture or setting picture, which are the really important pictures in fiction, and the verbal picture per se, such as metaphor. Picture words help, they do make the language more expressive, but we have to view them as an additional stylistic device and valuable in so far as they make the action and characterization and setting more vivid, and aid the reader in visualizing the larger pictorial units of the story.

The fiction writer today "shoots" life, and then cuts and edits his verbal films. The reader has to judge the story for himself, by what he sees projected on his mental screen.

Though indispensable in fiction, language is not the only means for re-creating human events. Pantomime can be full of meaning. The value of the word lies primarily in its image-making quality. The image, visual, auditory, tactile, etc., is more important than the word itself, if we could separate the two. Thus we can see the difference between narrative prose and other types of prose, between a pictorial and a conceptual language, between poetics and rhetoric.

Since no two writers have exactly the same perceptive ability nor the same sensory equipment, and differ in their sight and insight, we have a large variety of individual prose styles in fiction. The perceptive prose is personal prose, and original prose. An honest representation of reality is the fictional ideal. A false picture of life will falsify the language, and false language in turn will falsify life. The words are true when the events and characters are true.

A story is an event defined through language, and without this verbal definition the event is chaotic and incommunicable. Style means an intense search, through the word, of the event itself, what is the essence of it, and the best mimesis can do is to give an illusion of this essence. We have to resign ourselves to the shadows that veil so much of life, it is foggy country all around us, and who can say we are not face to face with a fake show, victims of some god or demon that will not let us see things as they are, as some eastern religions tell us? The writer rises in rebellion against this primordial nature of things that deceive most men and says in effect: I shall not be deceived. I see it clearly, this is the truth. And in this sense the writer is akin to the religious mystic or seer. But what is really the truth? Who knows? We have to bow our heads and not ask too many questions.

The perception of the world around him through sense data and insight and an awareness of the world within himself, of consciousness observing itself, the outer vision combined with the inner: this is what distinguishes the writer, and he stands or falls on his capacity for sense impressions and his imaginative insights, and on his ability to express them in words. If he is honest he will neither exaggerate nor minimize what he perceives, he will not fake it, he will not say something exists when it does not or deny that which exists. He will not knowingly misinterpret the facts as he knows them and mislead the reader. A good narrative prose is language that tells the truth and makes for a lucid presentation of the event.

This objective re-creation of experience is realized through subjective means. In writing *Ulysses* James Joyce was his own perceptive self, with startling results. His prose is realistic, it tells the truth about one day in Dublin as experienced and remembered by him, re-created through the most mimetic—and symbolic—prose we have ever had in the naturalistic tradition. Another writer, equally perceptive, would have given us another picture. This is Joyce's Dublin. The writer who is hopelessly enmeshed in the shadows to which most men are condemned and cannot see clearly cannot write clearly. He has to get out of the fog that dims our vision, the fatal mist that envelops the world. Perception makes for clearer vision, and the goal of narrative prose is to fight the fog. The writer has to clear the road to reality, and these private roads built by writers serve social purposes. As a road builder in foggy country the writer lights up the way for others through luminous language. This is not to deny the power of novel combinations to the scientist, who too is an imaginative person, but the scientist is not expected to excel in the mimetic faculty.

COMMON AND UNCOMMON WORDS

Style to be good should be clear, Aristotle says in his *Rhetoric* (Book III–1), and it should be appropriate, neither too low or mean, nor too high. Poetical language is not low but is not appropriate to prose. Clearness is gained by using words that are currently in common use, and distinction secured by using strange or foreign or unfamiliar words, metaphors, figures of speech, coined words, ornamental words, lengthened compound words, and by anything that differs from the usual idiom. Aristotle defended poets (*Poetics,* Ch. 22) for deviating from normal speech, and this deviation makes for distinction. Today fiction is not written in verse, but it is still poetry, and poetical language is by no means inappropriate to fictional prose. It needs some embellishment.

Aristotle was no poet like Plato, but like all Greeks he had a love for the beautiful, and we have to look upon beauty as the final perfection of both plot and language. Aristotle advised orators to give everyday speech an unfamiliar air, for people like what strikes them, he says, and are impressed by what is out of the ordinary. In both prose and poetry the language has to be heightened, or toned down, to avoid both lowliness and artificiality. "Naturalness is persuasive, artificiality is not." Strange words, compound words, invented words should be used sparingly, Aristotle warns his readers. A judicious mixture of ordinary language mixed with the extraordinary, of the common with the uncommon, sums up the Aristotelian theory of style. The exact proportion will vary from writer to writer and from story to story, and we might say from country to country and from age to age. How to make narrative prose non-prosaic is the real problem once clarity is attained. How to be simple and natural without being dull and mean. The dispute about the plain versus the ornamental or rich style has been going on for thousands of years and is not likely to be settled in our own age. The rich ornate Asiatic style was admired or dispised by the Greeks and the tendency for flowery figurative language persists to this day in the Mediterranean region. North Europeans, particularly Anglo-Saxons, prefer on the whole a plain and even an austere style of writing, though Shakespeare was no plain stylist, and Elizabethan prose charms us with its lavish verbal riches. Elizabethan writers were fascinated by English as though it were a newly discovered language for them.

The tendency in America is toward the plain style, which generally wears better. If Poe had written a more simple prose, less contrived, like his Gothic plots, his stories would be more readable today, and not so dated. Hemingway has been a more popular writer than Faulkner, partly because of the differences in their styles. Hemingway's lean prose, "cut down to the bone," is a highly disciplined, controlled language. Hemingway is always clear, Faulkner is not.

Stendhal, with his logical, scientific mind, though a romantic by temper, had a horror of eloquence and wrote his novels in a dry lucid prose. His rule of composition was to be always simple and clear. He wrote rapidly in a conversational style, without affectations, and he packed his prose with *"le petit fait vrai."* He wrote his masterpiece, *La Chartreuse de Parme,* at once a novel and a confession, in two months, and read the *Code Civil* to give it the right tone. This was the book that won Balzac's admiration. At its best the conversational style has the spontaneity of spoken speech, but this spontaneity is often achieved by much rewriting. A ballet dancer seems spontaneous, but endless hours of practice are behind her every motion. It took Salinger several years to write *Catcher in the Rye.*

Sterne's style in *Tristram Shandy* and other books is probably the happiest and most idiomatic conversational English written in his day, but like Thackeray's chatty language with its asides, it can be exasperating to the modern reader. Sterne let his pen lead him where it might. There is a danger of garrulity in the conversational style, especially in first person. It could be one long monologue on anything the writer happens to think of at the moment. *Tristram Shandy,* nevertheless, despite its terrible fluidity with dots and dashes, will repay close study. It has retained its merits as an original work of fiction, and as a forerunner of internal monologue.

The conversational style, no matter how rapidly or slowly written, is not at any rate undisciplined talk; it is stylized, like more formal ways of writing. The proportion of conversation in a story would naturally influence the style in which it is written, and dialogue by itself makes for plainness, if it is good realistic speech as in Joyce and Hemingway. Elaborate diction would obscure the dialogue. The more ornate stylists go for summary. If by a plain, simple style we mean a clear unaffected way of writing, no one can be against it, but it should not mean prosaic prose devoid of all emotion, without an internal glow, and become a refuge for non-writers, with no poetry, no madness in their makeup.

Wordsworth proposed to adopt the language of prose to poetry, asserting there is no *essential* difference between the language of prose and metrical composition. To him they were "almost identical, not necessarily differing even in degree." And to Flaubert writing prose was like writing poetry, and just as hard, just as demanding. Though today poetry, too, is written in a more colloquial style, prose and poetry remain different modes of composition, and what is appropriate for poetry might not be right for prose, and vice versa; yet they have so much in common as the language of poetics that they readily merge into each other. Elevated or strong emotions in prose, as in poetry, call for an elevated style, not in conventional poetic diction, but in extraordinary language, deviating from common speech. The extraordinary becomes normal in a state of emotional excitement. Love makes an ordinary man or woman a poet, as does grief or religious sentiment.

This deviation from ordinary language is the basic principle of style. In narrative prose we are adding the picture. Another characteristic of narrative prose is that some of it is in the author's language and some of it in character language —or it could be all in character language. It is not written in one voice. Dialogue and monologue are close to common everyday speech and create difficulties for the fiction writer aiming for stylistic distinction. How should he report speech? In character words, as in direct discourse, with quotation marks? In his own words, as part of the narrative, without quotation marks? Or through a combination of the two, as free indirect discourse, a method first perfected by Flaubert?

This last is an important stylistic device in *Madame Bovary*. Emma would often take out a green silk cigar case she found on her way home from the ball at La Vaubyessard, where she danced with the Vicomte, and look at it and sniff its lining, fragrant with tobacco and verbena.

> Whose was it? . . . The Vicomte's. Perhaps a present from his mistress. Embroidered on some rosewood frame, a pretty piece of furniture, hidden from all eyes, over which a pensive girl had worked for many hours, her soft curls falling over it. A breath of love had passed through the mesh of the canvas; every stroke of the needle had fastened there a hope or a memory; and all the interwoven threads of silk were but a continued extension of the same silent passion. Then, one morning, the Vicomte had taken it away with him. What words had they spoken as he stood leaning his elbow on one of those broad mantelpieces between flower vases and Pompadour clocks? She was at Tostes. He was in

Paris now; far away! What was this Paris like? Such a mighty name, with something so vast and measureless about it. She repeated it in a low voice, just for the thrill of it; it sounded in her ears like the great bell of a cathedral; it flamed before her eyes even on the labels of her jars of pomade.

These are Emma's thoughts given in third person, in Flaubert's language, but with her own intonation as it were, with question marks and exclamation points.

Her husband came home in the middle of the night, and she pretended to be asleep, he did not dare to wake her. He seemed to hear the breathing of his child. Flaubert gives us her husband's thought stream.

> Soon she would start growing fast; every season would bring rapid progress. He already saw her coming home from school at the end of the day, laughing, with ink stains on her blouse, and carrying her basket on her arm. They'd have to send her to boarding school; that would cost plenty; how would he manage it? He started thinking. He thought of renting a small farm in the neighborhood, and which he himself would supervise, every morning, on his way to see his patients. He would save the revenue from the farm, he would put it in a savings bank. Then he would buy some stocks, he didn't know which; besides, his practice would grow, he counted on it, for he wanted Berthe to be well educated, to be accomplished, to learn to play the piano. Ah! How pretty she would be later, at fifteen, when, resembling her mother, she would wear, like her, large straw hats in the summer; from a distance they'd be taken for sisters.
>
> (*Madame Bovary;* Translation is my own.)

If the language is not clear it fails in its primary function as a medium of communication, and with lack of communication, all the other effects, or nearly all, are lost. The stylist avoids unnecessary obscurities. Bad grammar will obscure the meaning of what is said, but would be accepted in dialogue or monologue. The fiction writer need not be an expert grammarian. He can, when in doubt, consult Fowler's *Modern English Usage* or some other reference work whose authority he respects. Mere correctness, of course, can never make a literary style, yet one cannot pretend to be a writer, let alone a stylist, without a workable command of English. Correct writing can be taught, and improve a writer's style, but the style itself is his own unique way of expressing himself, a sensory and imaginative achievement which cannot be taught. Even the study of models has at best a limited value.

Generally the best writers are clear. And we know that to write clearly one must think clearly, that confused thoughts make confused writing. In information prose, there should be no doubt in the reader's mind as to the meaning of what is said, and effective exposition means first of all clear writing. But in fiction, as in poetry, there might be a necessary ambiguity, and emotions are such ambiguous contradictory feelings anyway that their honest expression might be somewhat ambiguous, too, and by clarity we should not understand oversimplification. A state vehicle code is clear, but scarcely a model of good prose. "The Windhover" with its complex allusions seems ambiguous on a first or second reading, but when we realize that Gerard Manley Hopkins looks upon the windhover as a spiritual symbol of perfection and identifies this bird in its mastery of the skies with his ideal of Christ, the poem blazes out with meaning.

Let us take a story like "Seeds" by Sherwood Anderson. It is foggy writing. "You cannot be so definite without missing something vague and fine. You miss the whole point," says the psychoanalyst in it. This man has only one desire—to free himself. He is sick with the lives of the sick people he has treated. He has "rolled in offal." To the narrator the psychoanalyst is a fool. Love can't be understood. "It is given to no man to venture far along the road of lives." The doctor feels unclean, he is weary, and he wants to be made clean. We read about a young woman from Iowa, a music teacher, whose right foot is slightly deformed and who walks with a limp. She goes to Chicago, rents a room in a rooming house where all the other tenants are men, and she stands naked in the bathroom and leaves the door slightly ajar, hoping to entice some man, but she has crying spells and runs away when a man touches her. Tumbling on her knees she begs a painter to make love to her. "I can't stand the waiting. You must take me at once." In telling this woman's story the painter repeats some of the phrases the psychoanalyst used, word by word. "How smart we are. How aptly we put things. . . . You miss the whole point. . . . I am weary and I want to be made clean."

The painter has the same desperate desire for cleanliness after meeting this woman from Iowa and getting involved in her emotional problems, and he feels that he himself is like her, and cannot be her lover. What the woman suffers from is a universal disease. "What would cure her would cure the rest of us also. . . . We all want to be loved and the world has no plan for creating our lovers." The problem is too complicated for him. A writer cannot be too definite with a subject like this, and perhaps we would miss something fine and significant if it were made all clear to us. The narrator himself is wondering about its meaning as he goes along, exploring his theme, and he is almost as inarticulate as the characters in the story.

Yet "Seeds" is more believable and suggestive because of its ambiguity and vagueness, for leaving so much unsaid or half-said, and being inconclusive; it reads like a brooding tender commentary on life. The characterization, the language, the construction seem awkward, two men who have never met use exactly the same words and phrases, but the story somehow sticks in our minds. It is not the ambiguity we get from Hopkins' concentrated figurative language; this is loose, conversational, everyday English, almost too common and colloquial to be "literature" and to have stylistic distinction, but the author gives us a sense of the awesome separateness and solitudes of life in our crowded cities. He *is* talking about a universal disease, and we have an inkling of the subterranean hells found in men and women and which explain their conduct.

Thanks to Sherwood Anderson and a few other writers, notably Hemingway, the American vernacular became our literary language after the First World War. "All modern American literature comes from one book by Mark Twain called 'Huckleberry Finn'," says Hemingway in *Green Hills of Africa*. "If you read it you must stop where Nigger Jim is

stolen from the boys. That is the real end. The rest is just
cheating. But it's the best book we've had. All American
writing comes from that. There was nothing before. There
has been nothing as good since."

What happened in America has happened in other countries. A writer comes along and makes the common everyday
language, the spoken speech, literary prose. Dante made his
Tuscan dialect the literary language of Italy. Romance was
the vulgar tongue of France when the troubadours told their
courtly tales, and English was a rude speech in Chaucer's
time. Huck Finn's language, "You don't know about me without you have read a book by the name of *The Adventures of
Tom Sawyer:* but that ain't no matter. . . . Now the way that
book winds up is this: Tom and me found the money that the
robbers hid in the cave . . ." was his own personal language,
fresh, novel, surprising. As Twain says in an explanatory
note, "In this book a number of dialects are used, to wit:
the Missouri Negro dialect; the extremist form of the back-
woods Southwestern dialect; the ordinary 'Pike County' dialect; and four modified varieties of this last."

Jargon might be used in dialogue or for comic effect, and
it has a place in the specialized language of certain profes-
sions and academic disciplines, but a careful writer will not
use it without having a good reason for it. Slang is usually
short-lived and ugly and may disappear in a year or two; yet
some slang words and expressions eventually become good
English, and slang can be also the salt of language. Only a
pedant would never use slang, and pedants do not write
novels.

Like other living languages, English is changing, growing,
and what was good usage yesterday may not be so today, and
yesterday's current word is today's archaism, or what was
prosaic a generation ago is accepted into poetic diction. But it
would be a mistake to identify completely the written language with spoken speech. The style of written language has
always been appropriately more formal, and every language
would degenerate into dialect and jargon and would cease to
be the national tongue, a medium of communication among

all sections of the population, if it lacked a certain unity and permanence through its written form. Standard English is becoming increasingly standard.

Actually, English has undergone few changes since the beginning of the novel in English. Consider these opening paragraphs in *Robinson Crusoe*, which Defoe wrote fast for many, published in 1719. We would not call this style quaint or archaic, and it is perfectly comprehensible today. In first person this is a telling, not showing style.

> I was born in the year 1632, in the city of York, of a good family, though not of that country, my father being a foreigner of Bremen, named Kreutznaer, who settled first at Hull. He got a good estate by merchandise, and leaving off his trade, lived afterwards at York; from whence he had married my mother, whose relations were named Robinson, a very good family in that country, and after whom I was so called, that is to say, Robinson Kreutznaer; but by the usual corruption of words in England, we are now called, nay, we call ourselves, and write our name, Crusoe; and so my companions always called me.
>
> I had two older brothers, one of whom was lieutenant-colonel, to an English regiment of foot in Flanders, formerly commanded by the famous Colonel Lockhart, and was killed at the battle near Dunkirk against the Spaniards. What became of my second brother, I never knew, any more than my father and mother did know what was become of me.

Common words in English are generally of Saxon origin, and these are the words for the writer to cherish; they form the basic vocabulary of fiction. They name things and acts, they are connected with the home and the hearth, they have to do with "all trades, their gear and tackle and trim," to use a phrase by Hopkins, who loved these words.

The fiction writer can strengthen his style by increasing the proportion of short Saxon words in his stories, and there is a large stock of monosyllables to draw from. Saxon words make prose concrete and energetic. Concrete words are perceptive words, naming particular things, and particular things make the modern story. There is a naive primitive charm about many Saxon words. They are unpretentious, homely, true. They can knock the nonsense out of pedantic language, trim prose down, blow out the dust of libraries, tear off the ivy. Many of them are naturally mimetic words, with the sound suggesting the sense. Saxon words give us a sense of objects and acts as first perceived and named. We seem to be dealing with a newly created language that has the freshness of poetry in it.

Good narrative prose abounds in concrete nouns, active verbs, qualifying adjectives (in moderation), and the first personal pronoun I. Other pronouns are likely to make trouble, and we often wonder whom the writer means by *who or whom or he or him,* when he omits a name or will not repeat it. English bristles with adverbs, and the weeding out of adverbs might do more for style than the weeding out of adjectives. Such adverbs as *however, moreover, consequently, therefore, on one hand . . . on the other hand,* mean nothing by themselves and seldom justify the space given them. They are not used in poetry and make prose prosaic.

The adjective, though not as necessary as the noun, makes for more vivid concrete writing. Sometimes a noun is not enough; the idea remains indefinite and abstract and the descriptive adjective brings the object closer to us; it reinforces the idea by describing some special quality of it that makes it more particular and more easily grasped by the imagination. The adjective gives emphasis, finer shades of discrimination and more accurate writing, and accuracy sums up nearly all the virtues of good narrative prose. The tendency of the inexperienced writer to use many adjectives is basically a sound one; he is conscious of nuances and wants to express more clearly what he wants to say. The adjective operates on the principle of transferred meaning, like metaphor, and is its simplest variant. Economy in the use of adjectives might be carried to extremes and there is altogether too much prejudice against adjectives. *Smile* by itself does not arouse as clear an image as *crooked smile,* or *wistful smile,* and what is vague or general becomes vivid and particular through the adjective. *Rye green,* or *cherry red* is more vivid than just *green* or *red.* Many descriptive adjectives are nouns, or derived from nouns, and they are in general to be preferred, if they have not become clichés by overuse, such as *silver* stream, *iron* will, *milk*-white skin, *stone* heart, *silken* tresses, *willowy* figure, *mountainous* seas.

Nouns as adjectives reinforce the image. So do adjectives changed to nouns. "He stared at the transparent *whiteness* of her skin in the sunlight." "He savored the *sweetness* of her lips." "She observed the *pallor* of his face." We have a more expressive, impressionistic language in these sentences than we would have if we changed whiteness, sweetness, pallor to white, sweet, pale. "He stared at her transparent *white* skin in the sunlight." "He savored her *sweet* lips." "She observed his *pale* face." These are weaker, not so vivid. The particular quality of the skin, lips, and face is emphasized through the quality noun and draws the reader's attention to it. If overdone, this becomes an affectation and a conceit, but used in moderation it is a useful stylistic device.

The language of fiction should be kept at the perceptive level, in close contact with life and the senses. Abstract language withdraws a story from life. When concrete objects and acts are missing and we do not have the visible thing, we cannot see it, touch it, hear it, smell it, feel it; when it is not particular but general, and the specific sensation, the deed, the thought, the feeling condensed into an image is not there, we get a sort of lifeless, disemboweled prose.

The words in a story should spring from the immediate experience, the sensation, the apprehension of reality, and the best narrative style hits us with an almost physical impact. When the word gives us a vivid mental image, it is a good word. Saxon words are usually concrete picture words; they have the sense and sound of reality about them. Saxon English is not a conceptual language, and it has its roots deep in English idioms. The basic vocabulary of *Ulysses* is Saxon, and many of its polysyllables are compounds of monosyllables.

English has been the language of men of action, and probably no other European tongue has so many active verbs. Since drama means doing, English .is naturally dramatic. *Strike, break, slam, smash, gash, shake, shut, shatter, scatter, batter, roll, trundle, thunder, blare, blow*—each arouses a mental image and the sound fits the sense. Or consider *shimmer, glimmer, rustle, tussle, sway, swoon, swing*—they sound right to our ears, and we can visualize them. With Saxon words the writer is not likely to be precious and affected unless he goes to the other extreme and writes as a professional Saxonist, a nativist diehard. Generally it is better to say *start* than *commence, talk* than *converse, rise* than *ascend, go* than *proceed, ask* than *inquire*. The sophisticated like the plain word better, while the uneducated are often impressed by fancy flowery speech.

The Latin word has snob appeal, but not with real snobs. Yet the Latin word is not as alien as it seems, for English after all is a mixed language, with a rich Latin-French heritage. The Latin word might be just the right one for the sense, sound, and rhythm a writer is seeking, and sometimes the Latin word is more economical, too and can replace several Saxon words. *Conceive—be with child, become pregnant with, form in the mind. Remove—put out of the way.* There are fine sounds in Latin words also. The French title of Whitman's "Drum-Taps" is *"Roulement de tambour,"* which sounds more like drums rolling. The short Saxon words and the long Latin words blend together in good narrative prose and create pleasing rhythmic combinations, and Latin words can act as uncommon strange words, as lengthened forms, to give style distinction.

Shakespeare's vocabulary is predominantly Saxon, and it is charged with such powerful word poetry that Milton with his abstract Latinisms seems dull by contrast. Shakespeare is of course our supreme model in language, and we have to go back to him again and again to see how the King's English should be used. It is the most idiomatic concentrated image-packed concrete speedy language we have, and even the bombast is magnificent. Shakespeare will insert now and then a long Latin word in his dialogue, adding the uncommon to the common, with splendid results.

The excessively domestic look of prose would make it homely, and Saxon needs the Roman mantle as it were to gain dignity and grandeur. The strange words glamourize the language, and by balancing Saxon words with Latin words the writer gets the characteristic swing and flavor of English prose, and avoids monotony in language.

The Saxon word for sturdy peasant strength, the Latin word for elegance. The Saxon word for sensations, the Latin word for concepts. The Saxon word for the concrete and specific, the Latin word for the abstract and general. Exceptionally rich and varied in its vocabulary, English is the mighty hybrid among modern tongues.

SENTENCES AND PARAGRAPHS

We usually think in sentences or in groups of related words and write in paragraphs. Words were not divided in ancient manuscripts. The sentence is a rhythmic grammatically self-contained unit even if it consists of a single word, with a full stop; the paragraph is a rhythmic whole with a longer pause. Punctuation is as much a problem of rhythm and breathing as of grammar and makes for measured speech.

The stylistic principle of deviation from the norm applies to sentence structure also. Higher emotional or mimetic effects may be gained when the normal word order is altered. Evidently in *For Whom the Bell Tolls* Hemingway follows the Spanish word order to make the talk more authentic. In *Ulysses* the word order often follows the thought order. From Leopold Bloom's monologue: "The flow of the language it is. . . . Powerful man, he was. . . . It was a nun they say invented barbed wire. . . . Bad breath he has, poor chap. . . . Rather upsets a man's day, a funeral does." Inversions might be used for emphasis: "Deep grow the roots." "*Jim* I know." One of the most annoying tricks is inversion for elegant variation: *said he, answered he.*

Marcel Proust suffered from asthma but he had enormous breathing capacity in his sentences. A sentence should not be so long that we forget the beginning by the time we get to the end, but there are really no rules about sentence length, certainly not when written by a prose poet like Marcel Proust.

212

Sentences are likely to be longer in stories that are "told" rather than "shown," as we often find in older novels. H. G. Wells tells; Hemingway shows.

Now the unavoidable suggestion of that wide park and that fair large house, dominating church, village and the country side, was that they represented the thing that mattered supremely in the world, and that all other things had significance only in relation to them. They represented the Gentry, the Quality, by and through and for whom the rest of the world, the farming folk and the labouring folk, the tradespeople of Ashborough, and the upper servants and the lower servants and the servants of the estate, breathed and lived and were permitted. And the Quality did it so quietly and thoroughly, the great house mingled so solidly and effectually with earth and sky, the contrast of its spacious hall and saloon and galleries, its airy housekeeper's room and warren of offices with the meagre dignities of the vicar, and the pinched and stuffy rooms of even the post office people and the grocer, so enforced these suggestions, that it was only when I was a boy of thirteen or fourteen and some queer inherited strain of scepticism had set me doubting whether Mr. Bartlett, the vicar, did really know with certainty all about God, that as a further and deeper step in doubting I began to question the final rightness of the gentlefolks, their primary necessity in the scheme of things.

(H. G. Wells: *Tono-Bungay*)

Nick slipped off his pack and lay down in the shade. He lay on his back and looked up into the pine trees. His neck and back and the small of his back rested as he stretched. The earth felt good against his back. He looked up at the sky, through the branches, and then shut his eyes. He opened them and looked up again. There was a wind high up in the branches. He shut his eyes again and went to sleep.

Nick woke stiff and cramped. The sun was nearly down. His pack was heavy and the straps painful as he lifted it on. He leaned over with the pack on and picked up the leather rod-case and started out from the pine trees across the sweet fern swale, toward the river. He knew it could not be more than a mile.

He came down a hillside covered with stumps into a meadow. At the edge of the meadow flowed the river. Nick was glad to get to the river. He walked upstream through the meadow . . . The river made no sound. It was too fast and smooth.

(Ernest Hemingway, *Big Two-Hearted River*)

Short sentences are not always easier to read and understand, nor the most economical. The long sentence could give dignity to style, and beside a noble sentence of great length, a series of short sentences might look cheap and common though such a series might read like one long sentence. The long sentence, like the long scene, builds momentum, which might be dissipated in a series of short sentences. The long sentence might be necessary for recording an uninterrupted action and giving all the necessary details at once, and in sequence, without dividing the act by periods. It would make for variety in sentence structure and length, if not too obviously inserted for that purpose.

The short sentence, as in Hemingway, makes for forceful writing, and a story might end effectively with a few short crisp sentences. For the conclusion, Aristotle says in the *Rhetoric,* the disconnected style of language is right and will make the difference between the formal summing up of the argument and the oration proper, quoting from the Attic orator Lysias: "I have done. You have heard me. The facts are before you. I ask for your judgment." (It is shorter in Greek.)

Brevity is characteristic of masterful men. On defeating a king of Pontus, Caesar sent a message of only three words to the Roman senate: *Veni, vidi, vici.* (I came, saw, conquered.) Not many schoolboys today remember these words, which I used to shout as a young boy in Pontus, riding my broomstick horse. "Nuts!" said the American general in World War II when asked to surrender. Military commands are brief. Women, children, weak characters in a story might be expected to talk more than strong men. Western sheriffs in America conform to the popular image of the strong silent man and are laconic in speech. Brevity can make language more expressive, but it may also make for obscurity, and may not always be true economy. Condensed language like Bacon's is harder to read than the loose rambling style of Montaigne.

Proverbs are brief. The pithy statement is short, to the point. Long proverbs would be hard to remember and would lose their power through prolixity. And the proverb itself can be another stylistic device, making for tighter prose, particularly in dialogue, and through balanced clauses, or antitheses, for variety in sentence structure. *Birds of a feather flock together. Easy come easy go. One man's meat is another man's poison. Art is long, life is short.* Epigrams might serve the same purpose.

The extreme form of brevity is silence, and silence also can heighten language. The unspoken word might be far more expressive and moving than the spoken word, especially when the reader can guess what the unspoken word is. Silence is a figure of speech, it is not the direct way of saying it, and like other figures it can be a poetic device in prose.

The free-running style is natural to fiction, and we are reminded again of Hemingway with his *and . . . and . . . and* sentences, which make for an impressionistic style of writing, with the intellectual element or reflection taken out of it.

> After a while we came out of the mountain, and there were trees along both sides of the road, and a stream and ripe fields of grain, and the road went on, very white and straight and ahead, and then lifted to a little rise, and off on the left was a hill with an old castle, with buildings close around it and a field of grain going right up to the walls and shifting in the wind.
>
> (*The Sun Also Rises*)

This is the way most people talk, the *and* linking a series of clauses or statements of about equal value. This gives the continuity of the action or the thought stream in its natural order—or disorder. A sentence like this can go on indefinitely. With no particular idea emphasized, the meaning of the whole sentence is not always easily grasped, or remembered. There is no measure or number in this kind of sentence structure, and what is measured (as in verse) is easier to remember.

When an idea is emphasized and not all the clauses in the sentence are of equal value, and the main clause containing this idea is put at the end, as the climax of the whole statement, we have a periodic sentence. Logic comes in with emphasis and subordination, and in the periodic sentence the writer is organizing his language; it is tight, reasoned out, the subordinate clauses leading to the main one and to a definite end. The main idea is postponed to the end because it is the most strategic and emphatic position in the sentence and meanwhile the reader is kept in suspense until he reaches the end. The sentence comes to a stop with the revelation of the main idea and not before, and a full stop is required. The periodic sentence underlines what comes last. It disposes of other matters first to get to the final clause, the main idea, and by building to a climax it makes for unity.

The periodic sentence is generally a long complex one and is not often found in modern narrative prose. A very short sentence cannot be periodic, and to subordinate one clause to another means having more than one clause in the sentence. It is a complete unit in itself, and more coherent despite its length, but the trouble is this kind of sentence seems artificial in today's fiction and goes contrary to the principle of the invisible author. It might hold the attention of the reader better than a loose free-running sentence, but it does not always go well with plot. It makes the movement of the sentence closely connected or causal, but it brings a formal intellectual element into language, and is more appropriate to an essay. Yet it has a place in fiction, in giving, for instance, the step-by-step progress of an act and making for added suspense and drama:

> As a hawk that circles high over the canyons and pausing in midair surveys the lowlands, then shoots down like an arrow over a chick that has wandered away from the farm-yard and is pecking along the road, the Indian chief on his white horse, with one mighty movement of his arm, threw his lariat around Judge Brown's five-year-old daughter and carried her off to his camp.

The complex sentence may be necessary for complex thoughts, but with its elaborate subordinations, balance, and contrast, belongs to an older style of writing fiction. Sparingly used it might make for variety in sentence structure, score a point, tighten a loose style.

Narrative prose picks up speed when sentences and paragraphs are shorter and conjunctions omitted. Very long sentences and paragraphs, loaded with too many details, would tire the average reader. Long paragraphs go with a more leisurely life; ours is a fast-moving age and we are conditioned to speed. But the long sentence or paragraph can be more musical, give dignity to prose, make style more impressive.

A long paragraph, like a long sentence, might be more readable and intelligible than a short paragraph that is badly put together, and length by itself can never be an index of readability.

Let us have clarity by all means, but not at the expense of originality and charm. Once a writer is clear, style becomes a matter of distinction. The trouble with much plain talk is that it *is* mean. It might increase the readability of newspaper or business prose and improve the language of some government documents, which is all to the good, but plain talk can be banal, and what we are looking for in fiction is fresh suggestive language. We need more than the vocabulary of Basic English or its more recent variants in narrative prose, yet a writer like Hemingway can do fine things with short sentences and common one-syllable words, and we can say in his case that simplicity is the best ornament. But what would happen if we tried to simplify Shakespeare's language, colloquial as it is? Or Marcel Proust's? Or Henry James'? Complex sentences with polysyllables have their place in narrative prose.

In countries where English is the lingua franca or a second language, writers do not use Basic English or pidgin English. There are born poets among them, engaged in daring stylistic experiments and in new ways of writing English which should challenge us. The poet surmounts the color bar. We are living in an age of new literatures rising over vast areas of the world, in Africa, in Asia, in the West Indies. English is scarcely a foreign language to West African writers, and there is a growing demand for African fiction. Today we have a world literature in English.

10. NARRATIVE PROSE [II]

RHYTHM AND SOUND

Good narrative prose is rhythmic language. The rhythm, as we know, is regular in verse, irregular in prose. Meter is proper to poetry and not to prose, but it is by no means rare in fiction, and, if not too emphatic, a brief passage of metrical prose at a high moment in the action might be effective, and would be justified by the higher emotional content of the language. It is by little touches here and there that a writer makes his language more expressive and memorable.

Language is indefinite, formless without rhythm, and what is formless is hard to understand, or to remember. Verse is remembered more easily than prose because of its rhythm. The world's first stories were told in verse, orally, and remembered for generations; national epics in verse survived for hundreds of years in their spoken form before they were written down, and they might have been lost and forgotten if told in prose. Children easily learn poems by heart, but would have difficulty remembering a page of prose with its uncertain rhythm. Rhythm puts order in the disorder of words, organizes the language, makes it more comprehensible. Rhythm is the heartbeat of prose, as vital, distinct, and mysterious as the rhythm of the body. We breathe in measured movements, the heart pumps blood rhythmically, the stars move rhythmically in their course, there is a definite rhythm in the tides. Rhythm gives prose its breath, its forward movement, its vitality, and is a basic ingredient in all good writing, as it is indeed in all art.

Every language has its own characteristic speech rhythms. We do not speak words separately but group them together. A foreigner learning English has to learn also its rhythmic patterns, the stresses, slacks, pauses of English speech, how strong beats and weak beats affect the grouping of words; now four or five words spoken as though one word, now a single word or syllable emphasized.

Rhythm makes language more expressive, more meaningful, and it is a sort of speech itself. It does serve as a medium of mimesis. In narrative prose, particularly in dialogue, the rhythm should make the words move "trippingly" on the tongue, as Hamlet advised his players. The practiced writer instinctively regulates the speed or tempo of his prose, and terms used in musical composition might be useful in literature—*grave*, very slow, *andante*, slow but flowing, *allegro*, brisk, *vivo*, lively. There is a mysterious metronome in the writer's mind regulating his rhythm, and rhythms differ from writer to writer.

Good prose, like spoken speech, has plenty of movement in it, its pace determined largely by the action. At a climactic point the language, like the characters, might be a little breathless, the sentences and paragraphs shorter, conjunctions omitted, the dialogue brief, sometimes gasping, staccato. When the tension relaxes, the movement of the prose slows down, the sentences become longer, flowing. Problems of pace are among the most delicate in narrative prose.

Speech moving trippingly on the tongue should not come to a full stop where no stop is indicated, and a word that is strange and difficult to pronounce, such as a foreign word, would break the continuity of the rhythm. Sudden unwanted stops might have a shattering effect on prose; yet foreign words judiciously used add an authentic flavor to dialogue or monologue and might be an aid in characterization. Some of the characters in *War and Peace* occasionally speak in French. Hemingway sprinkles the dialogue in *For Whom the Bell Tolls* with Spanish words and expressions to indicate the conversation is taking place in Spanish.

> "Nay, *Inglés*," he said. "Do not provoke me." He looked at Pilar and said to her, "It is not thus that you get rid of me."

> *"Sin verguenza,"* Robert Jordan said to him, committed now in his own mind to the action. *"Cobarde."*
>
> "It is very possible," Pablo said. "But I am not to be provoked. Take something to drink, *Inglés,* and signal to the woman it was not successful."
>
> "Shut thy mouth," Robert Jordan said. "I provoke thee for myself."
>
> "It is not worth the trouble," Pablo told him. "I do not provoke."
>
> "Thou art a *bicho raro,"* Robert Jordan said. . . .
>
> "Very rare, yes," Pablo said. "Very rare and very drunk. To your health, *Inglés."* He dipped a cup in the wine bowl and held it up. *"Salud y cojones."*
>
> (For Whom the Bell Tolls)

Note that Hemingway does not translate these Spanish words. He keeps them uncommon, and they make for local color, an important stylistic device. Foreign words stop the average American reader dead in his tracks, and his fear of mispronunciation extends even to English words. It is a familiar sight in college classrooms to see a student stop while reading aloud and try to figure out how he should pronounce a word. The momentum, the cumulative power of the rhythm is lost. It is like singing a song and then stopping somewhere in the middle of it trying to figure out what comes next. But this risk might be worth taking. Foreign proper names not only add local color but might glamourize the language by their suggestive overtones or sonorities. It is scarcely necessary to point out the poetic value of place names. American place names sound tremendous to foreigners and Whitman's poetry would lose some of its distinctly American overtones and go flat without them. In *The Sun Also Rises,* Hemingway re-creates the atmosphere of Paris with a minimum of descriptive detail, by merely mentioning the names of streets, bars, restaurants. Dublin becomes more vivid through thousands of place names in *Ulysses.*

> Before Nelson's Pillar trams slowed, shunted, changed trolley, started for Blackrock, Kingstown and Dalkey, Clonskea, Rathgar and Terenure, Palmerston park and upper Rathmines, Sandymount Green, Rathmines, Ringsend and Sandy-

mount Tower, Harold's Cross. The hoarse Dublin United
Tramway Company's timekeeper bawled them off:
—Rathgar and Terenure!
—Come on, Sandymount Green!

Just as important are the names of the people in this novel.
Almost every page is studded with Irish names.

> —Gordon, Barnfield Crescent, Exeter; Redmayne of Iffley,
> Saint Anne's on Sea, the wife of William T. Redmayne, of a
> son. How's that, eh? Wright and Flint, Vincent and Gillett
> to Rotha Marion daughter of Rosa and the late George
> Alfred Gillett, 179 Clapham Road, Stockwell, Playwood and
> Ridsdale at Saint Jude's Kensington by the very reverend Dr
> Forrest, Dean of Worcester, eh? Deaths. Bristow, at White-
> hall lane, London: Carr, Stoke Newington of gastritis and
> heart disease: Cockburn, at the Moat house, Chepstow. . . .

Proper names have their own rhythm. Rhythm is the tom-
tom of poetry and prose and we all feel its hypnotic effect.
Rhythm can cause excitement among dancers, warriors, readers. Prose is easy to read when its rhythm is right and we go
from pause to pause without undue fatigue. But prose can be
too smooth, too flowing, and when the reader is gliding along
or floating down the stream of words with perfect ease he
might miss a lot on the way; and if he stumbles continuously
over words he cannot pronounce or because certain sounds
pile up, or because he is caught short by the rhythm, he becomes tense and nervous. The writer has to strike a balance
between these two extremes. He might have to trip the reader
on occasion to make him pause, look around, absorb the
scenery, as it were. If close attention to what is being said is
necessary, the style should not be too smooth and musical.
Let the writer occasionally throw a rock before the reader
to trip him up, to keep him on the alert.

Rhythm, rhyme, alliteration gain their mysterious effects
through repetition, a fundamental principle in all art. Children like to read stories in which words and sounds are repeated. Good prose has a recurrent rhythmic flow and its
sound patterns arouse an expectancy that is satisfied by the
repetition. Repetition makes for unity and emphasis. Gertrude
Stein is reported to have taught Hemingway the value of

repetition. There is no art without repetition, but repetition, without variety, becomes monotonous—insufferably so in Gertrude Stein's novel *The Making of Americans*.

English is not only a highly rhythmic but alliterative language, and the alliteration, or repetition of consonants, acts as a rhythmic device. *Clitter-clatter of clogs on cobblestones. The swish of silken skirts flaring on the village green. The snake slithered in the grass. The sun struck the icy crags of the Sierra Madre.* Alliteration creates images in our minds and is one of the great poetic resources of the English language. As everyone knows, English poetry began as alliterative verse; and this is true also in the medieval poetry of many other nations. Alliteration brings in the Saxon words and makes prose more concrete and vivid. Shakespeare's language delights us with alliterations and assonance, or the repetition of similar sounds, especially of vowels.

> Here lay Duncan,
> His silver skin lac'd with his golden blood;
> And his gash'd stabs look'd like a breach in nature
> For ruin's wasteful entrance: there the murderers,
> Steep'd in the colors of their trade, their daggers
> Unmannerly breached with gore. . . .
>
> What man dare, I dare:
> Approach thou like the rugged Russian bear,
> The arm'd rhinocerous, or the Hyrcan tiger.

But alliteration and assonance (which is less frequent in prose and not so useful) can be overdone. A virtue in prose becomes a vice when carried to excess, and there is more danger in too much than in too little. Too much melody might put us to sleep. Music could have a drowsy effect on the reader. Good prose need not be markedly musical, and too much music will soften the style. Like other Germanic languages, English is rather harsh in its sound patterns. This harshness is not altogether a disadvantage and makes for strength. Modern music is not very melodious, and dissonance has its attraction also in prose, although we do not want cacophony. Music sweetens the prose, but it should not be oversweet.

Like words, rhythm and melody also express thought and feeling. To make language more expressive the writer has to move in the direction of poetry, but poetry is a powerful spice. Too much of it will spoil the dish, and the food is tasteless without it.

"The delight in the richness and sweetness of sound, even to a faulty excess, if it be evidently original, and not the result of an easily imitable mechanism, I regard as a highly favorable promise in the compositions of a young man. The man that hath not music in his soul can indeed never be a genuine poet." So wrote Coleridge in *Biographia Literaria*. (Chapter XV.)

Without a fine ear for the acoustics of language, no writer can expect to be a stylist, for the stylist writes by the ear. He chooses his words for their sound as much as for their sense. Words in addition to delivering their meaning in an effective manner can be and should be a pleasure in their own right, and the best narrative style now walks, now dances toward its goal, with an occasional pirouette on the way, delighting in its own movements and grace. There is a free, spontaneous, winged quality about it; it is speech mixed with song. When the words are stripped of the rhythm and sound that music gives them and are bare, naked, without any sweetening, without color and imagery, we are perilously close to information, utilitarian prose, that of the newspaper. The musical note might come into summaries along with the picture, and by strengthening the summary with melody and image the writer avoids pedestrian prose and raises summary, as does Flaubert, to the power of scene or even above it; otherwise the scene will completely overshadow the summary, leaving dull gaps in the action.

With rhythm and music the power of words is multiplied. Like rhythm, music also is a kind of language, and in fact we call it the universal language. The rhythm and music in prose can create the most profound moods and cast a spell upon us. Like religion, literature cannot do without music, and both need it for permanence. Through music we can ascend to the sublime. Music could be valuable particularly at the beginning of the story when the reader is to be charmed into reading it before he is engrossed in the action; and at the end, when certain impressions, a particular tone or mood is to be emphasized for a poetic finale. Music will charm even a snake. The whirling dervishes of old Turkey worked themselves into a state of religious ecstasy by playing their pipes, and the Greeks were susceptible to the flute frenzy Aristotle mentions in the *Poetics*. We have rock 'n roll jam sessions, the Beatles. It is the same frenzy.

A rhapsodic dream vision when Thomas De Quincey was under the "tyranny of opium" produced the great organ notes in his prose. We are familiar with Thomas Wolfe's incantations. If we took the ecstatic element out of his loose lyrical novels we would no longer have his legend of youth glowing with the special intense quality of American living. It is overwriting, too metrical, too repetitious, too elevated, but necessary in this kind of mimesis. Thomas Wolfe poured it out like a volcano.

D. H. Lawrence was another ecstatic, with a prophet's gleam in his eyes. No one has described the English countryside better than D. H. Lawrence, and he does not have his equal in celebrating the life of the senses. But his characters are more like vibrating protoplasmic entities than recognizable, individual human beings. He stressed what people have in common with others—sex—more than what makes them different, and even a novel like *The Rainbow* is hard to read to the end. Despite the splendid language, the monotony of it wears the reader down. Lawrence produced strangely original works, we feel the power of his writing, we thrill to his descriptive prose. *The Rainbow* contains great writing, but can we call it a great novel in the sense that *Madame Bovary* is one? Compared to Flaubert, Lawrence seems formless in this family chronicle, but not even Flaubert could write descriptive prose so rich in sensations, in sight and insight.

> In autumn the partridges whirred up, birds in flocks blew like spray across the fallow, rooks appeared on the grey, watery heavens, and flew cawing into the winter.
> She hurried to the wood for shelter. There, the vast boom-

ing overhead vibrated down and encircled her, tree-trunks spanned the circle of tremendous sound, myriads of tree-trunks, enormous and streaked black with water, thrust like stanchions upright between the roaring overhead and the sweeping of the circle underfoot. She glided between the tree-trunks, afraid of them. They might turn and shut her in as she went through their martialled silence.

And again, to her feverish brain, came the vivid reality of acorns in February lying on the floor of a wood with their shells burst and discarded and the kernel issued naked to put itself forth. She was the naked, clear kernel thrusting forth the clear, powerful shoot, and the world was a bygone winter, discarded, her mother and father and Anton, and college and all her friends, all cast off like a year that has gone by, whilst the kernel was free and naked and striving to take new root, to create a new knowledge of Eternity in the flux of Time. And the kernel was the only reality; the rest was cast off into oblivion.

(D. H. Lawrence, *The Rainbow*)

Note the repetitions. This is a characteristic of D. H. Lawrence's style. He gains beautiful pictorial, symbolic or ironic effects through repetition; they add to the fire-power of his prose. This is not cool writing, but the impassionate language of a poet who is a seer. Lawrence is a novelist of ideas who stresses the vital importance of sex as communication. In a depersonalized fragmented industrialized society sex becomes a total encounter of two isolated personalities, an effort to bridge the gap between them. In *The Rainbow* we have men and women with the teeming life of earth pulsing in their veins. The Brangwens who had lived for generations on the Marsh Farm are fresh, blond, blue-eyed folk who felt "the rush of the sap in spring . . . knew the intercourse between heaven and earth, sunshine drawn into the breast and bowels, the rain sucked up in the daytime." They are landscape figures in the meadows where the sluggish Erewash separates Derbyshire from Nottinghamshire. This lack of communication Lawrence deplores is worse in those who are cut off from the soil and lead frustrated artificial intellectualized lives. He can be merciless with men like Michaelis writing smart society plays, who becomes Connie's lover in *Lady Chatterley's Lover,* before she meets a real man in Mellors, her lodge-keeper, and runs away with him. Connie's aristocratic husband, Clifford, injured in World War I and impotent, is another writer scorned by Lawrence, and so is the writer in "Two Blue Birds," to mention one of Lawrence's many excellent short stories.

Generally the short stories are not shapeless affairs and their characters emerge as distinct individualities we can remember. But in Lawrence's case we remember the complex relationships of people seeking communication and drawn sexually to each other; he stressed the relationship itself, that was his real subject, not the characters involved in the exchange. He wrote according to his own theory of fiction, reflecting his own philosophy of life, and his ideas with their mystical overtones are expressed in a sensory prose that his friend Aldous Huxley, another novelist of ideas, did not have.

Brevity does not make for music, and we might consider the terse style and the musical style opposites. Crisp dialogue is not melodic speech. Perhaps the ideal style, if we might risk another generalization here, is terse language sweetened with music; terse in scene, sweet in summary. The style as a whole should be a good acoustical blend, for again variety is very important. There are more common Saxon, one-syllable words in dialogue, and spoken speech, harsher in sound, should balance the melody that comes in with the long Latin word in long sentences. Melody in a way is alien to the native timbre of English speech, and a notably musical style will have a touch of Latinity in it; yet Hopkins shunned the Latin word, used Saxon words, and wrote some of the finest lyrics in English. And we can see in the most musical chapter of *Ulysses*, the Sirens episode, what might be done with Saxon sound patterns in prose, the tone of this chapter set by the first line, "Bronze by gold heard the hoofirons, steelyringing." Joyce did wonderful things with one-syllable words. And he used alliteration not only with mimetic, but satirical effects.

> Blazes Boylan's smart tan shoes creaked on the barfloor where he strode. . . . Jingle jaunted down the quays. Blazes sprawled on bounding tyres. . . . By Bachelor's walk jog jaunty jingled Blazes Boylan, bachelor, in sun, in heat, mare's

glossy rump atrot, with flick of whip, on bounding tyres:
sprawled, warmseated, Boylan impatience, ardentbold. Horn.
Have you the? Horn. Have you the? Haw haw horn.

Ulysses we might say is written in masculine prose, and
masculine prose is harsher in sound than feminine prose,
which is naturally more melodious and softer, and more emotional. The emotion heightens the language and brings in the
music. The exclamation point has all but vanished from rugged
masculine prose like Hemingway's, but women still use it.
Women should write like women and not like men. A distinctly feminine style in fiction might very well be its main
attraction, for male readers anyway, and women in turn respond to masculine prose.

Women writers need not imitate men. Since fiction has to
do with feelings rather than facts, women are naturals in this
art, and in language arts in general. Women, as mothers of the
race, are also mothers of language. They transmit language
from one generation to another, and as De Quincey remarks
in his essay on style, The Literature of Knowledge and the
Literature of Power, Greek, according to Byzantine writers,
was preserved in its purest form in the nurseries of Constantinople, and this was true also, he says, of the Latin language in Rome, according to the testimony of Latin authors.
Proust frequented the salons of Princess Mathilde, Mme.
Straus, Mme. de Caillavet, where, we may assume, certain
feminine influences seeped into his style. The best French no
doubt was spoken in the literary salons of France, presided
over by women.

Portrait of the Artist as a Young Man is in rhythmic melodious prose. The language is richer to the point of lushness
in the middle chapters and relatively dry and spare in the last
chapter, as Stephen Dedalus withdraws more and more from
his environment and his alienation deepens. The point of
view of the growing boy determines the verbal pattern in the
book. Joyce moved from sweet sounds to harsh sounds in his
next work, *Ulysses*. If the *Portrait* is written in three distinct
styles, *Ulysses* is written in a hundred or more different
styles. As the bulk of this novel is interior monologue and

dialogue, the short sentences have a disjointed effect and make us stumble as we go along. Except for brief intervals, it is stop and go, on a rocky road. The mellifluous sounds in the *Portrait* are missing. Stephen is more withdrawn and more bitter than when we left him in the *Portrait*, and the other characters are not poets like him. The irregularity, the jerky, chopped-up prose seem to express also the hustle and bustle of Dublin streets and we have a better imitation of life in a large city because of the language, seemingly chaotic, but rigorously designed for its particular task. Onomatopoeia is one of the persistent features of this complex prose.

> Grossbooted draymen rolled barrels dullthudding out of Prince's stores and bumped them up on the brewery float.

Joyce no doubt wrote by the ear. He was a trained singer, known for his voice before he became a writer.

SYMBOL AND METAPHOR

A fundamental difficulty in this craft, even in English, is sheer poverty of language. The literal meaning of words is not enough. What the writer cannot say directly he has to say indirectly, in a roundabout way, and often it is the roundabout way that gives life and beauty to style. The writer has to express one thing in terms of another to make his meaning clear, as we all do in ordinary conversation. Many words acquire symbolic meaning and express in visible and sensuous terms something intangible, invisible, immaterial. A symbol can give a vivid picture of what otherwise would remain inexpressible. Symbol, metaphor, analogy, allegory, irony, hyperbole, periphrasis are indirect ways of saying it. Writing about her father, a retired Iowa farmer in California, a college girl said, "Dad finally returned to his beloved soil," using a periphrasis, without knowing it, and this roundabout way is a more poetic and moving way of saying that her father died.

To get back to metaphor, it is an absolutely necessary part of language and not an ornament added from the outside, although it might also have ornamental value. A fresh metaphor is a new variation from ordinary speech, a new combination of things unconnected before, a new correspondence, to use a word made famous by Baudelaire in his sonnet, *Correspondances*. It is through new connections and combinations that a writer creates both his language and plot. The same perceptive faculty and imaginative sensitivity are at work in both, the same unifying vision shapes up both language and plot, and the word-maker is also the plot-maker. Symbol and metaphor are images, and their wide use emphasizes the importance of imagery in narrative prose.

Since the secret of style in fiction lies in new extraordinary uses of language by which a writer organizes an emotional experience into an integrated whole, nuances of thought or feeling, and many other details that have a bearing on the experience, might be left out if only the established dictionary meanings of words were used. Figures of speech make for a fuller and more precise mimesis.

The rhythm and music of prose also connect and express things that are not in the dictionary, and this extension of language through rhythm and music, and through symbol and metaphor, adds to the power of the word and gives it radiance. It is, to repeat, always by connecting, and by perceiving the like in the unlike, making dissimilars similar, reconciling and unifying opposites, that the writer fights his way through the fog and expresses the inexpressible. To Marcel Proust metaphor was the most important stylistic device and there can be, he said, no great narrative prose without it. He complained he could not find a single beautiful metaphor in all of Flaubert.

Metaphor operates on the principle of surprise. The reader is struck by the novelty and truth of it, he did not expect this particular connection; the combination is new, startling; and the unexpected, the striking is also the memorable and adds to our pleasure of reading fiction. We remember fresh metaphors; they register on our minds.

Metaphor is mimesis. It gives language a new turn and, if apt, will make the reader pause for a moment. It fills in the gaps in the dictionary. Prose gains both clarity and distinction through it. It says what cannot be said directly in straight language; it makes clear what would otherwise remain unsaid or obscure. Metaphor is as old as speech itself, and its value in both poetry and prose has been recognized since ancient times. In verse we have other means for making language more expressive, such as rhyme and meter. In prose metaphor has more to do in overcoming the limitations of the dictionary, not to say the limitations of mortality, and one fresh metaphor can elevate a page of prose to the level of literature. Being a picture, metaphor makes prose vivid, concrete. It is not abstract analogy. It adds to the pictorial qualities of language.

A child on occasion creates its own language, as does the poet. The "bright sayings" of children are often fresh metaphors. Even scientific writing, presumably farthest removed from the poetic, can be highly metaphoric, and a psychoanalyst describing human emotions uses many metaphors. Metaphor is insight, a perceptive act, an imaginative feat where the unconscious is at work, but it might also be consciously stimulated through an association or dissociation of ideas. Since nearly all children have a gift for it, and so many peasants in Ireland, Armenia, and other countries often speak like poets, a capacity for striking metaphors is not as uncommon as is generally supposed.

An orderly connected action presupposes a capacity for orderly connected language, and the two usually go together, but, as pointed out earlier, in the normal development of a creative writer the word-maker precedes the plot-maker. But they are related activities; the same combining power of the single vision is at work in both the choice and arrangement of the words and the choice and arrangement of the incidents. The plot and the style do not issue from separate compartments in the writer's mind. Without this imaginative ability to connect, through language and plot, it would be impossible to construct a story, and the writer would be lost in a jumble of fragments, in a multitude of disparate parts which do not add up to anything significant. What makes the metaphor makes also the plot, and the structure and texture of a story, its form and language, are two aspects of the same thing. They do not call for separate talents.

Figurative or metaphoric language cannot be a wild excursion into impossible analogies, and some resemblance, some connection no matter how tenuous or imaginative must exist for the comparison. It cannot be so farfetched that reason or imagination rebel against it. This is the reason why so many mixed metaphors are bad, with no basis for the comparison, one member of the analogy canceling out the other.

The metaphor might underscore the similarity in dissimilars: *the honeyed breath of the sage. The white-clad armor of the Russian winter stopped the German armies at Leningrad.* Or bring out the contrast in the parts: *eloquent silence.* A good metaphor should please the ear as well as the eye, add to the sight-and-sound pattern of prose. Metaphors should be the jewelry of language, not too conspicuous. The golden rule of metaphor, as of prose in general, is moderation. The metaphor stands out more sharply in a simple style. The surprise, if continuous, ceases to be a surprise. And the simple metaphors on the whole are best. An extended metaphor can be very beautiful, but is difficult to manage and might strike us as a conceit, forced, fancy writing.

Metaphor is such an intimate part of the structure of language that every language, one might say, is created by poets and is the result of innumerable strokes of genius, of insights into the inner essence and unity of things. Languages with no written literature are surprisingly metaphoric. When one learns a foreign language, one learns all kinds of new metaphors. Most idioms and idomatic expressions in English are nothing but metaphors. We are so familiar with them that we do not think of them as unusual. *Flying off the handle; water down the drain; falling for it hook, line, and sinker; steely grip; billing and cooing; splitting headache; right off the bat; talking through the hat; my feet are killing me; I haven't a thing to wear.*

Such common everyday expressions strike the foreigner by their aptness or vividness, or they might puzzle him, just as we would be delighted most likely, or bewildered, by certain expressions in Chinese or Japanese. Metaphors do not stay fresh forever; they become accepted language, part of current speech. The bedrock of English and other languages consists of dead metaphors. Some dead metaphors can be resurrected when given a new twist.

To Aristotle, a command of metaphor was by far the greatest thing in writing, and this alone he said cannot be learned from others. He stated clearly in the *Rhetoric* that it is of great value in prose, and indeed prose writers should pay specially close attention to metaphor because their other resources of language are more limited than those of poets. "Metaphor, moreover, gives style clearness, charm and distinction as nothing else can: and it is not a thing whose use can be taught by one man to another." (*Rhetoric*, III–2.)

Personification is a particularly useful metaphor and gives life and movement to prose. Is it not "pathetic fallacy?" It is neither pathetic nor a fallacy, and Ruskin, though an excellent stylist himself, was wrong in coining that expression. To ascribe human traits and feelings to inanimate objects is a perfectly natural, the human thing to do. Personification is widely used in folk tales and fables. Shakespeare was not worried about pathetic fallacy when he made King Lear speak these words:

> Slow, winds, and crack your cheeks! rage! blow!
> You cataracts and hurricanes, spout
> Till you have drench'd our steeples, drown'd the cocks!
> You sulphurous and thought-executing fires
> Vaunt-couriers to oak-cleaving thunderbolts,
> Singe my white head! And thou, all-shaking thunder,
> Strike flat the thick rotundity o' the world!
> Crack nature's moulds, all garments spill at once
> That made ingrateful man!
>
> . . . Rumble thy bellyful! Spit, fire! spout, rain!
> Nor rain, wind, thunder, fire, are my daughters:
> I tax not you, you elements, with unkindness;
> I never gave you kingdom, call'd you children,
> You owe me no subscription: then, let fall
> Your horrible pleasure; here, I stand, your slave,
> A poor, infirm, weak, and despis'd old man.

Some writers in their dread of being called poetic or affected will not be caught dead with a metaphor. There is no justification for such fear. Metaphor is nothing to dread or to mock at; the sinews of prose are metaphors. The dash and élan of a sharp mimetic style might be measured by its metaphoric content. It is a question of how much a writer wants to accomplish in writing a story. Journalistic prose leaves so much unsaid that we have at best a half-told tale.

What makes prose concrete and alive is the image. When the feeling or thought is not condensed in an image, it floats around, with no local habitation and name, we may get the rhetorical style, abstract prose. The condensation into image is a vital transformation of language and the difference between art and non-art, literature and journalism, poetic and rhetoric. It is when the image ties up the emotion, and there is no excess emotion left to float around that we get the true sober style in fiction. The verbosity and the vagueness in prose come with the absence of the image, which has an immediate sobering and clarifying effect on style. When a writer lacks the necessary sensory equipment in his makeup he has to rely on dialogue or write scenarios rather than full-blooded novels and short stories. If a writer cannot supply the vital sensuous details himself, he leaves too much to the reader's imagination and there is only a partial imitation of life, no matter how complete the documentation. In fiction, the image is the medium and the test. Without the thought or feeling condensed into an image, the style remains abstract, vaporous, remote from life, incomplete. Art is concrete, completed.

While narrative prose becomes more expressive by moving in the direction of poetry, it cannot go all the way, and we should remember that the language of prose is different from that of poetry, even though the difference is one of degree only. The writer moves closer to poetry or further away from it according to the requirements of his subject, and his own talents, his own tastes and temperament. He has to write in a style congenial to him, and indeed he cannot write in any other way. If he cannot think up fresh metaphors or doubts their value then he has to do without them, and may even propound a theory of No Metaphors, as does M. Robbe-Grillet.

SUITING THE WORD TO THE ACTION

Narrative prose at its best is the precise and complete expression of the subject matter in the story, and since the content is an event or action, narrative style is action prose, external or internal action. This fidelity to the experience, making it "the way it really was," is the responsibility of style, and to write truly means to write sincerely. Sincerity makes for mimesis. Good narrative prose is sincere prose, and the mystery of style is partly explained when we look at it as an expression of the writer's sincerity. Originality means sincerity. And it is sincerity that makes the writer search for the right word, which is the sincere word, and the sincere word is the persuasive word, good argument. Sincerity is not so much a moral issue here as a technical aspect of style. No sincerity, no style. The personality of the writer is blocked and cannot find free expression. Personal prose is sincere prose. It is free prose. It frees the writer.

If the original sensations and emotions were powerful, the style will be powerful; if they were weak, the style will be weak. If they are phony, the style is phony. An emotional experience sincerely expressed: that is what all good writers strive for.

With the re-creation of the experience being the writer's primary task, we know where we stand in the vast domain of prose, and we can distinguish narrative style from other styles. Most books and essays on style deal with these other styles, with rhetoric rather than poetic. Rhetoric *acted out* becomes poetic. If the style does not re-create the action, then it is not doing its job in fiction. A style is good in terms of what it does for the plot. In fiction even self-expression must be through the event.

The advice to "forget style and concentrate on the story" is meaningless, for there is no successful story without style. The style is the whole story, the complete expression of the content. It is not an extraneous ornament, something fanciful added to the story; not an affectation or mannerism. And even certain artificial styles, Michael Arlen's for instance, have an individual charm of their own. An Armenian boy, Dikran Kouyoumjian, went to London, changed his name to Michael Arlen, wrote *The Green Hat, These Charming People, Mayfair,* and other novels and short stories and made himself the spokesman of the "charming people" he met in Mayfair. An outsider writing as an insider, Michael Arlen became, in the twenties, the most fashionable author on both sides of the Atlantic, and his glittering mannered prose was the right language, one might say, for the artificial world celebrated in his work. He gave to Mayfair society the enchantment of *The One Thousand and One Nights.* A certain affectation is inevitable in the language of a writer who plays a role as a displaced person and has to live up to a legend he creates for himself, as did Michael Arlen, and as did Henry James before him. James also was an outsider among his "Europeans" and perhaps never wholly at home as a British subject. In fiction there is room for all kinds of style, the simple and ornate, the natural and artificial, the direct and the oblique, the metaphoric and cinematic.

The closer language clings to the originating experience the better. We need the language because of the story, and if there is no story, no significant event or at least a state of mind, a mood to begin with, there is properly speaking no style. The moment a writer deviates from his story he is in trouble stylistically, and instead of controlling his language, is controlled by it.

There is then no one best style in fiction. A style that is best for one story might be the worst possible kind of language for another story. Is the style right for *this* story? That is the question. Or is it right for this *part* in the story? The writer has to suit the word to the action, and when he does that, he might even add song to speech.

A good narrative style does not attract undue attention to itself. Its job is to keep the reader's mind on the story, on what is happening, the event, and not on the writer, no matter how personal the prose. The style of *Madame Bovary* does not detract the reader's attention from the story Flaubert is telling, it seems to be a part of it, and there we have an almost perfect union of subject matter and style, the form being the content.

A clear sharp impression of the event—that is what counts in style. Precision above all. The stylist weighs his words in milligrams. He has to choose the right word from among several synonyms, and the right word might well be the sonorous word, as it was with Flaubert and Poe. It might even be a vague, poetic word, not too precise in meaning, and the more suggestive for that reason. Ambiguity, too, can be a stylistic device and make language more expressive.

It is never easy to say what has not been said before, or to say it better, and it can be very hard on the health and nervous system of the writer. Art might be a prison to the writer, but it saves him from other prisons, and trapped by his words, he eludes other traps.

If the writer knows what to say, if he is clear about his subject, has explored all its angles, and the event he chooses glows in his vision with meaning and is crystallized into a significant picture of life, the problem of how to say it will be easier, but even then it can be rough going. When Flaubert wrote his first scenario of *Madame Bovary* he knew exactly what he wanted to say, and he made no important changes in it, but it took him four and a half years to write the novel.

When a writer starts out without an event, or without an event worth telling, relying on his gift for language, he is undertaking a hopeless venture. This is not a call for violent action, with the U. S. Navy coming to the rescue of the hero. The writer who has nothing important to say through an event, will be fussy and pretentious about his style, but his language, no matter how beautiful or poetic, would be a futile exercise in a vacuum. With an event to start with, everything can be organized around it. Something significant must happen, or language is helpless. We should recognize the limitations of style in fiction. It derives its power from the plot, from character and thought causing the action. After all we do enjoy reading novels in translation. Pity the stylist without a story, lost in the mires of self-expression. Neither language can make up for the deficiencies of plot, nor plot make up for deficiencies of language. The style cannot replace the action, nor the action replace the style.

Style should not be a strait jacket for the writer, but a free, bold adventure in language. The good style, like the good plot, has guts in it. That is what makes Joyce so interesting. The stylist in fiction is not afraid to try the new, to work out new combinations of words, to arrange them in new ways, to toss them around as it were, to play with them, fascinated by their sounds and shapes, by their overtones and associations. And he would rather be great than correct. He can risk a few mistakes, a few vices as excesses of his virtues.

Good writing is passionate writing, but with its passion controlled, dispassionate passion. It has to be hot to be cool. There is a deep earnestness and sincerity about a great style, and the reader feels it. It is like hearing the voice of a great and good person who is speaking about something that matters. Without this conviction of his subject's importance no writer can go very far as a stylist. Great subjects, great thoughts, make great language, and the stylist does not mouth platitudes. Great language comes out of a great heart and a great mind. The style is a true measure of the man. It is always in character, the authentic idiom of the writer himself.

VARIETIES OF NARRATIVE STYLE

Since the dramatic principle is well established in modern fiction, narrative style is partly or wholly character words. With the scene giving us a close imitation of the action as it occurs, we should keep in mind the superior mimetic qualities of scene style as against summary style. The voice structure, who is speaking, will determine the language in the story as a whole or in some part of it.

In exposition we have only one voice, the author's, but in a dramatic narration like the novel or short story we have character voices in addition, and the author's voice may be wholly absent, as in first person. Emotional experiences are usually rendered through a mixture of voices even if the over-all voice is the author's. In fiction the language varies; it is not a single integrated style. It might be more embellished in summaries, or more matter-of-fact, reportorial.

If all the characters talk alike, or like the author himself, the imitation is not very close. The writer has to discriminate between the speech of one character and another or his own speech. When the characters are presented from their own point of view, as independent entities and not as the author's puppets, they will express their thoughts and feelings in their own words, and by letting the characters speak for themselves the author underscores their individuality. A writer like James Joyce is a virtuoso of different styles, and we have an unforgettable world of voices and sounds in *Ulysses*.

The predominant qualities of modern American prose are movement, speed, sensation. We say jazz is physical music, and there is something physical about American prose, too; its sensuous impact is almost a national characteristic, as in the stories "The Open Boat" by Stephen Crane. Crane's language is vivid, alive, concrete. The American non-academic mind recoils from abstractions. The language of American fiction has a high, sometimes fantastic emotional content. The exaggerated style of our newspaper headlines is part of the American language, and the "tall tale" is part of our folklore. In a land of sudden changes and rapid transportation, and of immense distances, with an energetic population and a tradition of having the greatest this and that in the world, where "the sky's the limit," language is likely to be extravagant in tone and impatient with frills. And when innumerable demands are made on our attention, language has to be colorful and startling enough to make any impression on us. The drama of American living demands a dramatic language.

Foreign readers respond to the distinctive flavor of American prose; this is one reason why American fiction is popular abroad, and has started new literary movements in France and other countries. American novelists write in a new kind of language, and it is uncommon, even for us, within the covers of a book. Good prose, everywhere, has a national flavor. It clung to the wonderful prose of Thoreau. It clings to Hemingway's prose even when he changed the locale of his stories to Spain, Africa, Cuba. Willa Cather's prose is redolent with the prairies of Nebraska and the pure air of New Mexico. Thomas Wolfe's language throbs with North Carolina and night-time Virginia, the great red barns of Pennsylvania and the skyscrapers of his fabulous North. The Mississippi seeps in through Faulkner's style. Today we can sniff other odors in American prose, as the old farms and plantations had to make way for freeways, and jets roar continuously over our cities.

The American democracy mixes styles as well as peoples, and prose, like hybrid corn, can be more vigorous as a result of this mixing process. The American vulgate, like popular speech everywhere, is better adapted to fiction than the urbane prose that comforts American subscribers to the *Times Literary Supplement* and other British periodicals. Weary of all these engine noises and tough juvenile voices of arrogant misfits, a small minority look wistfully to old mother England for a taste of the King's English. But violence and vulgarity require a violent and vulgar language.

Today some of the better prose written in America is the work of writers whose mother tongue is not even English (Vladmir Nabokov, Anaïs Nin) or whose parents were immigrants, or who are descendants of the slaves on the old plantations. With the rise of America's submerged masses since the New Deal, American fiction is no longer a literature made exclusively by Anglo-Saxons, or by their American descendants. There has been an invasion from the lower depths, internal and external cross-fertilization.

Every age and every country has its own particular style of writing. Victorian prose differs from Elizabethan prose, American prose differs from British. What is modern today might be dated tomorrow. There is no absolute individual quality in style independent of time and place. Every writer worth his salt creates his own audience, if not in his own lifetime then posthumously, as did Henry James. But a writer cannot go too much against established—or changing—standards and tastes, for there is obviously a large unconscious component in the prose of every original writer, and the unconscious reflects time and place, there are deep social deposits in it. Poetry is the cry of the unconscious, breaking through the inhibitions imposed upon it, whether in Nigeria or in the nether-world of Jean Genet.

METHOD IN MADNESS

Style then cannot be a linguistic exercise in a vacuum, and since the language of fiction is controlled by plot and by the point of view, the style, we see, must vary. The style is good or bad according to the story, or the writer, or the period, or the place, or the purpose of it. Style has to be judged in its particular context and not as an independent entity in itself, or as isolated words and sentences. The good writer holds event and language, content and form, in closest union. When they are not, the transmutation of experience into fiction has not taken place; it is still sociology, psychology, journalism; still raw experience.

What kills writers is the difference between good and better, and in the end the writer has to resign himself to leaving his work unfinished, giving it up in despair because he cannot make it any better, there is no time.

Tolstoy, as his daughter Alexandra told me once, rewrote *War and Peace* seven times. "They say it is good, but it is just at this point that the real work begins." That was the way Tolstoy looked at the craft of fiction. In a letter to Leonid Andreyev, Tolstoy made these four points: (1) Write only when the thought you want to express is so persistent that it will not leave you in peace until you express it as well as you can. This need for expression and not money or glory should

240

be your reason for writing. (2) Simplicity makes for beauty. The simple may be artless and poor, but that which is artificial, mannered, can never be good. (3) No hurried writing. When there is a genuine need for expression the writer spares no time or effort to express it fully, definitely, clearly. (4) The desire to satisfy popular tastes ruins a literary work in advance. Significance is excluded from such writing. A story is not directly instructive like a sermon, but by revealing to men something new and unknown to them.

It is said Shakespeare never revised. Well, he was Shakespeare. There are no rules about revision, except to see the subject more clearly and clean up the prose. A short story might be written in a few hours and published without any changes, but a novel is a different matter. Novels are rewritten. At least good novels are. If my own experience is of any interest here, let me say that I am a slow writer—and reader —and I revise as I go along, after I do my "semi-automatic" writing in the note-taking stage and while the first draft is taking shape; then I have to give free rein to my unconscious and dredge up things I know I could not do so well by conscious effort. The intellect, the critical faculty, which inhibits the unconscious, comes in later, after my self-induced morning trance is over. But I wrote my first published story, "I Ask You, Ladies and Gentlemen," at one sitting, in two hours or less, and sent it to *Prairie Schooner* without changing a single word, a single comma in it. I wanted to prove to myself I could do it. Later it became the title story in my first book, an autobiographical non-fiction novel. I have not tried it again. I know I could not do it again. That just happened when I was in the mood for it. Narrative prose at its best has a spontaneous headlong quality that might be lost by too many revisions, and there is such a thing as the better being the enemy of the good, as the French say. So a writer must know where to stop, with a sigh.

In Greek philosophy there is of course nothing like Plato's prose, nor has any modern philosopher spoken to us in such charming tones. Plato had drunk from the honeyed fountains he describes in the *Ion*. According to Plato's theory the poet writes not by science or technique, not through any conscious artistry, but by inspiration or under the influence of some non-rational, supernatural influence; in short he is a poet because he is mad, and he does not always understand what he says; he is the medium of some higher spirit that gets into him. He is literally inspired.

No truth is in that tale which says that, when a lover may be had, one ought to accept the non-lover, rather than the lover, because the lover is mad, the non-lover in his senses. It would be right enough, if to be mad were simply and solely an evil. But in reality the greatest blessings come to us through madness, for there is a madness that is given from on high. The Delphic priestess, and the sacred women of Dodona, with their madness have wrought many noble things for many a house and many a state in Hellas, but when in their senses have accomplished meagre things or none. . . . To him who is rightly mad, rightly possessed, the madness brings release from his present ills.

Third is the kind of madness and possession coming from the Muses. It seizes on a delicate and virgin soul, awakes it, sets it raving in songs and every form of poetry, and thus, adorning countless deeds done by the men of old, provides instruction for posterity. But he who, wanting madness from the Muses, comes to the doors of Poesy, trusting to enter in, who thinks forsooth that art is adequate to make him poet, he remains outside, a bungler, and his poetry of common sense fades into nothingness before the poetry of the madmen.

(From *Phaedrus. Plato: Phaedrus, Ion, Gorgias, and Symposium, with passages from the Republic and Laws,* trans. by Lane Cooper)

In fact, all the good poets who make epic poems use no art at all, but they are inspired and possessed when they utter all these beautiful poems, and so are the good lyric poets; these are not in their right mind when they make their beautiful songs, but they are like Corybants out of their wits dancing about. As soon as they mount on their harmony and rhythm, they become frantic and possessed. . . . The poets, as you know, tell us that they get their honey-songs from honey-founts of the Muses, and pluck from what they call Muses' gardens, and Muses' dells, and bring them to us, like honey-bees, on the wing themselves like the bees; and what they say is true. For the poet is an airy thing, a winged and holy thing;

and he cannot make poetry until he becomes inspired and goes out of his senses and no mind is left in him; so long as he keeps possession of this, no man is able to make poetry and chant oracles.

(*Plato, Ion.* Copyright by John Clive Graves Rouse)

As rational human beings, we recoil in terror from the rule of the irrational, but no theory of fiction can ignore it—as no man can in his own life. The irrational is part of us and represents one side of the dual process in artistic creation.

Aristotle, who is more practical and matter-of-fact in his views on the nature of the poetic art and stresses the importance of technique, has a saying quoted by Seneca: "No great genius was ever without an admixture of madness." Flaubert's example does not seem to lend much credence to the theory of poetic inspiration, but I have no doubt that Flaubert was mad to begin with, all his life in holy raptures over the word.

> The lunatic, the lover and the poet
> Are of imagination all compact.

That poets are mad is an old belief persisting to this day. Few would care to dispute it. The reader, too, must be a little mad to enjoy great works of literature. The mania for mimesis, which we may consider a form of self-realization, gives lasting existence to the passions and deeds of mortals, holds nations in its thrall, makes a novel like *Tom Jones* or *War and Peace,* "the newspaper of the world" for generations. The poet is the truest historian, said Homer.

The writer knows not what mysterious power dwells within him. When roused by it, he is sometimes astonished by the things he says, and does. He cannot tell from where his best ideas come, what guides his fingers on a blank sheet of paper and casts a glow over his prose. He is in a state of continuous surprises, and what is new and delightful to his readers was new and delightful to him when he was fool enough to wrestle with chaos and the word came to his aid, the word put method in his madness and enabled him to impose order on the disorder of reality.

Other pleasures pale beside the creative surprises of the writer. He needs no other entertainment when carried away by this impulse. Spurred by inspiration; curbed by measure; cut, mutilated, writing out of his own bleeding wounds; knowing he is probably the most absurd of men; he cannot help himself, he does what he must. He attempts even the impossible. And he is often amazed by his success and the wonder of it all.

It is a loving and lovable madness. Perhaps there are good reasons why the writer is accorded the privilege of omniscience. Think of Shakespeare. It is a public recognition of the writer's all-knowing quality and the omnipotence of the word. There is a god in the poet, said the ancients. And so far no god has called the poet's bluff. The writer makes himself lord of language and converts a confused mass or agglomerate of experience to art. Nothing worthwhile can be done in this craft without a touch of genius, and by a touch of genius we mean a touch of madness, a touch of the poet. The wild beast of genius needs a sober driver. Hence the importance of measure. The making of a good novel or short story, once the writer's imagination is ignited by a fiery spark that strikes him seemingly from nowhere, is largely a problem of measure.

The writer's more conscious labors have to do with technique, with form, with measure. Measure itself may be an aspect of madness if we equate madness with the creative drive, but it is within the writer's control, and measure is most effective when there is madness in it. The writer can examine measure, he can study it, evaluate it for himself. He may master it. Through measure a story is given the structure and style that snatch it from the chaos of reality and fix it in the memory of men. We remember through measure. We move from the unrealized to the realized through measure. Through measure writing resists the ravages of time. Everything perishes save the written word, says an old eastern proverb.

SUGGESTIONS FOR FURTHER READING

This is not a comprehensive bibliography, but a list of books and essays the writer and reader of fiction might find useful and enjoyable. Works on formula fiction are not included, although a few contain valuable hints by practicing commercial writers. The more technical books and essays are listed first. Some general works contain much technical information. The reader is urged to explore also the related fields of drama and poetry. Few works dealing with individual authors are listed here; the available material is too vast, and constantly growing.

TECHNIQUE

Allott, Miriam, *Novelists on the Novel,* Columbia University Press; London: Routledge & Kegan Paul; Doubleday, 1959.

Ames, Van Meter, *Aesthetics of the Novel,* University of Chicago Press, 1928.

Aristotle, *Poetics,* Everyman's Library, Dutton. (Includes two other classics: Demetrius, *On Style;* Longinus, *On the Sublime.*)

——, *Poetics,* University of North Carolina Press, 1942. There are other good translations available in paperback. Butcher's includes the Greek text.

——, *The Rhetoric and the Poetics,* Modern Library, Random House, 1954.

Bates, H. E., *The Modern Short Story,* The Writer, Inc., 1950.

Beach, James W., *The Method of Henry James,* Albert Saifer, 1954.

Beach, Joseph Warren, *The Twentieth Century Novel: Studies in Technique,* Appleton-Century, 1932.

Bentley, Phyllis, *Some Observations on the Art of Narrative,* Macmillan, 1947.

Booth, Wayne C., *The Rhetoric of Fiction,* University of Chicago Press, 1961.

Bowen, Elizabeth, *Collected Impressions,* Knopf, 1950.

Brombert, Victor, *The Novels of Flaubert: A Study of Themes and Techniques,* Princeton University Press, 1967.

Brooks, Cleanth, Jr. and Warren, Robert Penn, *Understanding Fiction,* second edition, Appleton-Century-Croft, 1959.

Cather, Willa, *On Writing: Critical Studies on Writing as an Art,* Knopf, 1949.

Eisenstein, Sergei, *Film Form and the Film Sense,* Meridian Books, 1957.

Flaubert, Gustave, *The Selected Letters of Gustave Flaubert,* trans. Francis Steegmuller, Farrar, Strauss & Cudahy, 1953; Vintage, 1957.

Forster, E. M., *Aspects of the Novel,* Harcourt, Brace, 1927, 1947.

Friedman, Melvin, *Stream of Consciousness: A Study in Literary Method,* Yale University Press, 1955.

Friedman, Norman, "Point of View in Fiction: The Development of a Critical Concept," PMLA, December 1955.

Glasgow, Ellen, *A Certain Measure: An Interpretation of Prose Fiction,* Harcourt, Brace, 1943.

Gordon, Caroline, *How to Read a Novel,* Viking, 1957.

Grabo, Carl H., *The Technique of the Novel,* Scribner's, 1928.

Gwynn, Frederick L., and Joseph L. Blotner, eds., *Faulkner in the University: Class Conferences at the University of Virginia 1957–1958,* University of Virginia Press, 1959.

Hale, Nancy, *The Realities of Fiction: A Book about Writing,* Boston, Toronto: Little, Brown, 1961.

Hamilton, Clayton, *The Art of Fiction: A Formulation of Its Fundamental Principles,* Odyssey, 1939.

Hogarth, Basil, *The Technique of Novel Writing: A Practical Guide for New Authors,* London: John Lane, 1934.

Humphrey, Robert, *Stream of Consciousness in the Modern Novel*, University of California Press, 1954.

James, Henry, *The Art of the Novel: Critical Prefaces*, Introduction by Richard P. Blackmur, Scribner's, 1934.

———, *The Notebooks of Henry James*, eds. F. O. Matthiessen and Kenneth B. Murdock, Oxford University Press, 1947.

Kempton, Kenneth P., *The Short Story*, Harvard University Press, 1947.

Kronenberger, Louis, ed., *Novelists on Novelists*, Doubleday Anchor, 1962.

Liddel, Robert, *Some Principles of Fiction*, London: Cape, 1953.

———, *A Treatise on the Novel*, London: Cape, 1947.

Lubbock, Percy, *The Craft of Fiction*, Scribner's, 1921. With Foreword by Mark Schorer, paperback, Viking, 1957.

Macaulay, Robie, and George Lanning, *Technique in Fiction*, Harper and Row, 1964.

McHugh, Vincent, *Primer of the Novel*, Random House, 1950.

Matlaw, Ralph E., *The Brothers Karamazov: Novelistic Technique*, The Hague: Humanities Press (paperback), 1957.

Mendilow, A. A., *Time and the Novel*, London, New York: British Book Center, 1952.

Miller, James E., Jr., *F. Scott Fitzgerald: His Art and His Technique*, New York University Press, 1964.

Muir, Edwin, *The Structure of the Novel*, Hogarth Press, 1928, 1947.

Myers, Walter L., *The Later Realism: A Study of Characterization In The British Novel;* University of Chicago Press, 1927.

O'Brien, Edward J., ed., *Short Story Case Book*, Farrar & Rinehart, 1935.

O'Faoláin, Séan, *The Short Story*, Collins, 1948; Devin-Adair, 1951.

Romberg, Bertil, *Studies in the Narrative Technique of the First-Person Novel*, trans. Michael Taylor and Harold H. Borland, Stockholm: Almgvist & W. Rsell, 1962.

Schorer, Mark, "Technique as Discovery," *Hudson Review,* Spring 1948. Reprinted in Aldridge, *Critiques and Essays on Modern Fiction;* O'Connor, *Forms of Modern Fiction;* other collections of critical essays.

——, "Fiction and the 'Analogical Matrix,'" *Kenyon Review,* Autumn 1949. Reprinted in Aldridge.

Stang, Richard, *The Theory of the Novel in England, 1850–1870,* Columbia University Press, 1959.

Wharton, Edith, *The Writing of Fiction,* Scribner's, 1925.

Wolfe, Thomas, *The Story of a Novel,* Scribner's, 1936.

Writers at Work, The Paris Review Interviews, Vol. I, ed. Malcolm Cowley, 1959; Vol. II, ed. George Plimpton, Introduction by Van Wyck Brooks, Viking, 1963.

GENERAL

Abrams, M. H., *The Mirror and the Lamp: Romantic Theory and the Critical Tradition,* Oxford University Press, 1953, and Norton Library.

Aldridge, John, ed., *Critiques and Essays on Modern Fiction,* Foreword by Mark Schorer and Bibliography by Robert W. Stallman, Ronald Press, 1952.

——, *After the Lost Generation: A Critical Study of the Writers of Two Wars,* McGraw-Hill, 1951.

——, *In Search of Heresy,* McGraw-Hill, 1956.

Allen, Walter, *The English Novel,* London: Phoenix House, 1954; Dutton Everyman, 1958.

——, *Writers on Writing,* Dutton, 1949.

——, *Six Great Novelists,* London: Hamish Hamilton, 1955.

Anderson, Sherwood, *The Modern Writer,* Lantern Press, 1925.

——, *A Story Teller's Story,* Viking, 1924.

Auerbach, Eric, *Mimesis: The Representation of Reality in Western Literature,* trans. Willard R. Trask, Princeton University Press, 1953; Doubleday Anchor.

Balakian, Nona, and Charles Simmons, *The Creative Present: Notes on Contemporary American Fiction*, Doubleday, 1963.

Beach, Joseph Warren, *American Fiction, 1920–1940*, Macmillan, 1941.

Beebe, Maurice, *Ivory Towers and Sacred Founts: The Artist as Hero in Fiction, from Goethe to Joyce*, New York University Press, 1964.

Blackmur, R. P., *Eleven Essays on the European Novel*, Harcourt, Brace, 1964.

Blotner, Joseph L., *The Modern Political Novel 1900–1960*, University of Texas Press, 1966.

Bluestone, George, *Novels into Film*, Johns Hopkins Press, 1957.

Bone, Robert A., *The Negro Novel in America*, Yale University Press, 1958.

Booth, Bradford A., "Form and Technique in the Novel," *The Reinterpretation of Victorian Literature*, ed. Joseph E. Baker, Princeton University Press, 1950.

——, "The Novel," in *Contemporary Literary Scholarship: A Critical Review*, ed. Lewis Leary, Appleton-Century-Croft, 1958.

Brickell, Herschel, ed., *Writers on Writing*, Doubleday, 1949.

Brooks, Van Wyck, *The Opinions of Oliver Allston*, Dutton, 1941.

Burke, Kenneth, *The Philosophy of Literary Form: Studies in Symbolic Action*, Louisiana State University Press, 1941.

Caldwell, Erskine, *Call It Experience: The Years of Learning How to Write*, Duel, Sloan & Pearce, 1951.

Cary, Joyce, *Art and Reality*, Cambridge University Press, 1958; Doubleday Anchor.

Cassell's *Encyclopedia of Literature*, ed. S. H. Steinberg. 2 vols., Vol. I, London: Cassell, 1953.

Chase, Richard, *The American Novel and Its Tradition*, Doubleday, 1957.

Clark, Barrett H., *European Theories of the Drama*, Crown, 1959.

Conrad, Joseph, *Joseph Conrad on Fiction*, ed. Walter F. Wright, University of Nebraska Press, 1964.

Cooke, Albert, *The Meaning of Fiction*, Wayne State University Press, 1960.

Cowley, Malcolm, *The Literary Situation*, Viking, 1958.

——, *Exile's Return: A Literary Odyssey of the 1920s*, Viking, 1951.

Crane, Ronald S., ed., *Critics and Criticism: Ancient and Modern*, University of Chicago Press, 1952.

Daiches, David, *The Novel and the Modern World*, University of Chicago Press, 1960.

Dobrée, Bonamy, *Modern Prose Style*, Oxford Clarendon, 1934.

Edel, Leon, *The Psychological Novel, 1900–1950*, Lippincott, 1959.

——, and Gordon N. Ray, *Henry James and H. G. Wells: A Record of Their Friendship, Their Debate on the Art of Fiction, and Their Quarrel*, University of Illinois Press, 1958.

Ellmann, Richard, *James Joyce*, Oxford University Press, 1959.

Fiedler, Leslie, *Love and Death in the American Novel*, Stein & Day, 1966.

Ford, Ford Madox, *The March of Literature*, Dial, 1938.

——, *Joseph Conrad: A Personal Remembrance*, Octagon Press, 1924.

——, *The English Novel from the Earliest Days to the Death of Joseph Conrad*, Lippincott, 1929.

Frye, Northrop, *The Anatomy of Criticism*, Princeton University Press, 1957.

Geismar, Maxwell, *American Moderns: From Rebellion to Conformity*, Hill and Wang, 1958.

——, *Henry James and the Jacobites*, Houghton Mifflin, 1963.

——, *The Last of the Provincials: The American Novel, 1915–1925*, Houghton Mifflin, 1947.

——, *Rebels and Ancestors: The American Novel, 1890–1915*, Houghton Mifflin, 1953.

——, *Writers in Crisis: The American Novel, 1925–1940,* Houghton Mifflin, 1942.

Gelfant, Blanche Housman, *The American City Novel,* University of Oklahoma Press, 1954.

Goodman, Paul, *The Structure of Literature,* University of Chicago Press, 1954.

Graves, Robert, *Occupation: Writer,* Creative Age Press, 1950.

Guérard, Albert, Jr., *Thomas Hardy,* Harvard University Press, 1950.

Hackett, Alice P., *Sixty Years of Best Sellers: 1895–1955,* R. R. Bowker, 1956.

Hardy, Barbara, *The Appropriate Form: An Essay on the Novel,* Oxford University Press, 1964.

Hassan, Ihab, *Radical Innocence,* Princeton University Press, 1961.

Harvey, W. J., *Character and the Novel,* Cornell University Press, 1965.

Hicks, Granville, ed., *The Living Novel: A Symposium,* Macmillan, 1957.

Hoffman, Frederick J., *Freudianism and the Literary Mind,* Louisiana State University Press, 1957.

Howe, Irving, *Politics and the Novel,* Horizon Press, 1957.

Hughes, Carl Milton, *The Negro Novelist: A Discussion of the Writings of American Negro Novelists: 1940–1950,* Citadel Press, 1953.

James, Henry, *The Art of Fiction, and Other Essays,* ed. Morris Roberts, Oxford University Press, 1948.

——, *The Letters of Henry James,* ed. Percy Lubbock, Scribner's, 1920.

Jameson, Storm, *The Novel in Contemporary Life,* The Writer, Inc., 1938.

——, *The Writer's Situation and Other Essays,* Macmillan, 1950.

Johnson, Edgar, *Charles Dickens: His Tragedy and Triumph,* 2 vols., Simon & Schuster, 1952.

Kazin, Alfred, *On Native Grounds: An Interpretation of Modern American Prose Literature,* Reynal & Hitchcock, 1942; Doubleday paperback, 1956.

——, *The Open Form*, Harcourt, Brace & World, 1965.

Kennedy, Margaret, *The Outlaws on Parnassus*, Viking, 1958.

Kronenberger, Louis, ed., *Novelists on Novelists*, Doubleday Anchor, 1962.

Lauter, Paul, ed., *Theories of Comedy*, Doubleday Anchor, 1964.

Lawrence, D. H., *Selected Literary Criticism*, ed., Anthony Beal, Viking, 1966.

——, *Studies in Classic American Literature*, Doubleday, 1955.

Leavis, F. R., *The Great Tradition: George Eliot, Henry James, Joseph Conrad*, London: Chatto & Windus, 1948.

——, *D. H. Lawrence, Novelist*, London: Chatto & Windus, 1955.

Lesser, Simon, *Fiction and the Unconscious*, Beacon Press, 1957; Random House Vintage.

Levin, Harry, *The Power of Blackness*, Knopf, 1958.

——, *Symbolism and Fiction*, University of Virginia Press, 1956.

——, *The Gates of Horn: A Study of Five French Realists*, Oxford University Press, 1963.

Lewis, R. W. B., *The Picaresque Saint: Representative Figures in Contemporary Fiction*, Lippincott, 1959.

Lucas, F. L., *Style*, Macmillan; Collier Books, 1962.

Lukács, Georg, *Studies in European Realism*, trans. Edith Bone, Hillway Publishing Co., 1950.

——, *The Historical Novel*, trans. Hannah and Stanley Mitchell. Preface by Irving Howe, London: Merlin Press, 1962; Beacon paperback, 1963.

Murry, J. Middleton, *The Problem of Style*, Oxford University Press, 1922.

Maugham, W. Somerset, *Points of View*, Doubleday, 1958, and Bantam.

——, *The Art of Fiction: An Introduction to Ten Novels and Their Authors*, Doubleday, 1955.

——, *The Summing Up*, Doubleday, 1938, and Mentor Books.

Morris, Wright, *The Territory Ahead*, Harcourt, Brace, 1958.

Mott, Frank Luther, *Golden Multitudes: The Story of Best Sellers in the United States,* Macmillan, 1947.

Munson, Gorham, *The Written Word,* Creative Age Press, 1949.

Nowell, Elizabeth, *Thomas Wolfe: A Biography,* Doubleday, 1960.

O'Brien, Edward J., *The Advance of the Short Story,* Dodd, Mead, 1931.

——, *The Dance of the Machines: The American Short Story and the Industrial Age,* Macaulay, 1929.

O'Connor, Frank, *The Mirror in the Roadway,* Knopf, 1956.

O'Faoláin, Séan, *The Vanishing Hero, Studies of the Hero in the Modern Novel,* Atlantic-Little Brown; The Universal Library, Grosset & Dunlap; 1957.

Peyre, Henri, *The Contemporary French Novel,* Oxford University Press, 1955.

Porter, Katherine Anne, *The Days Before,* Harcourt, Brace, 1952.

Poulet, George, *Studies in Human Time,* trans. Elliott Coleman, Johns Hopkins Press, 1956.

——, *The Interior Distance,* trans. Elliott Coleman, Johns Hopkins Press, 1959.

Prescott, Orville, *In My Opinion: An Inquiry into the Contemporary Novel,* Bobbs-Merrill, 1952.

Rahv, Philip, *Image and Idea,* New Directions, 1949.

Rank, Otto, *Art and Artist: Creative Urge and Personality Development,* trans. C. F. Atkinson, Knopf, 1932.

Read, Herbert, *English Prose Style,* Pantheon Books; and Beacon paperback, 1955.

Reynolds, Paul, *The Writing and Selling of Fiction,* Doubleday, 1965.

Rideout, Walter B., *The Radical Novel in the United States 1900–1954: Some Interrelations of Literature and Society,* Harvard University Press, 1956.

Robbe-Grillet, Alain, *For a New Novel: Essays on Fiction,* trans. Richard Howard, Grove Press, 1965.

Sarraute, Nathalie, *The Age of Suspicion, Essays on the Novel,* trans. Maria Jolas, Grove Press, 1963.

Schorer, Mark, *Sinclair Lewis,* McGraw-Hill, 1961.

——, ed. *Modern British Fiction: Essays in Criticism,* Oxford University Press, 1961.

——, ed. with Foreword, *Society and Self in the Novel: English Institute Essays,* Columbia University Press, 1955.

——, ed. *The Story: A Critical Anthology,* Prentice-Hall, 1950.

——, *The Novelist in the Modern World,* University of Arizona Press, 1957.

Schucking, Levin L., *The Sociology of Literary Taste,* trans. E. W. Dickes, Oxford University Press, 1945.

Shipley, Joseph T., ed. *Dictionary of World Literature: Criticisms—Forms—Technique,* second edition, Littlefield-Adams paperback, 1954.

Sprigge, Elizabeth, *Gertrude Stein: Her Life and Work,* London: Hamish Hamilton, 1957.

Stoll, Elmer Edgar, *From Shakespeare to Joyce,* Doubleday, 1944.

Thompson, Stith, *Motif—Index of Folk Literature,* 6 vols. (1932–37), Indiana University Press.

Tindall, William York, *The Literary Symbol,* Columbia University Press, 1955.

Tolstoy, Leo, *What Is Art and Essays on Art,* Oxford University Press, 1930.

Trilling, Lionel, *The Liberal Imagination: Essays on Literature and Society,* Viking, 1950.

——, *The Opposing Self: Nine Essays in Criticism,* Viking, 1955.

Unwin, Stanley, *The Truth about Publishing,* seventh edition, London: George Allen & Unwin.

Van Ghent, Dorothy, *The English Novel: Form and Function,* Rinehart, 1953.

Warren, Austin, *Rage for Order: Essays in Criticism,* University of Chicago Press, 1948.

Warren, Robert Penn, *Selected Essays,* Random House, 1958.

Watkins, Floyd C., *Thomas Wolfe's Characters: Portraits from Life,* University of Oklahoma Press, 1957.

Wellek, René, and Austin Warren, *Theory of Literature,* Harcourt, Brace, 1956.

Wescott, Glenway, *Images of Truth: Remembrances and Criticisms,* Harper & Row, 1962.

West, Ray B., Jr., *The Short Story in America,* Henry Regnier, 1952.

——, and Robert Wooster Stallman, *The Art of Modern Fiction,* Rinehart, 1949.

Wilson, Angus, *The Wild Garden; Or, Speaking of Books,* University of California Press, 1963.

Wilson, Edmund, *Classics and Commercials: A Literary Chronicle of the Forties,* Farrar, Straus & Young, 1950.

——, *Eight Essays,* Doubleday Anchor, 1954.

——, *A Literary Chronicle: 1920–1950,* Doubleday, 1956.

——, *The Shores of Light: A Literary Chronicle of the Twenties and Thirties,* Farrar, Straus & Young, 1952.

——, *The Triple Thinkers: Ten Essays on Literature,* Harcourt, Brace, 1938.

——, *The Wound and the Bow: Seven Studies in Literature,* Houghton Mifflin, 1941.

Woolf, Virginia, *A Writer's Diary,* Harcourt, Brace, 1954.

——, *Granite and Rainbow,* Harcourt, Brace, 1958.

——, *The Common Reader,* First and Second Series, Harcourt, Brace, 1948.

——, *The Moment and Other Essays,* London: Hogarth, 1947.

Zabel, Morton Dauwen, *Craft and Character in Modern Fiction,* Viking, 1957.